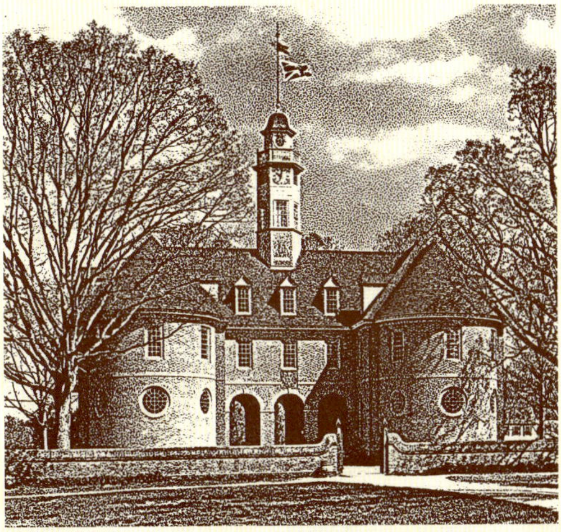

The Capitol *Colonial Williamsburg*

Unorthodox Strategies
for the Everyday Warrior

百戰奇略

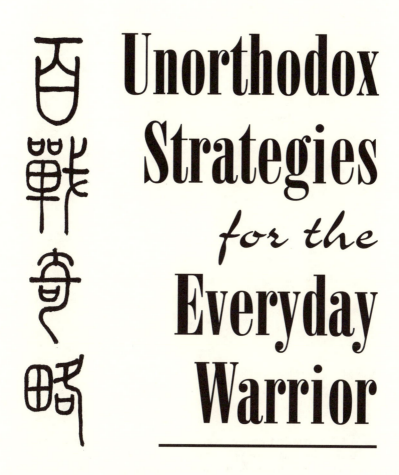

Unorthodox Strategies *for the* Everyday Warrior

Translated, with Historical Introduction and Commentary, by

Ralph D. Sawyer

With the collaboration of

Mei-chün Lee Sawyer

WestviewPress

A Division of HarperCollins*Publishers*

Published in 1996 in the United States of America by Westview Press, 5500 Central Avenue, Boulder, Colorado 80301-2877, and in the United Kingdom by Westview Press, 12 Hid's Copse Road, Cumnor Hill, Oxford OX2 9JJ

A CIP catalog record for this book is available from the Library of Congress.
ISBN 0-8133-2860-8

The paper used in this publication meets the requirements of the American National Standard for Permanence of Paper for Printed Library Materials Z39.48-1984.

10 9 8 7 6 5 4 3 2 1

Contents

Preface

The work originally known as *One Hundred Unorthodox Strategies—Pai-chan Ch'i-lüeh*—is a veritable compendium of tactical principles and historic battles, the latter being chosen to illustrate the individual lessons unfolded by the tactical discussions. Traditionally identified as Liu Po-wen, the book's author remains unknown but likely held a bureaucratic military position of some rank late in the Southern Sung dynasty and possibly completed the work early in the period of Mongol domination, as evinced by his grasp of the political factors affecting military affairs and his detailed knowledge of both military texts and historical writings. The *Unorthodox Strategies* thus provides a vibrant, systematic introduction not only to Chinese military thought but also to much of its military history. Moreover, while many prominent battles are recounted, others are rescued from obscurity, providing further evidence of the author's extensive knowledge and thoroughly analytic approach. (A few, however, prove somewhat puzzling because the critical factors presumably operative in a particular conflict's outcome appear less decisive than might have been expected.) The author's ability to discern abstract military principles within concrete contexts thus furnishes innumerable insights into the abstruse, often enigmatic Chinese military writings and an opportunity to study how tactical principles were actually employed by a hundred historical commanders over two thousand years.

As with our previous works, this book is intended for a general audience rather than just sinologists, military historians, or other specialists. Moreover, since the chapters are self-contained and self-explanatory, forming a tactical handbook for thoughtful study—whether centered on its original military intent or for more widespread application, including business, human relations, or the world at large—we have adopted a somewhat broader approach to its translation and presentation than previously. The introduction and appendices provide but a brief overview of the salient characteristics of Chinese warfare in the vast historic period under discussion and short summaries of the basic military writings frequently cited. No attempt has been made to fully discuss either of these, as they are covered in our other works, such as the *Seven Military Classics of Ancient China,* the *Military Methods,* and our forthcoming *History of Warfare in China.* Furthermore, while providing a few notes on the military contents for orientation, we have not undertaken a systematic, analytical overview, because the nature of the *Unorthodox Strategies* is inherently discrete and best explicated in concrete fashion in response to the numerous principles presented in the individual chapters. This is not to deny the existence of a systematic vision, one that might be said to underlie and characterize Chinese military science—based, for example, on the principles of maneuver warfare with all their ramifications, such as presently embodied in the U.S. Marine Corps Warfighting manuals—but in constructing such a synthesis the main thrust of the *Unorthodox Strategies* (to be flexible, variable, and formless) might also be overlooked. In fact, one of the critical lessons that must be painfully learned is that no single principle is ever applicable in all situations. Thus, while speed and swiftness are generally stressed, in some circumstances speed will not only exhaust one's forces but also uselessly throw them against overwhelming foes. Therefore speed and initiative are to be balanced with temporizing and defensive measures whose appropriateness (or domain of applicability) must be determined with respect to fixed parameters that characterize commonly recurring situational categories.

Insofar as the original texts are readily accessible and variations among the editions minimal, we have neither provided footnotes for our choice of one or another rendition nor systematically corrected the historical illustrations by comparative recourse to the original passages in the *Twenty-five Histories* and other sources. Rather, we have treated the book as a self-contained work, as virtually every Chinese reader has over the past few centuries. Scholars with competence in classical Chinese will readily note where alternative readings were selected or an explanatory phrase added, but may also wish to consult Chang Wen-ts'ai's excellent *Pai-chan ch'i-fa ch'ien-shuo* (Chieh-fang-chün ch'u-pan-she, Peking, 1987), which offers a carefully corrected text based on full research into the original passages and whose thoughtful conclusions regarding the text's authorship and date we generally follow. (Chang also points out that the book was originally called the *Pai-chan Ch'i-fa* and only acquired its present name of *Pai-chan Ch'i-lüeh* toward the middle of the Ch'ing period.)

In presenting this material there was a great temptation to extensively discuss the individual battles, setting them within their historical contexts and exploring the tactical implications. However, this would not only result in an unwieldy book, but further distract from the author's original purpose—to illustrate his tactical lessons with concrete examples rather than analyze concrete battles in terms of tactical principles. Insofar as the historical figures, while not unimportant, are merely actors in such illustrations, we have opted neither to explore nor expand them in cumbersome footnotes. Rather, our aim has been to produce a work equally accessible to those interested in military history, Asian history, and tactical thought in general, whatever their proposed domain of applicability. However, in the traditional Chinese manner we have appended brief observations to each chapter, sometimes commenting on the historical context or importance of the battles themselves but generally explicating the tactical principles with reference to the heritage of Chinese military thought as embodied by the *Seven Military Classics* and Sun Pin's *Military Methods.* We have emphasized concrete comparisons rather than general principles and frequently include divergent or alternative views. While the *Unorthodox Strategies* is therefore a self-contained, fully independent volume, it may also be viewed as a companion to our previous works, the *Seven Military Classics* and the *Military Methods.*

Apart from the abstract debt we owe to the historical commentators whose labors have illuminated China's innumerable texts, we would like to again acknowledge Zhao Yong's ongoing assistance in locating and obtaining obscure textual materials. In addition, we have benefited greatly from the wisdom and insightful comments of Peter Kracht, senior editor, as well as the expertise and commitment of the staff at Westview Press in making this book possible. As always, our thanks to Max Gartenberg for his generous efforts and to Lee T'ing-rong, who has once again honored the work with his calligraphy.

Ralph D. Sawyer

A Note on Pronunciation

As our views remain unchanged, we repeat our comments from our previous works: Unfortunately, neither of the two commonly employed orthographies makes the pronunciation of romanized Chinese characters easy. Each system has its stumbling blocks, and we remain unconvinced that the Pinyin *qi* is inherently more comprehensible to unpracticed readers than the Wade-Giles *ch'i,* although it is certainly no less comprehensible than *j* for *r* in Wade-Giles. However, as many of the important terms may already be familiar and previous translations of Sun-tzu's *Art of War* have mainly used Wade-Giles, we have opted to employ it throughout our works, including the *Unorthodox Strategies.* Well-known cities, names, and books—such as "Peking"—are retained in their common form, and books and articles published with romanized names and titles also appear in their original form.

As a crude guide to pronunciation we offer the following notes on the significant exceptions to normally expected sounds:

t, as in *Tao:* without apostrophe, pronounced like *d*

p, as in *ping:* without apostrophe, pronounced like *b*

ch, as in *chuang:* without apostrophe, pronounced like *j*

hs, as in *hsi:* pronounced *sh*

j, as in *jen:* pronounced like *r*

Thus, the name of the famous Chou dynasty is pronounced as if written "jou" and sounds just like the English name "Joe."

Chronology of Approximate Dynastic Periods

Dynastic Period	Years
Legendary Sage Emperors	2852–2255 B.C.
Hsia	2205–1766
Shang	1766–1045
Western Chou	1045–770
Eastern Chou	770–256
Spring and Autumn	722–481
Warring States	403–221
Ch'in	221–207
Former Han (Western Han)	208 B.C.–8 A.D.
Later Han (Eastern Han)	23–220
Six Dynasties Period	222–589
Three Kingdoms	222–280
Wei-Chin	220–316
Northern and Southern Dynasties	265–589
Sui	589–618
T'ang	618–907
Five Dynasties (Northern China)	907–959
Ten Kingdoms (Southern China)	907–979
Sung	960–1126
Southern Sung	1127–1279
Yüan (Mongol)	1279–1368
Ming	1368–1644
Ch'ing (Manchu)	1644–1911

Unorthodox Strategies
for the Everyday Warrior

Introduction

The history of China, ever portrayed in terms of its glorious culture and storied continuity, differs remarkably from general perceptions and common knowledge, being instead an interminable struggle between the forces of light and dark, culture and brutality, the civil and the martial. For five millennia China has tortuously suffered constant warfare, upheaval, and disintegration, untold millions repeatedly perishing whenever central authority waned and barbaric forces sundered the realm. Powerful generals forged personal domains then exploited the loyalty of troops enamored by promises of great rewards to contend for ultimate power. Millenarian leaders manipulated spiritual beliefs and wreaked havoc in purported quests to realize utopian visions, frequently destroying everything before them, oblivious even to the humanitarian constraints of their own religious precepts. Nomadic peoples repeatedly mounted incursions from out of the steppes, pillaging and plundering the border regions except during brief respites consequent to their decimation by powerful dynastic Chinese armies. Various tribes successively dominated North China for many centuries after the Han, and a few peoples, such as the Mongols and Manchus, conquered all of it through massively destructive campaigns long thereafter. In short, virtually every year witnessed a major battle somewhere in China, significant conflicts erupted nearly every decade, and the nation was consumed by inescapable warfare at least once a century.

Within this context of interminable strife, warfare truly became—as Sun-tzu, the famous general and strategist, asserted—"the greatest affair of state, the basis of life or death, the Tao to survival or extinction." Accordingly, as battlefield technology improved and combat forces escalated from a few hundred nobles venturing forth in their chariots to hundreds of thousands of infantry troops massed for protracted campaigns, military science—encompassing organization, tactics, command, and control—also developed and was studied by the professional military men who arose to cope with the growing complexity. Pondering their experiences, they formulated concepts and discerned principles to impose intellectual order upon the apparently chaotic nature of the battlefield. The resulting military manuals eventually furnished the officially sanctioned basis for systematically studying military doctrine, with seven such books, including Sun-tzu's famous *Art of War,* eventually being designated as canonical when compiled, edited, and published in the Sung dynasty as the *Seven Military Classics.*

Apart from the earliest periods of the Shang and Chou, and until the introduction of hot weapons and the impact of Western military practices, Chinese warfare showed remarkable tactical continuity. This continuity resulted from three factors: the slow evolution of the three component forces (chariots, cavalry, and infantry) with their relevant weapons groups; the systematic development of tactical doctrine that early assumed written form and was thereafter assiduously studied; and an innate reverence for tradition, for pondering the lessons and examples of the past. China's vaunted examination system, which really became effective in the T'ang, only to become stultifying from the Sung onward, reflected this penchant for revitalizing antiquity, for deliberately imitating the methods of the ancients in order to rectify contemporary shortcomings and deficiencies. This also proved true of the traditions embodied in the *Seven Military Classics,* although commanders could hardly ignore the ever-evolving nature of warfare and the pressing realities of the battlefield. They would also undoubtedly have been familiar with an incident in the *Tso Chuan* (reprised in Chapter 39 of the *Unorthodox Strategies*) where Duke Hsiang of Sung practiced the proper forms and thereby doomed his troops to defeat, and another later in the T'ang where an idealistic general slavishly emulated the ancient employment of battle chariots only to be destroyed by highly mobile cavalry and infantry.

Because imperial exams were also administered in technical subjects and the military arts, there was an added incentive to thoroughly study the orthodox military texts, particularly the *Seven Military Classics,* the designated basis for exam questions. The lessons derived from these writings not only provided a wide range of tactical knowledge but also furnished the concepts and vocabulary required for commanders to mutually communicate in their specialized area. Warfare thus became a Tao, a way of knowing or a science, encompassing battlefield analysis, enemy assessment, command and control, tactical decisionmaking, and numerous other important aspects of military activity. Analytic in nature, founded upon Sun-tzu's theoretical methods and parameters, Chinese military science was constantly augmented by the experience and ruminations of veteran generals and could be ignored by field commanders only at great peril.

The *Unorthodox Strategies* not only falls into this tradition but also constitutes a systematic summation of earlier military writings supplemented by historical illustrations that convert an otherwise conventional tactical manual into an astute casebook meriting close study. Composed perhaps at the very end of the Southern Sung dynasty or shortly thereafter, some decades subsequent to the publication of the *Seven Military Classics,* the unknown author availed himself of China's extensive dynastic histories to ferret out battles that would succinctly reveal the tactical principles in the context of concrete events. Many of these historical incidents preserve dialogues encompassing the commanders' own views, immediately revealing the vibrancy and continued relevance of the classical writings throughout Chinese history despite such important transitions as the shift from chariots to cavalry.

The author—sometimes claimed to be Liu Chi, also known as Liu Powen, of the early Ming dynasty—clearly ascribed to Sun-tzu's belief in the critical nature and importance of warfare. However, instead of initiating the book with this often-quoted thought, he commences with a chapter upon calculation and estimation, no doubt reflecting Sun-tzu's placement of "Initial Estimations" at the beginning of the *Art of War* to emphasize the analytic aspect of the Tao of warfare. Thereafter the *Unorthodox Strategies* proceeds with the consideration of some forty paired tactical concepts and a few individual principles, ending with two chapters on the essence of warfare whose concluding role equally stresses their importance. These last two chapters are premised upon a famous statement found in the *Ssu-ma Fa*—one perhaps still relevant in our troubled world—that states: "Even though a state may be vast, those who love warfare will inevitably perish. Even though calm may prevail under Heaven, those who forget warfare will certainly be endangered." No doubt the unknown author embraced the view that "when action should be taken one who hesitates and is quiet, without advancing, seriously injures all living beings. Weapons are inauspicious instruments, and the Tao of Heaven abhors them. However when their employment is unavoidable it accords with the Tao of Heaven."

Because the *Unorthodox Strategies* is founded upon Sun-tzu's concepts and adopts his tactics extensively, it almost merits being characterized as an explication of the *Art of War.* However, while the author obviously assimilated Sun-tzu's characterization of warfare as the Tao of tactics and command and quotes the *Art of War* in somewhat more than half his tactical discussions, he also fully takes cognizance of the dissimilar tactics and different concepts found in the other canonical military writings and even cites the *Analects* of Confucius and the earlier *Book of Documents* on a few occasions.

The essential vision is one of maneuver warfare intended to exploit a full array of possibilities, including deception, speed, and even temporizing, to attain the strategic advantage that ultimately translates into overwhelming force suddenly vanquishing a startled enemy. It thus fundamentally differs from the Western penchant for direct, immediate confrontation, for butting strength against strength just as imagized by Greek phalanxes of old clashing on the semi-arid plains or arrays of thousands moronically marching toward each other at measured pace in the nineteenth century. In contrast, while ordinary campaign forces in China eventually numbered 200,000 and probably peaked at a million or more for major invasions, immediately engaging in battle was never the norm.

Although the individual lessons contained in the *Unorthodox Strategies* clearly discuss the tactical principles, the historical incidents generally illustrate them well, and both have been amplified with our commentary, a few of the book's assumptions and organizing principles might prove useful for orientation. Foremost, all military activities—whether single battles, entire campaigns, or full national mobilizations—require carefully calculating the chances for success. The enemy must be evaluated, and, in accord with methods apparently prevailing from Sun-tzu's era onward, the probability for success quantitatively determined. Naturally this procedure requires intelligence-gathering activities, including the employment of spies, and attempts to undermine the enemy's strengths. Furthermore, the results of this assessment cannot be considered final until contemplated and modified in the context of strategic options that might minimize or even negate enemy advantages in supplies or manpower, such as fatiguing them through forced marches or coercing them onto constricted terrain.

These situational analyses probably proceeded by evaluating the parameters first suggested in the *Art of War,* structuring the tactical options in terms of paired opposites. The lessons in the *Unorthodox Strategies* are similarly centered upon complimentary tactical principles, although considerably expanded in their formulation beyond Sun-tzu's original categories. Among the most important might be the natural advantages of Heaven and Earth; quantities of supplies as relatively plentiful or scarce; numbers of men, as few or many; the state of the troops, as well-trained or not, fatigued or rested, hungry or well nourished, confident or fearful; the commander as experienced or not, capable or ignorant, self-controlled or easily angered, arrogant or humble; and the morale of the contending sides, as fervent or terrified. However, one fundamental conclusion repeatedly emerges from these studies: no single principle can ever dominate nor be applicable in every situation. At times the army should avoid warfare, yet at other times it should forcefully engage in battle even though numerically outnumbered and, except for one or two factors, enmeshed in a situation identical to one previously requiring restraint.

Having determined a battle or campaign to be necessary, the commander must then ponder the possible routes to conquest and strive to realize victory with a minimum expenditure of energy, even without fighting if possible. Among the methods for nonviolent conquest, overawing the enemy with superior military and economic strength represents the ideal, but thwarting the enemy's plans the most realistic. Efforts to achieve the latter would include alliance building, subverting enemy coalitions, assuming preemptory positions, and even refusing battle, an idea less favored by Sun-tzu's original doctrines. Moreover, campaign forces, of whatever size, should strive to confuse the enemy, deceiving them as to intentions and capability, and then strike when and where unexpected. According to Sun-tzu, the formless represents the highest realization of deception. By not revealing any intentions or presenting a discernible form the enemy will be baffled and forced to prepare against all eventualities, even foregoing planned assaults because of their inability to detect weaknesses or "vacuities." Slightly less transcendent, but still effective, would be deliberately creating facades and deceptions, such as feinting east to strike in the west, thereby compelling the enemy to inappropriately commit their defenses or balk their plans. However, although the *Unorthodox Strategies* discusses several concrete deceptive practices, the concept receives far less emphasis than in such writings as the *Art of War* and the *Six Secret Teachings*.

For engaging the enemy in battle, the *Unorthodox Strategies* presents a wide range of tactical possibilities founded on the operant principle of flexible response, of varying tactics to suit circumstances and situations. Preliminary to the actual engagement would be efforts designed to reduce the enemy's warfare capabilities, to stress and debilitate their forces. These focus on manipulating them in various ways, such as tempting them with apparently easy gains in order to destabilize them, to provoke them into motion and then capitalize upon their disorder and fatigue. Heavily entrenched, overwhelmingly strong, or fervently animated forces should never be directly engaged. Conversely, even when enjoying a vast superiority in troop strength or component forces, the commander should still shape the battle to greatest advantage, weakening and dividing the enemy's units to ensure victory at the least cost. The circumstances should be molded so that the army's strategic power—raw power coupled with positional advantage, an essential concept in Sun-tzu's doctrine—may be explosively employed, just like "the sudden release of a pent-up torrent down a thousand-fathom gorge." When such disproportionate advantages are thus achieved, even mediocre generals in command of average troops cannot fail to achieve shattering victories.

The doctrine of the unorthodox and orthodox, first formulated by Sun-tzu, appears in the *Unorthodox Strategies,* but in a much de-emphasized role, perhaps because of the difficulty commanders experienced in implementing such complex tactics with the large armies of their times. In essence, unorthodox tactics are realized through the flexible, imaginative, unconventional employment of forces, while orthodox ones are simply normal, conventional, by-the-book methods. The unorthodox and orthodox are thus inherently interrelated, mutually defining, and highly context dependent. While a number of chapters in the *Unorthodox Strategies* elucidate tactics that might prove to be unorthodox, depending upon their contextual application, the historical illustration for "Wind in Warfare" furnishes a striking example of the unorthodox because Fu Yen-ch'ing, the commanding general, finding himself downwind of the enemy, nearly blinded by blowing sand, adopted the unexpected but ultimately successful measure of attacking, rather than observing the oft-repeated prohibition never to attack against the wind.

Commanding massive forces capable of complex maneuvers and fully exploiting the numerous deployments articulated by traditional Chinese military science required not only acumen and expertise but also resilience, determination, wisdom, courage, and inspiration. Any general beset by personal weakness or flaws, given to emotional reaction or debilitating traits such as arrogance and greed, would doom his men to death and defeat even before the armies had clashed. Accordingly, the military writings generally devote extensive passages to the character and requisite abilities of generals and officers at every level, while history is replete with examples of successfully manipulating character flaws and exploiting professional weaknesses, including several found as historical illustrations in the *Unorthodox Strategies.*

Effective commanders must also master the psychology of warfare and always be cognizant of the army's morale, as well as their physical condition and remaining capabilities. Many of the military writings extensively pondered the question of spirit or *ch'i* (the vital *pneuma* of life), gradually evolving a comprehensive approach to stimulating and maintaining the soldier's morale, arousing their fighting spirit just before battle, and ensuring their commitment to fight to the death once engaged. However, the early *Tso Chuan* already contained a passage showing how the soldiers' fervor can be adversely affected by stimulating them too soon with the drums, while Sun-tzu expanded the concept further in passages that are extensively discussed in several chapters of the *Unorthodox Strategies.*

Underlying the issue of spirit was the fundamental problem of command and control—of organizing, directing, and successfully molding a unified force that would immediately respond to the commander's intent. A few chapters in the *Unorthodox Strategies* focus upon the issues of rewards and punishments and provide cursory discussions of the main problems. Training underpins every endeavor, but more significant is the army's hierarchical organization based upon the squad of five, coupled with the imposition of mutual responsibility obligations that link every man's fate to his fellows, thereby ensuring maximum effort in the face of danger. Besides fear, doubt constitutes the main problem that must be countered, for it is ever present in the tendency to perceive omens in natural phenomena and to question unfolding events. Once he vanquishes fear and doubt, the commander can direct a corps of completely responsive troops, enabling him to execute flexible tactics and exploit ongoing battlefield changes.

Although there was constant tension between professional military personnel and the literati staffing the bureaucracy, the latter often psychologically and educationally submerged into the effete world of hypocritical Confucianism (except early in the establishment of many dynasties when men of action dominated the court), most people still accepted the view that warfare was inherent to man and should therefore be studied and prepared for. This of course contradicted the late Confucian belief (originally espoused by Mencius) that human nature tends to be good, as well the prevailing view that overawing virtue alone could subjugate the world. The competition for scarce tax resources, coupled with an innate fear of strong generals, no doubt underlay much of the civil-martial conflict, while the opulent imperial lifestyle often drained the state's coffers, impoverishing the military and leaving the country at the mercy of nomadic powers. The *Huai-nan tzu*, a Former Han dynasty eclectic text, observed:

> When the ancients employed the military it was not to profit from broadening their lands nor coveting the acquisition of gold and jade. It was to preserve those about to perish, continue the severed, pacify the chaos under Heaven, and eliminate the harm affecting the myriad people.
>
> Now whatever beast has blood and *ch'i*, has teeth and bears horns, has claws in front and spurs in back—those with horns butt, those with teeth bite, those with poison sting, and those with hooves kick. When happy they play with each other; when angry they harm each other. This then is Heavenly nature.
>
> Men have a desire for food and clothes, but things are insufficient to supply them. Thus they group together in diverse places. When the division of things is not equitable, they fervently seek them and then conflict arises. When there is conflict the strong will coerce the weak, while the courageous will encroach

> upon the fearful. Since men do not have the strength of sinews and bone, the sharpness of claws and teeth, they cut leather to make armor, and smelt iron to make blades. In antiquity men who were greedy, obtuse, and avaricious destroyed and pillaged all under Heaven. The myriad people were disturbed and moved, none could be at peace in his place. Sages suddenly arose to punish the strong and brutal and pacify a chaotic age. They eliminated danger and got rid of the corrupt, turning the muddy into the clear, danger into peace.

Unfortunately the military thinkers frequently found themselves disparaged at court and disdained by the people at large, yet expected to successfully grapple with sudden predatory incursions by enemy states and the brutally aggressive actions of their military forces, both presumably stemming from man's inherent nature.

Although the *Unorthodox Strategies* focuses upon tactics and excerpts historical battles to concretely illustrate the discussion in a series of essentially self-contained lessons, some basic contextual information may prove useful for understanding the nature and capabilities of the military forces active in these periods. Irrespective of the period, Chinese military practice tended to be cumulative, always augmenting the past with new technologies and methods, yet essentially integrating them into a body of theory that had become canonical by the end of the Warring States. For example, when shifting from chariot-based forces to unified infantry and cavalry commands during the Han dynasty, the principles for maneuver warfare remained unchanged, although the speed with which they might be realized increased dramatically. While specific tactics might become outdated, the experience was never discontinuous, enabling the author of the *Unorthodox Strategies* to choose his examples from nearly two thousand years of history.

Certain recurrent themes stand out starkly. First, conflicts frequently arose between the emperor, the incarnation and wielder of centralized, despotic authority, and diffuse power centers, whether in remote provincial areas or simply subordinates in command of vigorous, perhaps victorious campaign armies. Second, millenarian movements constantly appeared that not only threatened established imperial rule, but also decimated much of the land in titanic struggles. Third, imperial China never resolved the ever-present problem posed by aggressive steppe peoples, generally but ineffectually trying to force their obedient conformance to the preconceived Chinese world order as tribute states; occasionally mounting external sweeps to diminish their power; and often bribing or otherwise buying them off, generally unsuccessfully, thus economically debilitating the country without ever increasing its defensive capabilities. Some periods also witnessed extensive efforts to contain the threat by employing "barbarians to control barbarians"—relying upon more Sinicized tribes to provide an active defense in the intermediate area along the border (eventually defined by the Great Wall) between the steppe and China proper. When mistreated or dissatisfied, these semisedentary tribes frequently rebelled and exploited their strategically advantageous position to easily plunder the empire.

The defining characteristics of traditional military forces in China remained largely unchanged from the late Spring and Autumn period—Sun-tzu's era—until the advent of hot weapons subsequent to the writing of the *Unorthodox Strategies.* Founded upon a strict hierarchical organization that made the squad of five the fundamental building block, armies as large as several hundred thousand were capable of segmenting and recombining, executing numerous deployments, varying unit formations within such deployments, and responding to ongoing battlefield commands. Their unity was attained through severe discipline, excellence in effecting measures for command and control, and powerful disincentives to disobedience. Only three significant changes occurred during the period covered by the *Unorthodox Strategies:* a shift from chariot-centered organization in the Spring and Autumn and early Warring States periods to massive infantry commands mired in prolonged engagements; a second shift in component force importance with the development of the cavalry at the end of the Warring States period and its increasing utilization to swiftly execute flexible tactics thereafter; and the gradual displacement of bronze weapons by iron versions over the centuries from the start of the Warring States period to the end of the early Han dynasty. While other changes are clearly discernible—many of them summarized in the Appendix—they are best characterized as evolutions rather than revolutions, easily encompassed within the vibrant tradition of Chinese military science.

Although warfare plagued China throughout its history, stimulating prodigious intellectual efforts to analyze its manifestations and fathom its principles, the number of extant military writings remains small. No doubt many early tactical treatises, being written on silk or bamboo slips before the invention of paper in the Han dynasty, perished before achieving the minimal circulation required to guarantee their survival, while other fragile manuscripts vanished prior to the adoption of printing in the T'ang. Moreover, the oft-remarked Chinese tendency to esteem the works of antiquity over contemporary writings contrived to designate the small number of the works that survived the innumerable cataclysmic events and centuries of interminable strife as canonical. However, because military science, including weapons and component forces, evolved only minimally from the Han dynasty onward, these older works retained an undiminished relevance that ensured their perpetuation. After much winnowing, revising, systematizing, commentary, and sustained growth in importance, seven important books were deemed fundamental expositions of doctrine and tactics—including Sun-tzu's famous *Art of War,* extensively drawn upon by the *Unorthodox Strategies*—and assembled into a standardized edition in the Sung dynasty entitled the *Seven Military Classics.* Although Ts'ao Ts'ao added a commentary to the *Art of War* during the Three Kingdoms period and wrote his own treatise, and many other generals and military officials did thereafter, none of them ever ranked in importance and influence with the *Seven Military Classics.* Numerous minor works, technical treatises, tactical manuals, and summary compilations appeared from the T'ang on, but, while undoubtedly known to the author of the *Unorthodox Strategies,* never received mention, thereby illustrating the continuing importance of the canonical texts in later theoretical thought.

One additional work requires mention: the *Military Methods,* a book probably composed in large part by Sun Pin—possibly Sun-tzu's great grandson—in the middle of the Warring States period. Because it was lost in the Han dynasty (and only rediscovered in the 1970s), the *Unorthodox Strategies* never incorporates any of its views into the tactical discussions. However, since the *Military Methods* preserves important early material and essentially constitutes an eighth military classic, a number of particularly illuminating passages are cited in our commentaries to the individual chapters.

The seven books of varying length and origin encompassed by the *Seven Military Classics* furnish the theoretical basis for virtually all the tactical discussions in the *Unorthodox Strategies,* with brief passages being quoted to summarily conclude each selection. The seven treatises, in their Sung dynasty canonical arrangement, are the *Art of War,* the *Wu-tzu,* the *Methods of the Ssu-ma* (*Ssu-ma Fa*), *Questions and Replies between T'ang T'ai-tsung and Li Wei-kung,* the *Three Strategies of Huang Shih-kung,* and *T'ai Kung's Six Secret Teachings.* Although uncertainty abounds regarding the authorship, dating, and extent to which these works are composites that draw upon common ground and preserve lost writings, the traditional order unquestionably is not chronological. For nearly a thousand years Sun-tzu's *Art of War* has generally been considered the oldest and greatest extant Chinese military work even though the purported author of the *Six Secret Teachings,* the T'ai Kung, was active five hundred years earlier than the historical Sun-tzu. The *Ssu-ma Fa* reputedly preserves materials dating back to the early Chou; the *Wu-tzu,* generally attributed to the great general Wu Ch'i, may have been recorded by his disciples and probably suffers from accretions; and the *Three Strategies* clearly postdates the *Wei Liao-tzu,* yet some traditionalists still vociferously associate it with the T'ai Kung. However, comparing the contents of these various works with actual historical battles, the likely evolution of warfare in China, and innumerable contemporary archaeological discoveries suggests (with many caveats and unstated qualifications) the following periodization and sequencing: initial period, the *Ssu-ma Fa* and the *Art of War;* second period, the *Wu-tzu;* third period, Sun Pin's *Military Methods,* the *Wei Liao-tzu,* the *Six Secret Teachings,* and finally the *Three Strategies;* and last, the T'ang or Sung dynasty *Questions and Replies.*

For the convenience of readers interested in the contextual background for material cited in the individual tactical discussions, extremely brief biographies of the purported authors—some of whom also appear in the historical incidents incorporated in the *Unorthodox Strategies*—and short discussions of the probable dates of composition, largely abstracted from the individual introductions found in our translation of the *Seven Military Classics,* are reprised in the introductory sketches below. However, much of the evidence for establishing composition dates remains tenuous, while the historical study of strategic thought and military concepts in China has only recently been systematically initiated.

T'ai Kung's Six Secret Teachings

The *Six Secret Teachings* purportedly records the T'ai Kung's political advice and tactical instructions to Kings Wen and Wu of the Chou dynasty in the mid-eleventh century B.C. Although the present book certainly dates from the Warring States period, some traditional scholars still believe it preserves at least vestiges of the oldest strata of Chinese military thought. The historic T'ai Kung has commonly been honored in China as the first famous general and the progenitor of strategic studies. A complete work that discusses not only strategy and tactics but also proposes the government measures necessary for forging effective state control and attaining national prosperity, the *Six Secret Teachings* is grounded upon, or perhaps projected back into, monumental historical events. The Chou kings presumably implemented many of these policies, enabling them to develop their agricultural and population base, gradually expand their small border domain, and secure the allegiance of the populace until they could finally launch the decisive military campaign that defeated the powerful Shang dynasty and overturned its six-hundred-year rule.

The *Ssu-ma Fa*

The *Ssu-ma Fa* is a terse, enigmatic text dating from about the fourth century B.C. (when it was probably compiled from materials originating in the Spring and Autumn period) that has traditionally been accorded far more authenticity than any of the other military writings. Virtually every account of its inception identifies it with the state of Ch'i, historically the fount of the innovative military studies that perhaps received their initial impetus from the T'ai Kung himself when he ruled as the first king of Ch'i and were subsequently advanced by Sun-tzu, Sun Pin, and Wei Liao-tzu. The title, *Ssu-ma Fa,* might be best translated as *The Methods of the Minister of War,* for the character *fa,* whose basic meaning is law, encompasses the concept of methods, standards, and techniques or art, as in the "art" of war. However, no single term adequately covers the content's scope because the *Ssu-ma Fa* discusses laws, regulations, government policies, military organization, military administration, discipline, basic values, grand strategy, and strategy.

One much disputed story associated with the book suggests that the famous general originally known as T'ien Jang-chü was instrumental in the great victories achieved by King Ching of Ch'i. Because he had held the post of Ssu-ma in this campaign, he was granted the privilege of assuming the title as a family surname. According to his brief biography in the *Shih Chi,* part of which provides the historical illustration for Chapter 14, "Awesomeness," when the *Ssu-ma Fa* was subsequently compiled under King Wei the book included his ideas and was thus initially entitled the *Military Methods of Ssu-ma Jang-chü.* Irrespective of this possible early evolution, the work probably assumed final form about the middle of the fourth century B.C., more than a hundred years after the death of Confucius. Unfortunately, the present book of 5 chapters merely preserves remnants of an extensive compilation that apparently once totaled 155 chapters in the Han dynasty. Fortunately these five seem to have been faithfully transmitted ever since the T'ang dynasty.

Sun-tzu's *Art of War*

Despite an extensive, extremely well known biography in the *Shih Chi,* because of the virtual absence of any other materials concerning his life and achievements, Sun-tzu continues to be an enigma. Not only are his background and early history completely unknown, it remains unclear whether he was born in Wu or Ch'i and whether he had studied military strategy and served in a command capacity before venturing to instruct the king of Wu or simply was a peripatetic thinker capitalizing upon an employment opportunity. However, it appears that he provided the king with the tactical methods and strategy for Wu's victorious campaign against the powerful state of Ch'u in 511 B.C. and may have played a similar role in subsequent victories over the aggressive states of Ch'i and Ch'in. Despite such highly visible successes, he certainly vanished from the historical stage by 500 B.C., reputedly of his own volition to avoid the inevitable death that seemed to befall all great military men in his era.

Traditionalists vociferously assert that the historical Sun-tzu portrayed in the *Shih Chi* biography actually composed the *Art of War*, but some skeptics have questioned his actions and existence on the basis of a few anachronisms coupled with the absence of any corroborative textual evidence. A balanced view that takes cognizance of the evolving nature of warfare, the rising need for military and bureaucratic specialization, the personalities involved, the complexity of the politics, and the fragility of recorded material might well conclude that Sun-tzu not only served as a strategist and possibly as a commander but also composed the core of the book that bears his name. Thereafter the essential teachings were probably transmitted within the family or a close-knit school of disciples, being improved and revised with the passing decades while gradually gaining wider dissemination. The early text may even have been edited by his famous descendant Sun Pin, who also extensively employed its teachings in his own *Military Methods*, simultaneously making the Sun name even more glorious.

Wu Ch'i's *Wu-tzu*

Unlike the semilegendary Sun-tzu, Wu Ch'i, the focal figure and speaker in the *Wu-tzu*, was a famous historical general who is even cited as an exemplar in several chapters of the *Unorthodox Strategies*. His military exploits and administrative achievements truly surpassed the ordinary, and shortly after his death his name became inextricably linked with Sun-tzu's. Born about 440 B.C. into the tumultuous era that witnessed the initial conflicts of the incessant warfare that would eventually reduce the number of powerful states from seven to one, he immediately realized that states could survive only if they fostered both military strength and sound government. While he attained great power and encouraged the development and preservation of distinctions, he personally eschewed the commanding general's visible comforts and shared every misery and hardship with his troops. Eventually he was murdered in Ch'u about 361 B.C., a victim of the enmity incurred by his draconian measures to strengthen central authority and the military.

According to subsequent historical writings, Wu Ch'i not only was never defeated in battle but rarely suffered the ignominy of a stalemate while compiling a remarkable record of decisive victories against the superior forces of entrenched states. Although often regarded as China's first great general, he equally garnered a reputation for impressive administrative reforms and innovations. Thus the work attributed to him, the *Wu-tzu,* not only numbers among the *Seven Military Classics* but has also long been valued as one of the basic foundations of Chinese military thought. Less strident than the *Art of War,* it seriously considers all aspects of war and battle preparation and suggests generally applicable techniques for resolving tactical situations. The core of the text was probably composed by Wu Ch'i himself then expanded and revised by his disciples, perhaps from their own memories or court recordings. Much of the original appears to have been lost, but what remains has been edited into a succinct, fairly systematic, and remarkably comprehensive work.

Sun Pin's *Military Methods*

In the centuries just before the founding of the first imperial dynasty in 221 B.C., four great military figures were commonly recognized as having been instrumental in strengthening their states and wresting power over the realm: Sun-tzu in Wu, Wu Ch'i in Wei, Shang Yang in Ch'in, and Sun Pin in Ch'i. Until recently only Sun Pin lacked his own work because one that had been identified with him in the Han imperial library, entitled *Military Methods,* had been lost, causing many scholars in later centuries to insist it had never existed. However, some two thousand years after its last recorded existence, remnants of his book were dramatically recovered in 1972 when a Han dynasty military official's tomb revealed a horde of bamboo strips that preserved numerous ancient writings on military, legal, and other subjects. Unfortunately, although many of the strips are perfectly preserved, over the centuries portions of others have suffered varying degrees of damage, ranging from complete physical disintegration to the partial obliteration of the brush-written ink characters. After long, painstaking reconstruction the contents have tentatively emerged, revealing incisive conceptions and integrated tactics that both draw upon and concretely expand Sun-tzu's earlier methods. Even in this overall imperfect condition the *Military Methods* remains a remarkable middle Warring States text, one that presumably embodies the views of the great strategist, probably a direct lineal descendant of Sun-tzu, who was active as Ch'i's chief tactician from 356 B.C. until 341 B.C.

and may have lived until near the end of the century. The victorious strategies for the two famous battles of Kuei-ling and Ma-ling, the latter recounted in the *Unorthodox Strategies* as the historical illustration for Chapter 30, "Knowledge," have always been attributed to Sun Pin.

The *Wei Liao-tzu*

The *Wei Liao-tzu* was named after a shadowy historical figure whose surname was Wei and personal name was Liao. (The character "tzu," meaning master and indicating respect, was added by the compilers of his book.) One view holds that Wei Liao probably lived in the last half of the fourth century B.C., an era when mendicant persuaders indiscriminately sought receptive ears among the various feudal lords, irrespective of their moral qualifications. Whatever his personal history, Wei Liao was a brilliant strategist and perceptive observer who realized that only by integrating the civil and martial could a state be assured of surviving in the tumultuous Warring States environment. Since he never illustrated his discussions with examples from personal military experience, he is not historically noted as a commander, and the book is almost devoid of actual tactics, it appears he was strictly a theoretician. However, his frequent citation of passages from numerous military writings and his detailed description of army organization and discipline provide evidence of his extensive military knowledge.

The style and historical content of the *Wei Liao-tzu* suggest it was composed about the end of the fourth century B.C. Based upon a partial bamboo-slip edition recently recovered, it clearly assumed present form before the Han dynasty in 206 B.C., contrary to skeptical claims denigrating it as a much later fabrication. Therefore, it might tentatively be concluded that the *Wei Liao-tzu* was based upon Wei Liao's court conversations with King Hui of Wei in the middle Warring States, perhaps with additional, detailed material about Ch'in's military organization appended by someone from his family or school within a century after his death.

The *Three Strategies of Huang Shih-kung*

Although there are numerous problems with the text of the *Three Strategies* and the usual questions about its authenticity, even if the book were a "valueless forgery" as claimed by the numerous Confucians who vehemently denounced its purported brutality from the Sung dynasty on, the work would still demand serious study because of its antiquity, complex content, and manifest influence on subsequent military thinkers in China and eventually

Japan. Based upon the concepts, language, and historical references incorporated in the text, it appears that the *Three Strategies* was written in reaction to the excesses of the Ch'in dynasty or possibly about the end of the Former Han dynasty, probably by a reclusive adherent of the Huang-Lao school who had expert knowledge of military affairs. This would account for the absence of many focal military topics, such as battlefield command and tactics, and the narrow focus upon government affairs in an age of peace.

Questions and Replies Between T'ang T'ai-tsung and Li Wei-kung

T'ang T'ai-tsung, who asks the questions and offers short observations in the classic, apparently received a Confucian education; therefore, he was thoroughly versed in the classics and histories, as well as being extremely skilled in the martial arts. He reportedly commanded troops by the age of fifteen and, after contributing to the establishment of the T'ang as both a strategist and heroic commander, was instrumental in subduing numerous challenges to the new state, including segments of the Western Turks. He finally became emperor by displacing his father in 627 A.D., although only after murdering his older brother, the designated heir. Stories of his prowess and famous horses abound in popular Chinese history, and he appears in several historical incidents in the *Unorthodox Strategies.*

As emperor he consciously cultivated the image of a proper ruler, one responsive to the needs of the people, willing to accept criticism and advice. The country was truly unified, both politically and culturally. Measures were enacted to reduce the plight of the people and stimulate the economy. Government expenditures were reduced, and effective administration was imposed throughout the nation. With the passage of time, and perhaps distance from the uncertainties of the initial period, he eventually became more independent, intolerant, and extravagant. However, the formative years of the T'ang saw the rebirth of thought and culture, the resurgence of a civilization that would dazzle Asia for three centuries.

Li Ching—also know by his honorific title of Li Wei-kung—who lived from 571 to 649, began his career under the Sui, serving in the northwest in a military capacity. One of T'ang T'ai-tsung's earliest associates and supporters, he also commanded T'ang troops in the suppression of both internal and external challenges, the great conquest of the Western Turks (for which he became famous), and the pacification of the South. Thus if the *Questions and Replies* preserves his conversations with T'ang T'ai-tsung, they had personally employed many of the book's concepts and strategies in critical battles. However, it differs significantly from the other classics, being more of a survey of earlier works together with a wide-ranging discussion and appreciation of their theories and contradictions, punctuated by lessons learned from personal experience.

The *Unorthodox Strategies,* an eclectic work that derives its tactical principles from the preceding military corpus, not only thus continued the vision of the *Questions and Replies,* but also provided a precedent for future writings, such as the incisive Ming dynasty *Essential Ruminations from a Straw Hut.* The unknown author has effectively abstracted the essential principles of Chinese military science, saving the reader innumerable pages of irrelevant and often redundant passages, while also presenting a syncretic theory of maneuver warfare that stresses flexibility, strategic power, and incisive tactics. Moreover, while commentators over the centuries frequently mentioned famous battles or well-known incidents in conjunction with their textual explications, the *Unorthodox Strategies* is unique in systematically illustrating the tactical principles with concrete events as part of the core discussion. In these illustrations the author's command of the historical literature may clearly be seen, for rather than being limited to famous battles his selections encompass the complete range, from the insignificant to the epoch-making. Regrettably his own name and military achievements will probably remain forever unknown.

1 Estimates 計

Tactical Discussion

In the Tao of warfare, calculation is foremost. Before engaging in combat first estimate the relative sagacity and stupidity of the generals, the enemy's strengths and weaknesses, the numerousness and paucity of the troops, the difficulty and ease of the terrain, and the fullness or emptiness of the provisions. If you send the army forth only after thoroughly analyzing such estimates, it will always be victorious. Sun-tzu's *Art of War* states: "Analyzing the enemy, taking control of victory, estimating ravines and defiles, the distant and near, is the Tao of the superior general."

Historical Illustration

At the end of the Later Han dynasty, Liu Pei of the kingdom of Shu occupied Hsiang-yang. Thrice he went to request Chu-ko Liang's strategic advice. Liang said: "Ever since Chung Chuo seized military power from the Han emperor, the number of heroes and valiants that have appeared to bestride the provinces and unite the commanderies is beyond counting. Compared with Yüan Shao, Ts'ao Ts'ao had little fame and few troops. However, Ts'ao Ts'ao eventually subjugated Yüan Shao by turning weakness into strength. It wasn't simply a question of the seasons of Heaven but must also have been due to human plans. Now that Ts'ao has already gathered a mass of a million, constricting the emperor and thereby exerting command over the feudal lords, you certainly cannot directly confront his forces. Meanwhile, Sun Ch'üan's family has occupied the region east of the Yangtze, the domain of the kingdom of Wu, for three generations. His kingdom's terrain is precipitous, the people are attached to the government, and the worthy and able assist him. His kingdom can be considered a potential basis of support but not an objective for conquest.

The province of Ching-chou to the north occupies the Han River region. Its strategic advantages extend throughout the south coastal region, and to the east it connects Wu and Hui. To the west it communicates with the regions of Pa and Shu. Ching-chou is martial territory, but the ruler is unable to defend it. Heaven has apparently provided it for you as a resource. General, why not think about it?

Furthermore, the province of Yi-chou to the southwest is precipitous and obstructed, encompassing fertile fields that extend a thousand kilometers. It is the earth of Heaven's warehouse. The founder of the Han dynasty relied upon it to establish his emperorship. Liu Chang, who occupies it, is obtuse and weak, while Chang Lu, who controls the region to the north, where the people are submissive and the state wealthy, does not know how to preserve the populace and mitigate their difficulties. The wise and capable officers there are hoping for an enlightened ruler.

Now you, general, are a descendant of the Han imperial family. Your credibility and righteousness are manifest throughout the four seas. Gather and unify the stalwarts of the realm; think of the worthy as a thirsty man thinks of water. Then extend your grasp over the provinces of Ching-chou and Yi-chou, securing their cliffs and passes; establish harmonious relations with the various barbarians in the west and be conciliatory to those in the south; and externally form an alliance with Sun Ch'üan while internally rectifying your own administration. When revolution transforms the realm, order one of your superior generals to command Ching-chou's forces in an advance toward Wan and Lo while you personally lead the troops from Yi-chou. If you go forth through Ch'in-chou, who among the common people will not welcome you with baskets of rice and pots of wine? If it is truly thus, hegemony can be achieved and the house of Han will flourish."

"Excellent," exclaimed Liu Pei. Events subsequently unfolded as foretold.

Commentary

Although the quotation summarizing the tactical discussion stems from Sun-tzu's tenth chapter, "Configurations of Terrain," the title for this opening selection—"Estimates"—mirrors the *Art of War*'s leading chapter, "Initial Estimations." For Sun-tzu, warfare was the "greatest affair of state, the basis of life or death, the Tao to survival or extinction," and had therefore to be analytically approached to determine whether any war, as well as individual engagements, would be feasible. Careful deliberations focused upon comparatively evaluating the enemy and oneself according to a score of parameters, calculating weighted values for each of them with some sort of tally board to assess the overall probability for success, not unlike Western military intelligence procedures in recent decades. The following key sentences from Sun-tzu's "Initial Estimations" indicate the critical parameters:

> Structure warfare according to the following five factors, evaluate it comparatively through estimations, and seek out its true nature. The first is termed the Tao; the second, Heaven; the third, Earth; the fourth, generals; and the fifth the laws for military organization and discipline.
>
> Thus when making a comparative evaluation through estimations, seeking out its true nature, ask: Which ruler has the Tao? Which general has greater ability? Who has gained the advantages of Heaven and Earth? Whose laws and orders are more thoroughly implemented? Whose forces are stronger? Whose officers and troops are better trained? Whose rewards and punishments are clearer?

Historically, the region of Shu (part of modern Szechwan) proved essential not only to Liu Pei's efforts to forge a viable kingdom amidst the turmoil of the Later Han dynasty's final years but equally in Ch'in's meteoric rise to found the first, brief imperial dynasty. Rich in materials and resources, this remote region also formed a natural bastion whose forbidding terrain allowed a few entrenched troops to easily withstand vastly superior foes. Chuko Liang's strategic analysis epitomizes the developed stage of grand strategy and political thought at the end of the Later Han dynasty, providing evidence of a willingness to simultaneously form alliances and exploit weaknesses to achieve long-range objectives. Through his well-known perspicacity the kingdom of Shu managed to survive for nearly three decades in the face of Ts'ao Ts'ao's overwhelmingly superior forces and continue for another three after his death, largely due to the economic achievements brought about by his administrative skills. However, while garnering fame for tactical foresight and military acumen, his actual combat record was undistinguished at best, notwithstanding the incident recounted in Chapter 9, "Trust," his cleverness in Chapter 43, "The Vacuous," and his unspectacular death recorded in Chapter 49, "Security." However, the weakness of the resulting nominal alliance between Liu Pei and Sun Ch'üan was subsequently exploited by Ts'ao Ts'ao, as recounted in the historical incident for Chapter 22, "Alliances."

2 Plans 謀

Tactical Discussion

If you attack the enemy just after they have formulated their strategy, it will ruin their plans and force them to submit. The *Art of War* states: "The highest realization of warfare is to attack plans."

Historical Illustration

During the Spring and Autumn period Duke P'ing of Chin wanted to attack the state of Ch'i, so he dispatched Fan Chao to observe Ch'i's government. At a feast in his honor Duke Ching of Ch'i presented him with a cup of wine, but Fan Chao asked to drink from the ruler's goblet. The duke ordered that his cup be brought to his guest. Fan Chao had already drunk from it when Yen Tzu seized the goblet and exchanged it for another cup. Later Fan Chao, pretending to be drunk, unhappily rose to dance. He asked the Music Master: "Can you perform the music of Ch'eng-chou for me? I want to dance to it." The Music Master said: "Your ignorant servant is not familiar with it."

When Fan Chao went out Duke Ching said: "Chin is a great state. He came to observe our government. Now that you have angered this great state's emissary, what will we do?" Yen Tzu said: "I observed that Fan Chao was not ignorant of the proper forms of court behavior but sought to embarrass our state, so I did not comply." The Music Master said: "The music of Ch'eng-chou is the music of the Son of Heaven. Only the ruler of men can dance to it. Now Fan Chao, although a subject, wanted to dance to the music of the Son of Heaven. Therefore I did not perform it."

Fan Chao returned to Chin and reported to Duke P'ing: "Ch'i cannot yet be attacked. I tried to insult their ruler but Yen Tzu realized it. I wanted to act contrary to their forms of court behavior, but the Music Master perceived it." Confucius subsequently said: "The saying, 'to shatter an enemy a thousand miles off without going beyond the banquet hall' refers to Yen Tzu."

Commentary

The thrust of this selection derives from Sun-tzu's chapter entitled "Planning Offensives," where he states: "Subjugating the enemy's army without fighting is the true pinnacle of excellence. Thus one who excels at employing the military subjugates other people's armies without engaging in battle, captures other people's fortified cities without attacking them, and destroys other people's states without prolonged fighting. He must fight under Heaven with the paramount aim of 'preservation.' Thus his weapons will not become dull, and the gains can be preserved. This is the strategy for planning offensives."

Despite the passage's orientation, neither Sun-tzu nor the other ancient military strategists ever advocated avoiding battle when it proved necessary. However, they first directed their efforts toward wining through intimidation, to simply overawing the enemy, whether by military power, economic might, or surpassing Virtue. Thereafter they focused upon thwarting the enemy rather than confronting them head-on in a battle of attrition, particularly when venturing beyond their own state's borders. The enemy's plans might be frustrated by severing their supply lines, prepositioning holding forces along a projected route of march, deploying in unexpected strength, or simply refusing to give battle, remaining ensconced within heavily fortified positions as discussed in Chapters 38 and 77, "Defense" and "Refusing Battle" respectively.

The historical illustration reflects the widespread belief that it would be both difficult and costly to assault a state effectively ruled by a virtuous monarch supported by capable advisers. Naturally other criteria, such as military strength, organization, and expertise were also important, but the presence of competent administrators and talented generals tended to deter precipitous attacks, requiring instead that psychological measures be employed to distance the ruler from his advisors, as well as corrupting the latter through various inducements, such as riches and beautiful women, as espoused by the T'ai Kung in the much excoriated portions of the *Six Secret Teachings.* Numerous ruses and tests were formulated to evaluate other men, especially commanders and the ruler's assistants; many are still preserved by the various military writings. Yen Tzu himself gained a reputation as a statesman and diplomat, numerous stories and other disparate material eventually coalescing around his name some centuries after his death.

3 Spies 間

Tactical Discussion

Whenever planning to conduct a major military expedition, you should first employ spies to determine the enemy's troop strength, emptiness or fullness, and movement and rest, and only thereafter mobilize the army. Great achievements can then be attained, and you will always be victorious in combat. The *Art of War* states: "There are no areas in which one does not employ spies."

Historical Illustration

In the sixth century, during the Northern and Southern Dynasties period, general Wei Shu-yü of the Northern Chou, whose personal name was Hsiao K'uan, succeeded in defending and protecting the area about Yü-pi through his virtuous actions. Hsiao K'uan excelled in pacifying and governing the people and was able to gain their willing allegiance. All the spies he dispatched into Northern Ch'i fully exhausted their abilities. Moreover, Hsiao K'uan also bribed many Northern Ch'i citizens with gold for information and reports and thus knew all about Ch'i's actions and court affairs.

Ch'i's minister Hu Lü-kuang, whose style name was Ming Yüeh (Bright Moon), was worthy and courageous. Hsiao K'uan was deeply troubled about him. Northern Chou's chief of military planning, Ch'ü Yen, who was thoroughly versed in milfoil divination, advised Hsiao K'uan: "Next year Ch'i's court will certainly be marked by mutual killing." Thereupon Hsiao K'uan ordered Ch'ü Yen to fabricate a prophetic verse that said: "A 'hundred pints' will fly up to Heaven, a 'bright moon' will shine on Ch'ang-an." At that time a "hundred pints" was equal to a "hu," Hu Lü-kuang's surname. Additional verses read: "The high mountain, unpushed, will crumble of itself, the hu tree, unsupported, will become established by itself." Hsiao K'uan then ordered several spies to memorize these lines and spread them about Ch'i's capital. When Tsu Hsiao-cheng, who had recently clashed with Hu Lü-kuang, heard them he further embellished the lines, and Hu Lü-kuang, known as "Bright Moon," was eventually executed because of it. When Emperor Wu of the Northern Chou learned about Lü-kuang's death, he declared a general amnesty, fully mobilized the army, and subsequently exterminated the Northern Ch'i.

Commentary

Sun-tzu's chapter entitled "Employing Spies," from which the tactical quotation derives, berates rulers for their reluctance to offer the generous rewards necessary to attract and motivate spies. Sun-tzu emphasized the need for comprehensive military and political intelligence, as did most of the other military writers, and was appalled by the vast expenditures wasted in mounting inadequately conceived and planned campaigns. The chapter states: "The means by which enlightened rulers and sagacious generals moved and conquered others, that their achievements surpassed the masses, was advance knowledge. Advance knowledge cannot be gained from ghosts and spirits, inferred from phenomena, or projected from the measures of Heaven, but must be gained from men for it is the knowledge of the enemy's true situation." To counter the prejudice that wise monarchs neither need nor retain spies he cited famous examples from among the great sages and moral paragons of antiquity, asserting that they played a vital role in the rise of the earliest dynasties.

General Wei Shu-yü achieved a lasting historical reputation for his skill in employing secret agents, essentially confirming Sun-tzu's view that "Unless someone has the wisdom of a Sage, he cannot use spies; unless he is benevolent and righteous, he cannot employ spies; unless he is subtle and perspicacious, he cannot perceive the substance in intelligence reports." However, the historical incident also illustrates the power of rumor and prophetic verse throughout Chinese history. Several dynasties, including the Han and T'ang, arose in part because of such prophecies, while many men were condemned because they were mentioned in rumors or were said to have sought confirmation of their prospects for revolutionary acts through divination.

The verses themselves illustrate the nature of Chinese word play. In the Northern Chou's era a "hu" was a large measure for corn and grain equal to "a hundred pints," but was also Hu Lü-kuang's surname, so the "hundred pints" was immediately understood as referring to him. The "bright moon" of the first couplet, simply being his style name, reinforced the identification. The second couplet turns upon the emperor's surname being "kao," translated as "high" in "high mountain," implying that the emperor would perish by himself, while the second half asserts that the "hu" tree—a tree name formed by adding a "wood" signifier to the Chinese character identical with Hu Lü-kuang's surname and similarly pronounced—would gain its position even without external support. Naturally the emperor assumed the worst and reacted precipitously, as desired.

4 Elite Forces 選

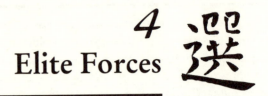

Tactical Discussion

Whenever engaging in combat with an enemy, you must select courageous generals and fierce troops, forming them into an advance front. On the one hand this will strengthen their resolve; on the other it will suppress the enemy's awesomeness. The *Art of War* states: "An army that lacks a properly selected vanguard is termed 'routed.'"

Historical Illustration

In the twelfth year of the Chien-an reign period (207 A.D.), Yüan Shang and Yüan Hsi fled to Shang-ku commandery, where the Wu Huan, a minority people, had mounted several harmful border incursions. Ts'ao Ts'ao went forth on a punitive campaign against them. By midsummer he had reached Wu-chung, but in early autumn there was extensive flooding, rendering the road along the marshes impassable. T'ien Ch'ou offered to act as their local guide, to which Ts'ao Ts'ao agreed. T'ien led the troops forth from Lu-lung Pass, but the road was blocked by the overflowing waters. Therefore they cut into the mountainsides to fill the valley lowlands for some five hundred miles. They passed through Pai-t'an district, traversed P'ing-kang and the Hsien-pei administrative region, and penetrated Liu-ch'eng district in the east. However, before they had advanced two hundred miles their barbarian enemies had learned of their coming. Yüan Shang and Yüan Hsi, together with others, such as T'a-tun, khan of the Wu Huan; Lou-pan, khan of the Liao Hsi; and Neng-ch'en-ti-chih, khan of the Yu Pei-p'ing, in command of several tens of thousands of cavalry, came forth to counter them. In midautumn Ts'ao Ts'ao's forces ascended Mt. Pai-lang and suddenly encountered the enemy's multitudes. As Ts'ao Ts'ao's supply train was far behind and his mailed soldiers few, those about him were all afraid. Ts'ao Ts'ao then climbed up higher and observed that out in the distance the barbarian troops had not yet deployed into ordered formations, so he loosed his troops to suddenly strike them, deputing Chang Liao's forces to act as an advance front. The barbarian masses were horrendously shattered and Ts'ao Ts'ao's forces beheaded T'a-tun together with numerous high-ranking individuals. More than 200,000 Han and barbarian soldiers surrendered to Ts'ao Ts'ao.

Commentary

Sun-tzu's chapter entitled "Configurations of Terrain" discusses two topics—specific configurations of terrain and issues of command and control. The quotation abstracted above, embedded in a discussion of major command failures, in full runs as follows: "If a general, unable to fathom his enemy, engages a large number with a small number or attacks the strong with the weak while the army lacks a properly selected vanguard, it is termed 'routed.'" In the historical illustration, Ts'ao Ts'ao succeeded despite attacking a numerically superior foe because he seized the moment and exploited the enemy's unpreparedness by suddenly assaulting them with elite troops, as advocated by this selection's tactical principle.

In addition to the importance of a strong advance front or vanguard, the ancient military writers often stressed the general need for elite troops that could penetrate deployments or otherwise throw an enemy into chaos. For example, the great general Wu Ch'i asserted:

> The ruler of a strong state must evaluate his people. Among the people, those who have courage and strength should be assembled into one unit. Those who take pleasure in advancing into battle and exerting their strength to manifest their loyalty and courage should be assembled into another unit. Those who can climb high and traverse far, who are nimble and fleet, should be assembled into a unit. Officials of the king who have lost their positions and want to show their merit to their ruler should be assembled into a unit. Those who abandoned their cities or left their defensive positions and want to eradicate the disgrace should

> also be assembled into a unit. These five will constitute the army's disciplined, elite troops. With three thousand such men, from within one can strike out and break any encirclement or from without break into any city and slaughter the defenders.

In the *Six Secret Teachings* King Wu states: "In general, when employing the army it is essential to have military chariots, courageous cavalry, a first-assault wave, a hand-picked vanguard, and then a perceived opportunity to strike the enemy." Moreover, an entire chapter of the book—"Selecting Warriors"—is devoted to the characteristics that mark naturally courageous warriors and the background of others who, shamed by past experience, might also be expected to serve valiantly.

5 The Infantry 步

Tactical Discussion

Whenever infantry units engage chariot or cavalry forces in combat, they must rely upon mounds and hills, ravines and defiles, forests and trees in order to be victorious. If they encounter level, easy roads they must deploy into a square formation and erect palisades around the perimeter. When the horses, baggage wagons, and infantrymen are all inside, the infantry forces should be divided into holding and assault forces. While the holding forces defend the formation, the assault forces should go forth to engage the enemy in combat. When the assault forces defend the formation, the holding forces should go out to fight.

If the enemy attacks one side, then two of your units should send forth troops, proceeding by way of their flanks to overwhelm them. If the enemy attacks two sides, you should divide your forces and harass them from the rear. If the enemy attacks all four sides, you should redeploy into a circular formation, dividing your troops into four in order to attack them on all fronts. If the enemy flees in defeat, you should employ cavalry to pursue them and have your infantry forces follow behind them. This is the method for certain victory. The *Six Secret Teachings* states: "When infantry engage in combat with chariots and cavalry, they must rely on hills and mounds, ravines and defiles. If you lack ravines and defiles, then order our officers and troops to set up barriers and caltrops."

Historical Illustration

In the Five Dynasties period, General Chou Te-wei of the Chin, who held the post of Military Commissioner for Lu-lung, relying upon courage alone, disparaged the enemy and neglected defensive measures along the border. Consequently, he eventually lost the strategic Yü-kuan pass. Moreover, every time the Khitan grazed their flocks in the area between Ying-chou and P'ing-chou, they launched incursions into Hsin-chou. When General Chou again tried to capture them he was not victorious and was even forced to flee to Yu-chou. The Khitan besieged him there for two hundred days, so the situation within the fortified city became perilous and distressed.

Li Ssu-yüan heard about the siege and arranged with Li Ts'un-hsü to assemble seventy thousand infantrymen and cavalry at Yi-chou in order to rescue him. From Yi-chou they went out northward, their route of march passing over the heights of Mt. Ta-fang and along the torrents down to the east. Li Ssu-yüan had his adopted son Ts'ung-k'o take command of three thousand cavalrymen and form the vanguard. They advanced as far as the mouth of the mountain where the Khitan intercepted them with ten thousand cavalrymen, causing all the generals and warriors to turn white.

Li Ssu-yüan then advanced with a hundred cavalrymen, removed his helmet, brandished his whip, and addressed the Khitan in their native language: "Without cause you have violated our border area. The king of Chin has therefore ordered me to take command of this mass of a million cavalrymen, go out to directly assault your city of Hsi-lou, and obliterate your race." Thereupon he reared his horse, whipped him fervently, and thrice penetrated the Khitan formation, killing one of their leaders. To his rear the army advanced in unison, and the Khitan soldiers retreated. Thus Chin's besieged forces were at last able to get out.

Li Ts'un-hsü next ordered his infantrymen to cut down some trees to fashion the wooden stakes needed for the deer-horn formation. Each man held a long wooden stake in order to create a palisade. When the Khitan encircled the temporary stockade, Li's soldiers fired ten thousand crossbows at them from within. Their falling arrows obscured the sun, while the dead and wounded Khitan soldiers and horses blocked the road.

Thereafter they proceeded toward Yu-chou where the Khitan had assumed formation and awaited them. Li Ts'un-hsü ordered his infantrymen to deploy to his rear and remain alert without initiating any movement. He further ordered his weary and weak soldiers to drag firewood and burn grass while advancing. The smoke and dust covered the Heavens, so the Khitan, unable to determine their strength, drummed an advance into combat. Li Ts'un-hsü then raced his forces forward from the rear to exploit the opportunity, going on to severely defeat the Khitans. Gathering up their multitudes like rolling up a mat, the Khitan departed via the northern mouth of the mountain, their captured and slain being counted by the tens of thousands. Subsequently they lifted the siege of Yu-chou.

Commentary

This chapter and the following one focus upon a common tactical problem—combat units suddenly encountering an enemy consisting of different, generally superior, component forces. In antiquity it would have been infantry confronted by more mobile chariots or cavalry, while today it might be a light infantry company overwhelmed by tanks or suppressed by helicopter gunships. In such situations the beleaguered unit, irrespective of contemporary advanced weaponry, such as antitank rockets and hand-held ground-to-air missiles, must inevitably shape the battle to exploit the immediate terrain, especially narrows and heavy growth, and thereby diminish the enemy's mobility and firepower advantage while executing the tactical maneuvers necessary to bring their own weapons to bear.

The tactical quotation is derived from two paragraphs found in a chapter entitled "The Infantry in Battle" in the *Six Secret Teachings.* As they explicate parts of the historical illustration, they merit quoting in full:

> The T'ai Kung said: "When infantry engage in battle with chariots and cavalry, they must rely on hills and mounds, ravines and defiles. The long weapons and strong crossbows should occupy the fore; the short weapons and weak crossbows should occupy the rear, firing and resting in turn. Even if large numbers of the enemy's chariots and cavalry should arrive, they must maintain a solid formation and fight intensely while skilled soldiers and strong crossbowmen prepare against attacks from the rear."
>
> King Wu said: "Suppose there are no hills or mounds, ravines or defiles. The enemy arrives, and it is both numerous and martial. Their chariots and cavalry outflank us on both sides, and they are making sudden thrusts against our front

> and rear positions. Our Three Armies are terrified and in chaotic defeat. What should we do?"
>
> The T'ai Kung replied: "Order our officers and troops to set out spiked horse barriers and wooden caltrops, arraying the oxen and horses by units of five in their midst, and have them establish a four-sided martial assault formation. When you see the enemy's chariots and cavalry are about to advance, our men should evenly spread out the caltrops and dig ditches around the rear, making them five feet deep and wide. It is called the 'Fate of Dragon Grass.' Our men should take hold of the spiked horse barriers and advance on foot. The chariots should be arrayed as ramparts and pushed forward and back. Whenever they stop set them up as fortifications. Our skilled soldiers and strong crossbowmen should prepare against the left and right flanks. Afterward, order the Three Armies to fervently fight without respite."

In "Strategic Military Power" Sun-tzu also comments about the employment of circular formations when under duress: "Intermixed and turbulent, the fighting appears chaotic, but they cannot be made disordered. In turmoil and confusion, their deployment is circular and they cannot be defeated." Moreover, the T'ai Kung advocated the tactical employment of "dust screens": "Have our older and weaker soldiers drag brushwood to stir up the dust, beat the drums, and shout. In this situation the enemy will not dare come forward." Of course square formations, such as those used by the famous Swiss pikemen, were also employed in European warfare to counter the disruptive potential of direct cavalry assaults.

6 The Cavalry 騎

Tactical Discussion

Whenever cavalry units engage infantry forces in combat, should they encounter mountains, forests, ravines, defiles, bodies of water, or wetlands, they must urgently proceed through them and quickly depart. These six constitute terrain on which defeat is certain; do not engage in combat on them. If you want to fight, you must secure level, easy terrain where the cavalry will be unobstructed in both advancing and retreating. Then when you engage an enemy infantry force, you will invariably be victorious. A tactical principle states: "Employ cavalry on easy terrain."

Historical Illustration

In the Five Dynasties period, about 910 A.D., King Chuang-tsung of Chin, soon to become emperor of the Later T'ang, wanted to rescue Chao and thus ended up opposing Liang's forces about five miles from Po-hsiang. The king's forces encamped north of the Yeh River. Although Chin's troops were few, Liang's soldiers under the command of General Wang Ching-jen, while numerous, included few elite forces. When Chin's forces spied the enemy in the distance they blanched. General Chou Te-wei exhorted his troops: "They are nothing but ordinary men from Pien and Sung, soon to be defeated." He then withdrew and informed the king of the situation. King Chuang-tsung said: "We have brought our army out a thousand miles, so it would be advantageous to quickly engage in battle. If we do not exploit our strategic power to quickly attack them, it will allow the enemy to learn our true numbers, after which it will no longer be possible to implement our plans." General Chou replied: "Not so! The people of Liang excel at fighting from fortified defenses and are not adept at open field combat. Our own strength in seizing victory lies with the cavalry. Cavalry are adept in warfare on broad plains and expansive wilds. Right now our army is encamped upriver, perilously close to the enemy's position, hardly terrain that would be advantageous to us."

Displeased, King Chuang-tsung retired to lie down in his tent. None of the generals dared to go in to see him. General Chou then spoke with the Supervisor of the Army, Chang Teng-yeh: "The king is angry that his old general has not quickly engaged in battle. It is not that I am afraid but that our troops are few and we are within the river's width of the enemy's gate. Liang's forces may have obtained boats and oars to cross the river, but we lack similar equipment. It would be better to withdraw the army to Hao-yi and thereby entice the enemy to leave their encampment, disrupting and laboring them. With such a strategy we can be victorious." Teng-yeh went in and spoke with King Chuang-tsung: "General Chou is an old general who well understands military affairs. I ask that you do not precipitously dismiss his words." King Chuang-tsung hastily got up and said: "I just realized it."

Shortly thereafter General Chou's soldiers captured a Liang reconnaissance patrol and interrogated them about General Wang Ching-jen's activities. They advised that he was constructing several hundred boats to form a pontoon bridge. General Chou then brought them in to see King Chuang-tsung. The king laughed: "Liang is acting just as you expected." Thereupon they withdrew the army to Hao-yi.

Subsequently, General Chou dispatched three hundred cavalrymen to provoke firefights with Liang's encampment, personally following after them with three thousand elite cavalrymen. Enraged, General Wang came forth with all his forces and fought running battles with General Chou over several tens of miles. When they reached south of Hao-yi both sides deployed into fixed formation, and Liang's army then stretched across the fields for six or seven miles. King Chuang-tsung whipped his horse, ascended the heights, looked out and happily said: "Level plains and shallow grass—we can advance and withdraw. Truly this is terrain where we can wrest victory." Thereupon he dispatched someone to inform General Chou, "We should now engage them in battle."

General Chou again remonstrated with him: "Without any preparation Liang's forces hastily came forth and have now traveled far. Moreover, they have fought running battles with us. Since they came forth so quickly, they certainly did not have any time to prepare rations; even if they have any rations, they have not had the leisure to eat them. By mid-day their men and horses will be hungry and thirsty, and their army will certainly withdraw. If we attack them while they are withdrawing, we will inevitably be victorious." About midafternoon heavy dust began to arise within Liang's deployment. General Chou ordered the beating of the drums, and with a tumultuous clamor they advanced to attack, Liang's army then suffering a great defeat.

Commentary

The Chinese military writers were acutely aware that terrain imposes inescapable constraints on component forces and the essential baggage train. Although the tactical principle cited above indirectly derives from the great T'ang general Li Ching (to whom the *Questions and Replies* is nominally attributed), the most extensive, clearly formulated analyses are preserved in the *Six Secret Teachings,* a late Warring States work. For example, the chapter entitled "Cavalry in Battle" enumerates "ten situations that can produce victory and nine that will result in defeat." Among those conducive to defeating cavalry is the presence of numerous obstacles; inherently difficult terrain, such as wetlands or muddy ground; and constricted passages that sufficiently reduce mobility to allow destructive firepower to be effectively employed. Among these, the T'ai Kung emphasized mountains, deep valleys, heavy vegetation, forests, gullies, ravines, hillocks, and quagmires.

The historical illustration reprises the famous battle of Pai-hsiang where the great Chin general Chou Te-wei applied several fundamental tactical principles to ultimately wrest victory even though being severely outnumbered. First, despite the king's impatience, he refrained from committing his forces to combat until the conditions for victory had been achieved. As Sun-tzu said, "The victorious army first realizes the conditions for victory and then seeks to engage in battle. The vanquished army fights first and then seeks victory." Second, he understood the enemy's strengths and weaknesses, having previously led successful cavalry attacks against overwhelming odds when Liang's commander mounted an awesome display of some thirty thousand men arrayed in terrifyingly shining armor and thus compelled them to cross the river to assume their position at Pai-hsiang.

Since Liang's forces were apparently composed mainly, if not exclusively, of infantry and had proven themselves less capable in open-field fighting, General Chou chose to provoke them into abandoning their entrenched position to recklessly race out onto the nearby open wilds. By deliberately manipulating and destabilizing them just as advocated by most of the military writers from Sun-tzu on, he exploited General Wang's arrogance and short temper, two well-known character flaws predisposing any commander to likely defeat. Thereafter, instead of hastily mounting his own attack, General Chou waited for the enemy's spirits to flag and their hunger to grow, thus implementing another of Sun-tzu's fundamental concepts, manipulating spirit or *ch'i.* (The psychology of *ch'i* is extensively discussed in the *Unorthodox Strategies,* particularly in Chapters 73 and 74, "Anger" and "Spirit" respectively.) Finally, knowing that armies become most vulnerable when attempting to disengage and withdraw, he loosed his well-rested and well-fed cavalry forces to capitalize upon the disorganization brought about by their wheeling about and overwhelm them. Throughout, the battle was a paradigm exercise in rational command and control.

Sun Pin, in his chapter entitled "Ten Questions" in the *Military Methods,* essentially advocated the same tactics for such situations:

> Suppose our army encounters the enemy and both establish encampments. Our chariots and cavalry are numerous, but our men and weapons are few. If the enemy's men are ten times ours, how should we attack them?
>
> To attack them, carefully avoid ravines and narrows; break open a route and lead them, coercing them toward easy terrain. Even though the enemy is ten times more numerous, easy terrain will be conducive to our chariots and cavalry, and our Three Armies can attack. This is the Tao for striking infantry.

7 Amphibious Strategies 舟

Tactical Discussion

Whenever you engage an enemy in combat along or on rivers and lakes, it is necessary to have boats and oars. Moreover, you should assume a position upwind or upstream. One who is upwind can, by exploiting the wind, employ an incendiary attack to set the enemy afire. One who is upstream can utilize the current's strategic power to ram the enemy with high-walled war vessels. In such cases you will always be victorious in battle. The *Art of War* states: "One who wants to engage in combat does not go contrary to the current's flow."

Historical Illustration

In the Spring and Autumn period Ho-lü, future king of Wu, attacked the state of Ch'u. Ch'u ordered their prime minister to divine about the battle's outcome, which turned out to be inauspicious. Prince Tzu Yü, the Minister of War, said: "We have gained a superior position upstream, so how can it be inauspicious?" Ch'u subsequently engaged Wu in battle, employing massive, high-walled vessels to suddenly penetrate Wu's flotilla. Wu's strategic power was therefore weakened, and their army found it difficult to fend off Ch'u's land forces. Eventually Wu's army was badly defeated.

Commentary

Although Chinese civilization largely developed along the Yellow and Yangtze River basins, warfare in the ancient period tended to be concentrated on the central plains and in the nearby mountains. Accordingly, despite China's numerous lakes and smaller rivers, the classic military writings of the Warring States period, include Sun-tzu's *Art of War,* virtually ignore amphibious engagements. Even the lengthy *Six Secret Teachings* devotes only a few paragraphs to the problems raised by fighting along rivers or across lakes and generally echoes many other works in advocating that armies avoid such terrain except in desperate circumstances. However, everyone knew how to exploit the current's strategic power and launch a downstream attack, as may be seen in the Spring and Autumn conflict between Ch'u and Wu, which coincidentally witnessed the extensive use of ships to transport invasion-bound troops. Moreover, the southeastern part of the country, site of the states of Wu and Yüeh, was a particularly wet area along the coast containing great marshes and lakes that made chariot warfare almost impossible but simultaneously stimulated the development of infantry forces. Generals necessarily developed tactics for river confrontations, such as those sketchily preserved in the early *Tso Chuan*, but the military theoreticians apparently avoided the subject. Apart from some brief lines in Sun Pin's *Military Methods*, one of Sun-tzu's paragraphs constitutes the fullest expression in any of the classical writings:

> After crossing rivers you must distance yourself from them. If the enemy is fording a river to advance, do not confront them in the water. When half their forces have crossed, it will be advantageous to strike them. If you want to engage the enemy in battle, do not array your forces near the river to confront the invader but look for tenable ground and occupy the heights. Do not confront the current's flow. This is the way to deploy the army where there are rivers.

Sun-tzu also devoted a full chapter to incendiary warfare, otherwise undiscussed in the military classics even though incendiary attacks were obviously employed in antiquity, as evidenced by the advice provided in the *Six Secret Teachings* and the *Military Methods* for defending against them, as will be discussed in Chapter 27, "Preparation" and again in Chapter 66, "Incendiary Strategies."

8 Chariots 車

Tactical Discussion

Whenever engaging cavalry or infantry in battle on broad plains or expansive wastes, you must employ rectangular, enclosed chariots and deer-horn chariots in square formations. Then you will be victorious because they will furnish the means to control the expenditure of energy, provide a defense to the fore, and organize and constrain the regiments and squads of five. A tactical principle from the *Questions and Replies* states: "On expansive terrain employ chariot formations."

Historical Illustration

In 279 A.D., during the Western Chin dynasty, Yang Hsin, Inspector General for Liang-chou commandery, fell into discord with the Ch'iang and Jung peoples and was slain. The region west of the Yellow River was then cut off. Whenever the emperor gazed westward and became troubled, he would come down into the court and sigh, saying: "Who can go out through Liang-chou to undertake a punitive campaign against these brigands?" None of his court ministers responded.

Commandant Ma Lung came forward and said: "If your majesty were able to entrust me with the responsibility, I could pacify them."

The emperor said: "If you are able to exterminate these bandits, how would I not entrust it to you? It is only a question of your strategy."

Ma Lung said: "If your majesty is willing to entrust me with the task, you should allow me to determine the strategy."

The emperor said: "Discuss it."

He replied: "I request permission to levy three thousand valiant warriors, selected without questioning their origins, and lead them on a campaign to the west. Embracing your majesty's awesome virtue, it will hardly be worth the effort to exterminate these miscreants."

The emperor assented, appointing Ma Lung as Protectorate General for Wu-wei commandery. Ma Lung then recruited men capable of using waist-drawn crossbows with a pull weight of thirty-six catties, and set up targets to test them. Commencing early in the morning, by midday he had obtained 3,500 men, a number he pronounced sufficient for the task.

Ma Lung then led his troops westward to ford the Wen River. Mu-chi-neng and other barbarian leaders, with more than ten thousand cavalry, took advantage of the ravines in order to intercept Lung's front, and established ambushes to cut off his rear. Then, in accord with the Diagram for Eight Formations, Ma Lung had rectangular chariots constructed. Where the terrain was expansive, he employed deer-horn chariots; where the road was narrow he added protective wooden structures on top of the chariots. Thus he was able to fight and advance, and wherever their arrows fell, for every draw of the bowstring a man dropped. Fighting running battles for a thousand miles, the dead and wounded were counted by the thousands.

When Ma Lung arrived at Wu-wei, he captured the great barbarian leader Ts'ui-pa-han. Ch'ieh-wan-neng and others, leading more than ten thousand troops, then gave their allegiance. Thus the numbers that Ma Lung executed and killed, together with those who surrendered and submitted to Chin rule, were several tens of thousands. Moreover, he led friendly Jung leaders, such as Mu-ku-neng, to engage Mu-chi-neng and his allies in battle and slew him. Thereafter, Liang-chou was pacified.

Commentary

Chariots, which first appeared in China during the Shang dynasty, provided the organizational focus for military activities not only during the Shang and Western Chou periods but also well down into the Warring States period, when their numbers were great but their role vastly reduced, having been increasingly supplanted by massive infantry forces. In the Shang and early Chou, when combat was limited to the nobility and campaign armies numbered several thousand to perhaps twenty or thirty thousand, engagements were limited and frequently resolved into clashes between individual warriors. Military organization was based upon chariot-centered platoons and companies, with only a hundred to a thousand chariots participating in early encounters. However, by the time of Ma Lung's barbarian campaigns in the mid–third century A.D., chariots had ceased to play any role except on such distant marches into hostile, inhospitable lands, just as under the immediately preceding Han dynasty. Ma Lung's achievements were remarkable, requiring years to attain, and became justifiably famous, particularly in the context of China's interminable conflict with nomadic steppe peoples.

The tactical discussion not only cites a principle from the *Questions and Replies* but also quotes extensively from the book's opening discussions, as may be seen from the following key paragraphs:

> The T'ai-tsung said: "When Ma Lung of the Chin dynasty conducted a punitive campaign against Liang-chou, it was also in accord with the 'Diagram of Eight Formations,' and he built narrow chariots. When the terrain was broad he employed encampments of 'deer-horn chariots,' and when the road was constricted he built wooden huts and placed them upon the chariots so they could both fight and advance. I believe it was orthodox troops that the ancients valued!"
>
> Li Ching said: "When I conducted the punitive campaign against the T'u-chüeh we traveled west for several thousand miles. If they had not been orthodox troops how could we have gone so far? Narrow chariots and deer-horn chariots are essential to the army. They allow controlling the expenditure of energy, provide a defense to the fore, and constrain the regiments and squads of five. These three are employed in turn. This is what Ma Lung learned so thoroughly from the ancients."

The degree of chariot specialization developed by the middle Warring States period may be found in a chapter entitled "The Army's Equipment" in the *Six Secret Teachings,* while "Battle Chariots" in the same work preserves a detailed analysis of advantageous and disadvantageous terrain for chariot operations.

9 Trust 信

Tactical Discussion

Whenever engaging an enemy in combat, if the officers and troops tread without fear or regret where ten thousand will die for every one that survives, it is always because trust has caused them to do so. When superiors esteem trust and employ the lower ranks with sincerity, they will exhaust their emotions without any doubts and never fail to be victorious in battle. A tactical principle from the *Six Secret Teachings* states: "One who is trustworthy will not be deceitful."

Historical Illustration

During the Three Kingdoms period, Emperor Ming of Wei personally led his troops on a campaign against Shu and then proceeded to Ch'ang-an. He deputed Ssu-ma Yi to supervise Chang Ko's armies and an additional 200,000 stalwart troops from Yung-chou and Liang-chou. Ssu-ma Yi concealed these armies and stealthily marched forward, seeking an opportunity to assault Chien-ko. At that time Chu-ko Liang, Shu's prime minister, was ensconced on Mt. Ch'i. His flags were well arrayed, his war implements all sharp, and his defenses occupied all the ravines and strongpoints. Just then Shu was about to rotate some of its troops, so the number present amounted to about eighty thousand. When Wei's troops first deployed into battle formation, it happened that Chu-ko Liang's replacements arrived to implement the rotation. His staff felt that as the enemy's troops were strong and numerous, beyond what their standing strength could control, it would be best to delay releasing the current troops for a month in order to combine their power with that of their replacements.

Chu-ko Liang said: "When I united these stalwart men and marched forth on this campaign, I emphasized trust as the foundation. 'To gain an objective but lose one's credibility' was considered regrettable by the ancients. Those about to depart have bundled up their clothes and are waiting for the moment to leave. Their wives, stretching their necks, watch for them and count the days. Even though we confront great hardship on this campaign, righteousness cannot be abandoned." He then insisted they all depart.

Thereupon, those scheduled to leave were all elated and wanted to remain for one more battle, while the ones who had just arrived were stimulated to be courageous and willing to obey his orders even unto death. They said among themselves, "Even our deaths will not repay Duke Chu-ko Liang's beneficence." As the time for battle approached, they all drew their swords and competed to be first to fight. With every one of them becoming a match for ten enemy soldiers, they killed Chang Ko and forced Ssu-ma Yi to retreat. The great victory of this single battle stemmed from trust.

Commentary

The quotation cited in the tactical discussion, drawn from "A Discussion of Generals" in the *Six Secret Teachings,* actually refers to a commander's requisite traits and qualifications, defined in part with respect to the ruler. However, virtually every military writer emphasized the general importance of trustworthiness (or good faith), sincerity, and credibility in commanders—otherwise orders would be doubted and the soldiers undisciplined. The original paragraph typifies Warring States' discussions: "Generals have five critical talents. What are referred to as the five talents are courage, wisdom, benevolence, trustworthiness, and loyalty. If he is courageous, he cannot be overwhelmed. If he is wise, he cannot be forced into turmoil. If he is benevolent, he will love his men. If he is trustworthy, he will not be deceitful. If he is loyal, he will not be of two minds." However, the *Six Secret Teachings* also noted that a pronounced weakness of the trustworthy is their tendency to trust others, leaving them open to deceit and the ignominy of defeat.

The historical illustration recounts a third-century A.D. event in which Chu-ko Liang echoes a famous incident from the Spring and Autumn period with his observation that "'To gain an objective but lose one's credibility' was considered regrettable by the ancients." In 634 B.C., Duke Wen of the state of Chin discontinued his siege of Yüan and departed when he failed to effect the city's fall within the three predetermined days even though its collapse appeared imminent. He explained his actions by saying: "Trust is the state's treasure, what the common people rely upon for preservation. If we gain Yüan but lose their trust, what will we employ to preserve the people? What we would lose would be exceedingly great." The people of Yüan were so impressed by his trustworthiness that they surrendered immediately thereafter.

10 Instructions 教

Tactical Discussion

Whenever the army is to be mobilized, the soldiers must first be instructed in combat. In ordinary times the warriors of the Three Armies should be well practiced in the methods for segmenting and reuniting, assembling and dispersing, and thoroughly prepared in silently sitting, rising, advancing, and withdrawing to commands. Ensure that they will look to the flags and pennants when they meet the enemy in order to respond to battlefield changes and will obey the gongs and drums for advancing and withdrawing, for then they will always be victorious in combat. A principle from the *Analects* states: "To engage in warfare with an uninstructed populace may be considered abandoning them."

Historical Illustration

During the Warring States period, general Wu Ch'i of Wei said: "Now men constantly perish from their inabilities and are defeated by the unfamiliar. Thus among the methods for employing the military, training them and causing them to be alert are primary. One man who has been trained in warfare can instruct ten men. Ten men who have studied warfare can train one hundred men. And one hundred men who have studied warfare can train one thousand men. One thousand men who have studied warfare can train ten thousand. Ten thousand who have studied warfare can train the Three Armies. [As Sun-tzu said,] 'With the nearby await the distant; with the well-ordered await the labored; with the surfeited await the hungry.' Have them deploy in circular formations, then change to square ones. Have them sit, then get up; move, then halt. Have them move to the left, then the right; forward and to the rear. Have them divide and combine, unite and disperse. When all these changes are familiar, provide them with weapons. Being spiritual and enlightening them, these are what are termed 'the general's affairs.'"

Commentary

In this selection the author has substituted Wu Ch'i's overview, originally found in the chapter entitled "Controlling the Army," for the usual historical incident. Additional brief discussions of the necessity and importance of training and instruction are scattered throughout the classic military writings, but the topic is particularly prominent in the *Six Secret Teachings* and the *Questions and Replies,* both of which reprise essential methods for drilling men to execute fundamental formations. The *Ssu-ma Fa,* a work probably composed early in the Warring States period from more ancient materials, also preserves important fundamental insights. For example, the author—perhaps Ssu-ma Jang-chü—observed that men differ in temperament and customs and therefore need to be transformed even before basic military activities can be undertaken:

> In general, in warfare it is not forming a battle array that is difficult, it is reaching the point that the men can be ordered into formation that is hard. It is not attaining the ability to order them into formation that is difficult, it is reaching the point of being able to employ them that is hard. It is not knowing what to do that is difficult, it is putting it into effect that is hard. Men from each of the four quarters have their own nature. Character differs from region to region. Through teaching they come to have regional habits, the customs of each state thus being different. Only through the Tao (of instruction) are their customs transformed.

Molding men to a common understanding, values, and predictable behavior is accomplished through education, as this passage from the *Ssu-ma Fa*—which coincidentally echoes the quotation from Confucius's famous *Analects* found in the tactical discussion—indicates:

> Only after effective instructions have been provided to the people can the state carefully select and employ them. Only after government affairs have been thoroughly ordered can the hundred offices be sufficiently provided. When instructions are thoroughly examined, the people will manifest goodness. When practice becomes habit, the people will embody the customs. This is the pinnacle of transformation through education.

The *Wei Liao-tzu,* a late Warring States work, summarized the experience and viewpoint of war-weary military thinkers:

Today if the people turn their backs to the border gates and decide the issue of life and death, if they have been taught to die without hesitation, there is a reason. Training and instructions have caused the defenders to inevitably be solid; those engaged in battle to inevitably fight; perverse plans not to be put into action; perverse people not to speak; orders to be effected without any changes; the army to advance without doubt; and the light units to be like a clap of thunder, to rush at the enemy like the terrified. Raise those of merit, distinguish those of virtue, making their distinction as clear as black and white. Cause the people to follow the orders of their superiors just as the four limbs respond to the mind.

If the forward units break up the enemy's ranks, throw his formation into chaos, and crush his hardness like water bursting through, there is a basis for it. This is termed the Army's Instructions. They provide the means to open sealed borders, preserve the altars of state, eliminate disaster and harm, and complete Martial Virtue.

11 Large Numbers 衆

Tactical Discussion

In warfare, if your forces are numerous and the enemy's few, you should not engage them in battle amid ravines and defiles but must secure level and easy, broad and expansive terrain. Then, if your soldiers advance when they hear the drums and halt when they hear the gongs, they will always be victorious. A tactical principle from the *Ssu-ma Fa* states: "When employing a large mass, advance and halt."

Historical Illustration

In 383 A.D., during the T'ai-yüan reign period of the Eastern Chin dynasty, Emperor Fu Chien of the rival Ch'in advanced his army and encamped at Shou-yang. Thereafter he deployed his forces along the Fei River, resulting in a standoff with Chin's general Hsieh Hsüan. Hsieh Hsüan addressed Fu Chien: "You have come from afar, crossed our border, and are now deployed along the river, indicating that you do not quickly intend to do battle. We request that you withdraw somewhat to allow our generals and warriors a little space to put their feet, after which we will bludgeon ourselves against you exalted gentlemen. Wouldn't it be pleasant to relax your constraints a little and observe it?"

Fu Chien's staff officers all objected: "We should stop them at the Fei River. Do not let them ascend the embankment! We are numerous while they are few and must fully preserve our strategic power." However, Fu Chien said: "If we withdraw but a little and let them cross, with our several hundred thousand resolute cavalrymen we can press them toward the river and then exterminate them." His brother Fu Jung thought similarly, so they signaled their soldiers to withdraw. The troops became disordered and were unable to halt. Thereupon Hsieh Hsüan, Hsieh Yen, Huan Yi, and others, accompanied by eight thousand elite cavalrymen, forded the Fei River. Chang Hao, commanding the army on the right, fell back somewhat. However, Hsieh Hsüan and Hsieh Yen continued to advance their soldiers and engaged Fu Chien's army in a major battle on the south bank of the Fei River. Fu Chien's massive forces were shattered.

Commentary

Over the centuries much energy has been devoted to the problem of relative numbers in their five possibilities: overwhelming superior, slightly superior, equal, inferior, and vastly inferior. The next chapter addresses the question of inferior numbers, the most difficult situation to confront commanders, while others expand upon both situations. However, superior numbers, particularly after infantry forces became important and often totaled several hundred thousand or more, posed not only command and logistics problems, but also the difficult issue of physical deployment so that they might be effective rather than just bunched together uselessly. It was generally felt that large forces require more space in which to maneuver and fight, whereas inferior numbers invariably benefit from constricted terrain, as discussed in the next chapter. Even Sun Pin noted that pondering how to manipulate superior numbers marked an enlightened general:

> King Wei inquired: "If we are strong while the enemy is weak, if we are numerous while the enemy is few, how should we employ them?"
>
> Sun Pin bowed twice and said: "This is the question for an enlightened king! To be numerous and moreover strong yet still inquire about employing them is

the Tao for making the state secure. The method is called 'Inducing the Army.' [Feign] disruption in your companies and disorder in your ranks to apparently accord with the enemy's desires. Then they will certainly engage you in battle."

The laconic *Ssu-ma Fa* quotation incorporated in the tactical discussion appears in an important overview of the general question of relative numbers:

> In general, as for the Tao of warfare: When you employ a small number, they must be solid. When you employ a large mass, they must be well ordered. With a small force it is advantageous to harass the enemy; with a large mass it is advantageous to use orthodox tactics. When employing a large mass, advance and stop; when employing a small number, advance and withdraw. If your large mass encounters a small enemy force, surround them at a distance, but leave one side open. Conversely, if you divide your forces and attack in turn, a small force can withstand a large mass. If their masses are beset by uncertainty, you should take advantage of it. If you are contending for a strategic position, abandon your flags as if in flight and when the enemy attacks turn around to mount a counterattack. If the enemy is vast, then concentrate your troops and let them surround you. If the enemy is fewer and fearful, avoid them and leave a path open.

However, other possibilities are raised in Chapter 19, "The Strong."

The historical illustration recounts the infamous battle of Fei River in which Fu Chien foolishly fated his overwhelmingly superior force—often claimed to have numbered a million men—to ignominious defeat while he himself was killed shortly thereafter by another enemy. Not only did he stupidly induce chaos in his own ranks, but he probably erred in setting their initial disposition by ignoring Sun-tzu's well-known admonition not to deploy near rivers but instead seek tenable, higher ground. (However, see Chapter 65, "Rivers," for further discussion of the basic principles for deploying near rivers.) Perhaps he recalled another of Sun-tzu's instructions, one ironically found in the first part of the same paragraph. In full, Sun-tzu said:

> After crossing rivers you must distance yourself from them. If the enemy is fording a river to advance, do not confront them in the water. When half their forces have crossed, it will be advantageous to strike them. If you want to engage the enemy in battle, do not array your forces near the river to confront the invader but look for tenable ground and occupy the heights. Do not confront the current's flow. This is the way to deploy the army where there are rivers.

12 Small Numbers 寡

Tactical Discussion

In warfare, if you oppose a numerous enemy with only a few, you must do so when the sun is setting, through ambushes concealed by deep vegetation or by intercepting them on a confined road. Under such circumstances you will invariably prove victorious. A tactical principle from the *Wu-tzu* states: "When employing a few, concentrate upon narrows."

Historical Illustration

In the third year (537 A.D.) of the Ta-t'ung reign period of the Western Wei during the Northern and Southern Dynasties period, general Kao Huan of Eastern Wei crossed the Yellow River and pressed Hua-chou. Wang Pa, Regional Inspector for the area, strongly defended it, so Kao's army forded the Lo River and encamped west of Hsü-yüan. The Western Wei dispatched general Yü Wen-t'ai to resist them. When general Yü arrived at Wei-nan, south of the Wei River, the soldiers from the nearby districts had not yet assembled. His own generals, citing the inability of their few troops to be a match for the more numerous enemy, suggested that they wait for Kao Huan to move farther west while keeping him under observation.

General Yü said: "If Kao Huan reaches Hsien-yang, everyone will be put into consternation. Now he has just arrived so we can launch a sudden attack against him." Then he had a floating bridge erected at Wei-nan, ordered the army's soldiers to pack three days' rations, the light cavalry to ford the Wei River, and the heavy baggage train to proceed westward along the river from Wei-nan. On the first of October they reached Sha-yüan, somewhat more than sixty miles from the Eastern Wei forces.

General Kao Huan led the Eastern Wei army forth to meet them. General Yü's reconnaissance cavalry reported that the Eastern Wei army would shortly arrive, so he summoned his generals for a strategic discussion. Li Pi said: "They are numerous while are few; we cannot simply engage them in battle but should just deploy our forces. Ten miles east of here is a sharp bend in the Wei River. We can assume a position there and await them." Thereupon they advanced as far as the bend and deployed from east to west with their backs to the river. Li Pi held the right flank, Chao Kuei the left. General Yü ordered his generals and officers to conceal themselves and their weapons amid the new growth and arise when they heard the sound of the drums.

The Eastern Wei army arrived as the sun was setting. From afar they observed but a small force and so their soldiers competed with each other to rush into battle, their troops becoming disordered and their formations disrupted. Just when the soldiers were about to clash, General Yü called for the drums, and his officers and troops all rose up. Yü Chin joined the battle with his main force, while Li Pi and the other commanders led elite cavalry units in striking across the Eastern Wei army, breaking it into two. They then went on to extensively destroy it.

Commentary

Confronting a stronger, especially numerically superior foe has long been warfare's most challenging problem. The classic Chinese solution was to avoid immediate clashes until the enemy could be manipulated to create a localized, relative advantage, whereupon a limited battle might be advantageously fought. The fundamental objective thus became enticing the enemy onto constricted terrain, thereby reducing their mobility and compressing their forces, as Wu Ch'i advised in the full passage from which the tactical quotation is drawn:

> Avoid the enemy's forces on easy terrain; attack them in narrow quarters. Thus it is said for one to attack ten nothing is better than a narrow defile. For ten to attack a hundred nothing is better than a deep ravine. For a thousand to attack ten thousand nothing is better than a dangerous pass. Now if you have a small number of troops, should they suddenly arise, striking the gongs and beating the drums, to attack the enemy on a confined road, then even though their numbers are very great they will all be startled and move about. Thus it is said, when employing larger numbers, concentrate upon easy terrain; when using small numbers, concentrate upon naturally confined terrain.

Creating ambushes to disorient the enemy and inflict heavy casualties was also deemed critical. In a paragraph largely paraphrased by the chapter's tactical discussion, the T'ai Kung advised methods for assaulting a superior foe:

> If you want to attack a large number with only a few, you must do it at sunset, setting an ambush in tall grass, pressing them on a narrow road. Select our skilled soldiers and strong crossbowmen and have them lie in ambush on both sides, while the chariots and cavalry deploy into a solid formation and assume position. When the enemy passes our concealed forces, the crossbowmen should fire en masse into their flanks. The chariots, cavalry, and skilled soldiers should then urgently attack their army, some striking the front, others striking the rear. Even if the enemy is numerous, they will certainly flee.

Should the immediate terrain lack confined roads or dense vegetation, the T'ai Kung advocated luring the enemy onto conducive ground:

> You should set out specious arrays and false enticements to dazzle and confuse their general, to redirect his path so that he will be forced to pass tall grass. Make his route long so you can arrange your engagement for sunset. When his advance units have not yet finished crossing the water, or his rear units have not yet reached the encampment, spring our concealed troops, vehemently striking his right and left flanks, while your chariots and cavalry stir chaos among his forward and rear units. Even if the enemy is numerous, they will certainly flee.

However, in all cases the fundamental principle enunciated by Sun-tzu and Sun Pin remains—"Attack where they are unprepared, go forth where they will not expect it."

13 Love 愛

Tactical Discussion

Whenever engaging an enemy in combat, if the officers and troops would rather advance unto death than retreat and live, it is always because the commander's solicitude and beneficence have brought it about. When the Three Armies know that their superiors love them as sincerely as their sons, they will love their commanders as fervently as their fathers and penetrate deadly terrain without begrudging their deaths in order to repay their commander's virtue. A tactical principle from the *Art of War* states: "When one regards the people as beloved children, they will be willing to die with you."

Historical Illustration

In the Warring States period General Wu Ch'i of the state of Wei, who served as Protector of the West Ho region, wore the same clothes and ate the same food as the men in the lowest ranks. When sitting he did not set out a mat; while on the march he did not ride a horse. He personally packed up his leftover rations and shared all labors and misery with the troops. Once, when one of his soldiers had a blister, he personally sucked out the pus. The soldier's mother heard about it and wept. Someone said to her: "Your son is only an ordinary soldier, while the general himself sucked out the pus. What is there to weep about?" The mother retorted: "That isn't it. In years past General Wu also sucked his father's blister. His father went off to war without any hesitation and subsequently died at the hands of the enemy. Now General Wu Ch'i again sucks my son's blister, so I do not know where he will die. For this reason I weep." Because Marquis Wen felt that Wu Ch'i was scrupulous and fair handed in employing the army and had gained the allegiance of his officers and troops, he appointed him as Protector for the West Ho region. In this capacity he fought seventy-six battles with the other feudal lords, winning sweeping victories in sixty-four of them.

Commentary

Unlike contemporary military practices—except in the Marine Corps, which stresses leading from the front—the Chinese believed that the commander should set a personal example for his troops and provide visible leadership, even though only directing the battle rather than personally fighting, as was prevalent in ancient Greece. Only then would he win their emotional allegiance and be fully aware of their hardships and miseries. The *Wei Liao-tzu*, a very late Warring States work, summarized this view:

> Now when the army is toiling on the march the general must establish himself as an example. In the heat he does not set up an umbrella; in the cold he does not wear heavier clothes. On difficult terrain he must dismount and walk. Only after the army's well is finished does he drink. Only after the army's food is cooked does he eat. Only after the army's ramparts are complete does he rest. He must

> personally experience the same toil and respite. In this fashion even though the army is in the field for a long time, it will be neither old nor exhausted.

Historically, Wu Ch'i stood out and became the exemplar for these observances, although he commanded armies early in the Warring States of generally less than a hundred thousand men. Centuries thereafter the *Wei Liaotzu* still cited him as the model for emulation:

> When Wu Ch'i engaged Ch'in in battle, wherever he encamped the army did not flatten the paths between the fields. Young saplings provided protective covering against the frost and dew. Why did he act like this? Because he didn't place himself higher than other men. If you want men to die, you don't require them to perform perfunctory acts of respect. If you want men to exhaust their strength, you don't hold them responsible for performing the rites. Thus in antiquity an officer wearing a helmet and armor didn't bow, showing people that he is not troubled by anything. To annoy people yet require them to die, to exhaust their strength, from antiquity until today has never been heard of.

The *Huang Shih-kung*, an even later work written about the turn of the millennium, delimited the essentials for prospective commanders:

> Now those who command the army must share tastes and attitudes with the officers and men and confront both safety and danger with them, for then the enemy can be attacked. Thus the army will attain full victory, and the enemy will be completely destroyed. The *Military Pronouncements* states: "When the army's wells have not yet been completed, the general does not mention thirst. When the encampment has not yet been secured, the general does not speak about fatigue. When the army's cook stoves have not yet been lit, the general does not speak about hunger. In the winter he doesn't wear a fur robe, in the summer he doesn't use a fan, and in the rain he doesn't set up an umbrella." This is termed the proper form of behavior for a general.
>
> He is with them in safety; he is united with them in danger. Thus his troops can be combined but cannot be forced apart. They can be employed but cannot be tired out. With his beneficence he ceaselessly gathers them together; with his plans he constantly unites them. Thus it is said that when you cultivate beneficence tirelessly, with one you can take ten thousand.

Chapter 87, "The Difficult," expands this concept further, requiring that the commanding general equally confront all the dangers facing his troops rather than safely ensconcing himself away from the battlefield.

14 Awesomeness 威

Tactical Discussion

Whenever engaging an enemy in battle, if the officers and troops courageously advance rather than risk retreat, it is because they fear their commanders instead of the enemy. But if they risk retreat rather than advance, they fear the enemy instead of their commanders. When generals can force their officers and troops to rush into water and tread on fire without flinching, it is their awesomeness and severity that caused it. A tactical principle from the *Book of Documents* states: "When awesomeness exceeds love, affairs will be successful."

Historical Illustration

In the Spring and Autumn period, during the time of Duke Ching of Ch'i, the state of Chin attacked the major cities of A and Chüan, and the state of Yen invaded the river district of Ho-shang. Ch'i's army was badly defeated, sorely troubling Duke Ching. Yen Ying then recommended Ssu-ma Jang-chü, saying: "Even though Jang-chü is descended from a concubine, still in civil affairs he is able to attach the masses and in martial affairs is able to overawe the enemy. I would like my Lord to test him."

Duke Ching summoned Ssu-ma Jang-chü and spoke with him about military affairs. He was greatly pleased and appointed him as General of the Army to lead the soldiers in resisting the armies of Yen and Chin. Jang-chü said, "I was formerly lowly and menial. If my Lord pulls me out from amidst my village and places me above the high officials, the officers and troops will not be submissive and the hundred surnames will not believe in me. Since I am insignificant and my authority light, I would like to have one of my Lord's favored ministers, someone whom the state respects, as Supervisor of the Army. Then it will be possible." Duke Ching assented, deputing Chuang Chia to go forth.

Ssu-ma Jang-chü, who had already taken his leave, made an agreement with Chuang Chia, saying: "Tomorrow, at midday, we shall meet at the army's gate." Jang-chü raced ahead to the army, set up the gnomon and let the water drip in the water clock, awaiting Chuang. Chuang, who had always been arrogant and aristocratic, assumed that since the general had already reached the army while he was only the supervisor, it was not extremely urgent. His relatives from all around, who were sending him off, detained him to drink. Midday came and Chia had not arrived. Jang-chü then lay down the gnomon, stopped the dripping water, and went into the encampment. He advanced the army and took control of the soldiers, clearly publicizing the constraints and bonds. When the constraints had been imposed it was already evening, and then Chuang Chia arrived.

Ssu-ma Jang-chü said: "How is it that you arrive after the appointed time?" Chuang Chia acknowledged his fault, saying, "High officials and relatives saw this simple one off, thus he was detained." Jang-chü said: "On the day a general receives the mandate of command he forgets his home; when he enters the army and takes control of the soldiers he forgets his loved ones; when he takes hold of the drumsticks and urgently beats the drum he forgets himself. At present, enemy states have already deeply invaded our lands, while within the state there is unrest and movement. Officers and soldiers lie brutally cut down and exposed on the borders. Our ruler neither sleeps soundly nor enjoys the sweet taste of his food. The fate of the hundred surnames hangs upon you, so what do you mean by being seen off?"

He summoned the provost marshal and inquired: "What is the army's law regarding those who arrive after the appointed time?" The reply: "They should be beheaded!" Chuang Chia was terrified, and he ordered a man to race back and report to Duke Ching, asking to be saved. The messenger had already left, but not yet returned, when Jang-chü beheaded Chuang in order to publicize the enforcement of discipline within the Three Armies. All the officers within the Three Armies shook with fear.

Somewhat later an emissary that Duke Ching had dispatched, bearing a tally to pardon Chia, raced into the army. Ssu-ma Jang-chü said: "When the general is with the army, there are orders of the ruler which are not accepted." He queried the provost marshal, "What is the regulation regarding racing into the army?" The provost marshal said: "He should be beheaded." The emissary was terrified. Ssu-ma Jang-chü said, "We cannot slay the ruler's emissary." Then he beheaded the emissary's attendant, severed the carriage's left stanchion, and beheaded the horse on the left in order to instruct the Three Armies. He dispatched the Duke's emissary to return and report and then moved the army out.

The officers and soldiers next encamped, dug wells, lit cookfires, and prepared their drink and food. He asked about those with illnesses, had physicians prescribe medicine, and personally looked after them. In all cases when he took the emoluments of office and his rations, he presented them to the officers and troops, personally dividing them equally. He compared the strong and weak among them and only after three days took control of the soldiers. The sick all sought to go on the march, fighting fervently to go into battle on his behalf. Chin's army heard of it, abandoned their position, and departed. Yen's army heard of it, crossed over the river, and dispersed. Thereupon he pursued and attacked them, subsequently retaking all the territory within the borders of the old fief, and returned with the soldiers.

Commentary

The ability to have commands obeyed in battle is not easily achieved, as many officers have learned to their regret over the centuries, but depends upon earning both the fear (or respect) and allegiance of the soldiers. Until recent decades, most armies—including Germanic forces in the late eighteenth and nineteenth centuries and Japanese units in World War II—functioned because their soldiers feared their own NCOs and officers more than the enemy, just as the tactical discussion indicates. However, in general the Chinese military thinkers believed that awesomeness alone would merely force men to go forth into battle; only emotional factors coupled with the prospect of glory and rewards would motivate them to heroic action. Moreover, the commander's personal charisma also counts for much, as Huang Shih-kung pointed out:

> When the general lacks awesomeness, then the officers and troops will disdain punishment. When they disdain punishment, the army will lose its organization into squads of five. When the army loses its squads of five, the officers and soldiers will abandon their positions and run off. When they flee, the enemy will take advantage of the situation. When the enemy seizes the opportunity to profit from the situation, the army will inevitably perish.

The essential question became how to balance the commander's solicitude for his men with the severity necessary to instill discipline and effect command. Sun-tzu provided a highly regarded solution, as these passages from the T'ang dynasty *Questions and Replies* indicate:

> The T'ai-tsung said: "Severe punishments and imposing laws make men fear me and not fear the enemy. I am very confused about this. In antiquity the Han

Emperor Kuang Wu opposed Wang Mang's mass of a million with his solitary force, but he didn't use punishments and laws to approach the people. So how did his victory come about?"

Li Ching said: "An army's victory or defeat is a question of the situation and a myriad factors and cannot be decided by one element alone. In the case of Ch'en Sheng and Kuang Wu defeating the Ch'in army, could they have had more severe punishments and laws than the Ch'in? Emperor Kuang Wu's rise was probably due to his according with the people's hatred for Wang Mang. Moreover, Wang Hsün and Wang Yi did not understand military strategy and merely boasted of their army's masses. Thus in this way they defeated themselves.

According to Sun-tzu, 'If you impose punishments on the troops before they have become emotionally attached, they will not be submissive. If you do not impose punishments after the troops have become emotionally attached, they cannot be used.' This means that normally a general should first bind the soldiers' affection to him and only thereafter employ severe punishments. If their affection has not yet been developed, few would be able to conquer and be successful solely by employing severe laws."

The T'ai-tsung said: "In the *Shang Shu* it says, 'When awesomeness exceeds love, affairs will be successful. When love exceeds awesomeness there will be no achievement.' What does this mean?"

Li Ching said: "Love should be established first and awesomeness afterward—it cannot be opposite this. If awesomeness is applied first and love supplements it afterward, it will be of no advantage to the prosecution of affairs. The *Shang Shu* was extremely careful about the end, but this is not the way plans should be made in the beginning. Thus Sun-tzu's method cannot be eliminated for ten thousand generations."

Accordingly, in a passage essentially paraphrased by the tactical discussion above, the *Wei Liao-tzu* earlier concluded that love coupled with severity yields victory:

Now the people do not have two things they fear equally. If they fear us, then they will despise the enemy; if they fear the enemy, they will despise us. The one who is despised will be defeated; the one who establishes his awesomeness will be victorious. In general, when the general is able to implement the Tao to awesomeness, his commanders will fear him. When the commanders fear their general, the people will fear their commanders. When the people fear their commanders, then the enemy will fear the people. For this reason those who would know the Tao of victory and defeat must first know about the balance of power of "fearing" and "despising."

Now one who is not loved and cherished in the minds of his men cannot be employed by me; one who is not respected and feared in the minds of his men cannot be appointed by me. Love follows from below, awesomeness is established from above. If they love their general, they will not have divided minds; if

> they are awestruck by their general, they will not be rebellious. Thus excelling at generalship is merely a question of love and awesomeness.

However, Chapters 16 and 96, "Punishment" and "Fear" respectively, also focus on the problem of fear in the ranks and ponder ways to stem cowardly desertions, concluding that severe punishments are essential for battlefield discipline and control.

15 Rewards 賞

Tactical Discussion

In general, if despite high walls, deep moats, and a hail of stones and arrows the officers and troops are to compete with each other to ascend the walls, or when the naked blades first clash they are to contend with each other in rushing forth, they must be enticed with heavy rewards. Then every enemy will be conquered. A tactical principle from the *Three Strategies* states: "Beneath heavy rewards there will certainly be courageous fellows."

Historical Illustration

At the end of the Later Han, every time the great general Ts'ao Ts'ao successfully attacked and destroyed a fortified city, he rewarded the meritorious with all the spoils. If it were appropriate to reward a man's efforts, he would not begrudge even a thousand catties. However, for wantonly bestowing rewards upon those without significant accomplishments he would not allow a penny. Thus he was able to be victorious in every battle.

Commentary

As noted in the previous commentary, rewards were thought to provide the incentives for action, the stimulus to brave an enemy's defenses and seize his position. The military writers actually devoted far more space to the nature and employment of punishments, particularly as it was assumed that the ruler would make the people's welfare a priority, allowing them adequate means to live. Rewards would, however, appeal to every man's desire for personal profit and the riches that would distinguish him from his fellows, and they became increasingly important as warfare became more violent and the tasks of combat fell to the masses rather than the nobility, as in antiquity. The psychology of rewards was well enunciated and required that their credibility be maintained. Moreover, they had to be universally applied, as the T'ai Kung noted: "In rewarding value the lowly. When rewards extend down to the cowherds, grooms, and stablemen, these are rewards penetrating to the lowest." He also said: "Honored ranks and generous rewards are the means by which to encourage obeying orders." The *Wei Liao-tzu* tied them to credibility, stating: "When rewards are like the sun and moon, credibility is like the four seasons, orders are like the axes of punishment, and regulations are as sharp as the famous sword Kan-chiang, I have never heard of officers and troops not following orders." The *Wu-tzu* devotes one of its six extant chapters to the importance of publicly honoring the valiant with a magnificent feast to stimulate them and others to heroic deeds, while also showing visible solicitude for their families and the families of those who died in service. The philosophers, such as Hsün-tzu, Lord Shang, and Han Fei-tzu, discussed the psychology of rewards and punishments far more extensively than the military writers, perhaps establishing the common understanding in the Warring States period. However, most of the philosophers and many of the military writers felt that other factors—especially shame, loyalty, and innate courage—were more important, and even the great Sun Pin deemphasized rewards and punishments somewhat, saying: "Rewards are the means by which to give happiness to the masses and cause soldiers to forget death. Punishments are the means by which to rectify the chaotic and cause the people to fear their superiors. They can be employed to facilitate victory, but they are not urgent matters."

16 Punishment 罰

Tactical Discussion

In general, in warfare you must cause the officers and troops to brave advancing rather than dare to retreat. Anyone who withdraws even an inch must be subjected to the severest punishment, for then you can seize victory. A tactical principle from the *Ssu-ma Fa* states: "In punishing, do not change their ranks."

Historical Illustration

During the Sui dynasty, the great general Yang Su commanded with strictness and attention to order. Anyone who disobeyed a command was immediately executed, leniency never being granted. Whenever they were about to face the enemy, the general would abruptly seek out soldiers who had contravened military regulations and behead them. In the most numerous case the number amounted to more than a hundred; in the least, not less than several tens. Even when their blood overflowed before him, his speech and laughter remained unchanged. When the army deployed for battle, he would first order three hundred men to rush forth into the enemy. If they penetrated the enemy's formation, their task was complete; however, if they returned without having been successful, he would not inquire how many had failed but would execute all of them. Thereafter he would again order two or three hundred men to advance, treating them on their return just as before. The thighs of his generals and soldiers trembled, but they were consumed with a commitment to fight to the death. As a result Yang Su proved victorious in every engagement.

Commentary

This selection, which completes the pair "rewards and punishments," emphasizes the need for visibly imposing extreme punishments in order to frighten the soldiers into obeying orders and fighting fervently. This approach essentially embraces the views and policies of the famous statesman and Legalist philosopher Lord Shang—one of the early architects of Ch'in's meteoric rise to found the first, harsh imperial dynasty—who advocated severely punishing minor offenses in order to prevent major crimes from being committed. Although the military writers essentially concurred, in general their view was somewhat more balanced and stressed appropriateness, punishing minor infractions by lesser means, such as reductions in rank, extra guard duty, and flogging. However, to ensure a deterrent effect, they all insisted upon strictness, impartiality, and promptness in imposing punishments, as well as death for desertion in combat. The *Six Secret Teachings* contains a summary expression of this philosophy:

> The general creates awesomeness by executing the great. Prohibitions are made effective and laws implemented by careful scrutiny in the use of punishments. Therefore, if by executing one man the entire army will quake, kill him. In executing, value the great. When you kill the powerful and the honored, this is punishment that reaches the pinnacle. When punishment reaches the pinnacle, your awesomeness has been effected.

The T'ai Kung also said: "Severe punishments and heavy fines are the means by which to force the weary and indolent to advance."

Punishments must be consistently applied, during ordinary times, and on the basis of uncovering all evil, so that people will not dare to commit offenses or disobey orders even if they might go undetected. The system was further reinforced by making all the members of the squad of five mutually responsible for each other, thereby exploiting the emotional basis of shame in conjunction with the threat of implicating one's comrades while also making the latter his policemen and potential executioners. The second half of the *Wei Liao-tzu,* which preserves several chapters of army regulations that probably reflect Ch'in dynasty practice, enumerates a variety of punishments specifically tailored to the mutual responsibility system and asserts that punishments are the means to military power:

> If you cause the people to fear heavy punishments within the state, then outside the state they will regard the enemy lightly. Thus the Former Kings made the regulations and measures clear before making their awesomeness and punishments heavy. When punishments are heavy, then they will fear them within the state. When they fear them within the state, then they will be stalwart outside it.

Obviously, without the threat of pain and death, the army would be unable to discipline its soldiers and ensure their performance in combat.

17 The Host 主

Tactical Discussion

In warfare, someone who invades your territory is cast in the tactical role of a "guest," while you are the "host" and so cannot lightly engage in battle. Rather, since the officers and troops are concerned about their homes, you must stabilize the army, assemble the people, occupy the valleys, protect the cities, make preparations in the narrows, and sever the enemy's supply route. If the invaders try to provoke you into combat, they will not succeed; meanwhile, supplies thought to be en route will not arrive. If you then wait for them to become distressed and fatigued before attacking, you will certainly be victorious. A tactical principle from the *Art of War* states: "When one fights on his own territory, it is 'dispersive terrain.'"

Historical Illustration

During the Northern and Southern dynasties period, Emperor Wu of the Later Wei personally commanded an assault on Mu-jung Te of the Later Yen in the city of Yeh, but his forward army was badly defeated. Mu-jung Te immediately wanted to counterattack, but Han Chuo, Cavalry Assistant to the Regional Military Inspector, came forward and said: "Only after first achieving victory in the court did the ancients actually attack an enemy in combat. At the moment there are four reasons why it would not be appropriate to attack Wei and three why it would not be appropriate for us in Yen to initiate any movement at all."

Mu-jung Te inquired: "What reasons?"

Han Chuo said: "Wei's army is hung up far inside our borders, so it is to their advantage to fight in the wilds, the first reason they cannot be attacked. They have deeply penetrated the territory near our capital, reaching fatal ground, the second reason they cannot be attacked. Their vanguard has already been defeated so their rear formations will certainly be solid, the third reason they cannot be attacked. They are numerous while we are few, the fourth reason they cannot be attacked.

Our officers and troops will be fighting in their own territory, the first reason it would not be appropriate for us to initiate action. If we engage them in combat but are not victorious, it would be difficult to stabilize the people's morale, the second reason it would not be appropriate to initiate action. Since the walls and moats have not yet been properly repaired, if the enemy comes up we will be unprepared, the third reason it would not be appropriate to initiate action.

Strategists all shun such circumstances, so it would be better to deepen the moats, raise the heights of walls, and then, being well rested, await the fatigued. Wei's forces are transporting grain a thousand miles and have been unable to forage in the wilds, so as the time becomes prolonged, their Three Armies will be wasted and reduced, and many of their officers and troops will perish. When their army has thus grown 'old' and prays just to survive, if you implement wise strategic plans against them, you can wrest a victory." Mu-jung Te said: "Han Chuo's words truly embody the wisdom of the famous strategists Chang Liang and Ch'en P'ing."

Commentary

This selection and the one that follows discuss the tactics appropriate to an invader, termed a "guest,"and the defender, termed the "host." Generally speaking, the concept of a host was not restricted simply to a defender locked within his home state, but equally characterized any army occupying a position and mounting an active defense against an aggressor. Sun-tzu initially articulated the concept, but it appears in other works as well, including Sun Pin's *Military Methods* and the *Questions and Replies,* which itself emphasizes the relative nature of the definition.

Since the next selection focuses upon the "guest's" tactics and psychology, our comments here are limited to the role and experience of the host. The Chinese military writers felt that soldiers engaging in battle near their homes would, contrary to modern expectation, tend to be distracted, concerned about their families, perhaps overconfident, but equally hesitant and dispirited rather than determined to fight to the death in defense of their native state. Sun-tzu termed this "dispersive terrain"—because the men had a tendency to disperse, returning to their own home towns—and analyzed the emotional and tactical aspects in a passage long preserved outside the extant text of the *Art of War,* but included in our translation of Sun-tzu under the chapter title of "Nine Configurations." The author of the *Unorthodox Strategies* in fact incorporated much of it in the tactical discussion above:

> The king of Wu asked Sun-tzu: "On dispersive terrain the officers and troops are thinking of their families. As we cannot engage in battle with them, we must solidly defend our positions and not go forth. If the enemy attacks our small cities, plunders our fields, prevents us from gathering firewood, blocks our major roads, and awaits our emptiness and depletion to urgently advance and attack, what should we do?"
>
> Sun-tzu replied: "When the enemy has deeply penetrated our capital region, putting numerous fortifications and cities behind them, their officers and men regard the army as their family, are focused in their intentions, and lightly enter into battle. However, our troops are in their native state; they feel secure on their territory and embrace life. Therefore in battle formation they are not firm; when they engage in battle they are not victorious. We should assemble the people and gather the masses; collect the foodstuffs, livestock, and cloth; defend the walled cities and prepare to defend the passes; and dispatch light troops to sever their supply routes. If they are not able to provoke us into battle, their provisions fail to arrive, and there's nothing in the countryside that they can plunder, their Three Armies will be in difficulty. Take advantage of the situation to entice them, and then we can be successful.

Ancient states and modern countries being invaded by superior foes bent upon long-term occupation rather than simple raiding, such as China in World War II, have often been compelled to employ a scorched-earth policy just to deny the enemy necessary materials and supplies. However, in the case of raiding parties Wu Ch'i advised temporizing only until they were hindered and slowed by their burdens:

> If a savage raiding force appears, you must carefully consider its strength and well maintain your defensive position. Do not respond to their attacks by going out to engage them. When they are about to withdraw at the end of the day their packs will certainly be heavy and their hearts will invariably be afraid. In withdrawing they will concentrate upon speed, and inevitably there will be stragglers. You should then pursue and attack them, and their troops can be overcome.

In either case, the defenders must overcome a disadvantageous situation to finally mount an effective response.

18 The Guest 客

Tactical Discussion

When engaging in warfare, if the enemy is cast in the role of the host while you are acting as the guest, you should concentrate upon penetrating deeply. When you have made a deep penetration of their borders, the enemy, being the host, cannot be victorious because you will have attained the situation of the terrain being heavy for the guest and dispersive for the host. A tactical principle from the *Art of War* states: "When you penetrate deeply, the troops will be unified."

Historical Illustration

At the beginning of the Han dynasty, Han Hsin and Chang Erh, in command of several tens of thousands of soldiers, were about to go eastward down through Ching-hsing to attack the state of Chao. The king of Chao and Chen Yü, Lord of Ch'eng-an, assembled their soldiers at the mouth of Ching-hsing, their combined troops numbering about 200,000 men. The Lord of Kuang-wu, Li Tso-chün, advised the Lord of Ch'eng-an: "I have heard that when Han Hsin crossed the Yellow River and went west to capture Wei-pao and eliminate Hsia Shui, the blood flowed as far as Kuan-yü. Now he has obtained Chang Erh's assistance and they are discussing a campaign down here to Chao. This will be a situation in which, to exploit their previous victories, they will venture far from their state. Wherever their reputation precedes them, the people will quake; their front cannot be withstood. However, I have heard that when provisions are transported a thousand miles the soldiers have a famished look, and that when they light their cookfires only after gathering firewood the army does not sleep on a full stomach. At present the road to Ching-hsing cannot accommodate two chariots side by side or cavalry properly deployed several abreast. Their supplies and provisions must be behind them. Therefore, I would like your majesty to allow me to personally lead thirty thousand cavalrymen to proceed along the bypaths and sever their supply route. Meanwhile, your majesty should deepen the moats and heighten the fortifications without engaging them in battle. When they are uable to advance or retreat, while there is nothing in the wilds for them to forage upon, before ten days have elapsed, you will be able to suspend the heads of these two generals beneath your pennants. I would like your majesty to pay heed; otherwise, you will be captured." The Lord of Ch'eng-an, priding himself on being well versed in military affairs, ignored him and indeed was slain.

Commentary

This selection characterizes the tactical effects achieved by an invading force deeply penetrating enemy territory in terms of the conceptual pair introduced in the last selection, "guest" (or invader) and "host" (or defender). The analysis turns upon Sun-tzu's configurations of terrain as defined in several passages found in the *Art of War:*

> When the feudal lords fight in their own territory, it is dispersive terrain. When they enter someone else's territory but not deeply, it is light terrain. When one penetrates deeply into enemy territory, bypassing numerous cities, it is heavy terrain. Where if one fights with intensity he will survive but if he does not fight with intensity he will perish, it is fatal terrain.

Sun-tzu discerned distinct psychological stages as the troops proceeded out from their native states, where they are mentally distracted, through crossing the enemy's border into light terrain, and finally deep onto heavy terrain where there is no alternative to fighting. (One of his basic tenets, as discussed in Chapters 50 and 51, "Danger" and "Fighting to the Death," holds that being cast onto fatal terrain will elicit desperate efforts from the soldiers rather than provoke a complete collapse of will in the face of an impossible situation.) Extensive passages nominally attributed to him—preserved only in the *T'ung Tien* and largely ignored—systematically analyze these tactical situations and describe the psychological stages:

> The king of Wu asked Sun-tzu: "Suppose we have reached light terrain and have just entered the enemy's borders. Our officers and men are thinking of turning back. It's hard to advance but easy to withdraw. We do not yet have ravines and defiles behind us, and the Three Armies are fearful. The commanding general

wants to advance and the officers and troops want to retreat, so above and below are of different minds. The enemy is defending his walled cities and fortifications, putting his chariots and cavalry in good order. Some occupy positions to our fore; others strike our rear. What should we do?"

Sun-tzu replied: "When we have reached light terrain, the officers and men are not yet focused because their task is entering the border, not waging battle. Do not approach his famous cities nor traverse his major roads. Feign doubt; pretend confusion. Show him that we are about to depart. Then initially select elite cavalry to silently enter their territory and plunder their cattle, horses, and other domestic animals. When the Three Armies observe that our cavalrymen were able to advance, they will not be afraid. Divide our superior soldiers and have them secretly prepare ambushes. Should the enemy come up, strike without hesitation; if they do not come up, then abandon the ambushes and depart."

Sun-tzu also said: "Suppose the army has entered the enemy's borders. The enemy solidifies his fortifications without engaging in battle. Our officers and troops are thinking of returning home, but even if we want to retreat it would also be difficult. This is referred to as light terrain. We should select elite cavalry to establish ambushes on the strategic roads. When we withdraw, the enemy will pursue us; when they come up, strike them."

The king of Wu asked Sun-tzu: "Suppose we have led the troops deep into heavy terrain, bypassing a great many places so our supply routes are cut off or blocked. Suppose we want to return home but cannot get past their strategic configuration of power. If we want to forage on the enemy's land and maintain our troops without loss, then what should we do?"

Sun-tzu replied: "Whenever we remain on heavy terrain the officers and troops will readily be courageous. If the supply routes are no longer open, then we must plunder to extend our provisions. Whatever the lower ranks obtain in grain or cloth must all be forwarded to the top, and those that collect the most will be rewarded. The warriors will no longer think about returning home.

If you want to turn about and go forth, urgently make defensive preparations. Deepen the moats and raise the ramparts, showing the enemy our determination to remain indefinitely. The enemy will suspect we have an open route somewhere and will remove themselves from the critical roads. Then we can order our light chariots to sally forth silently, the dust flying up, using the cattle and horses as bait. If the enemy goes forth, beat the drums and follow him. Prior to this secretly conceal some warriors in ambush, setting the time with them so that our forces within and without can launch a coordinated attack. The enemy's defeat can then be known."

Ensuring a continuous flow of supplies would invariably be critical for deep operations in hostile territory. However, more important would be the size of the invading force, for it is not simply a question of penetration alone, but of the relative power being brought to bear, as Germany's Russian campaign in World War II clearly showed. The *Ssu-ma Fa* adopted a conservative perspective in this regard:

> In general, in warfare: If you advance somewhat into the enemy's territory with a light force, it is dangerous. If you advance with a heavy force deeply into the enemy's territory, you will accomplish nothing. If you advance with a light force deeply into enemy territory, you will be defeated. If you advance with a heavy force somewhat into the enemy's territory, you can fight successfully. Thus in warfare the light and heavy are mutually related.

19 The Strong 強

Tactical Discussion

In general, if you want the enemy to engage your stronger, more numerous troops in battle, you should feign fear and weakness in order to entice them into it. When they carelessly come forth, you can suddenly assault them with your elite troops and their army will invariably be defeated. A tactical principle from the *Art of War* states: "Although capable, display incapability."

Historical Illustration

In the Warring States period General Li Mu of Chao long held the command responsible for defending Yen-men against the nearby Hsiung-nu. He stressed convenience in assigning his officers to posts and had all the taxes and duties directly brought into their military headquarters to be expended for the troops. Every day he would have several cattle butchered for his officers' enjoyment. He drilled the troops in horsemanship and archery, strictly regulated the signal fires, and employed numerous spies. Thereafter he constrained the soldiers with specific orders: "Whenever the Hsiung-nu launch a raid, quickly assemble in the fortress and protect it. Anyone who dares to fight the enemy will be beheaded." Events unfolded as he had dictated for several years without them suffering any losses or deaths. Accordingly, the Hsiung-nu thought Li Mu was afraid and even Chao's own border soldiers felt their general was a coward. The king of Chao upbraided him, but Li Mu persisted in his policies.

The king summoned Li Mu back to the court and replaced him with another general. For slightly more than a year, every time the Hsiung-nu came forth, the border forces went out to engage them in battle but were unsuccessful and several times suffered extensive losses. Farming and herding therefore became impossible in the area. Consequently, the king once again asked Li Mu to assume responsibility for its defense. Li Mu declined on account of illness, shut his door, and did not go out. The king again earnestly entreated Li Mu to undertake command of the army. Li Mu said: "If you want to employ me, I must proceed as before; only then will I dare accept your mandate." The king assented, so Li Mu went forth to his post. Immediately after arriving, he imposed the same restrictions on his forces as before.

Whenever the Hsiung-nu appeared they failed to seize anything and concluded that Li Mu was afraid. Meanwhile, as the border soldiers received their daily pay and other rewards but were unused, they all wanted to fight. Li Mu then picked the best chariots, some thirteen hundred, and cavalrymen, totaling about thirteen thousand, and other elite warriors worth a hundred catties of gold each, some fifty thousand, together with a hundred thousand skilled archers. He assembled them all somewhat farther away for additional combat training and also had all the livestock released to graze. The common people filled the wilds. When a Hsiung-nu raiding party came, he pretended to be defeated and abandoned the few thousand holding troops to them. After the khan heard about it, he led a massive number of horsemen to invade the border. Li Mu employed numerous unorthodox formations, extended his left and right flanks in order to assault them, and severely defeated them, killing more than a hundred thousand Hsiung-nu cavalrymen. The khan fled, and for more than ten years thereafter the Hsiung-nu did not dare to encroach on Chao's border.

Commentary

This selection considers a problem similar to the one posed in Chapter 11, "Large Numbers." The latter focuses upon simple numerical advantage, while presumably here the advantage is compounded: not only more troops, but also greater power, whether generated by better trained and equipped forces, greater mobility in the component arms, or perhaps concentrated firepower from the crossbow, the most advanced weapon of the times. Since few commanders would foolishly risk an open battle against markedly superior forces, the tactical discussion advises resorting to deceit and deception, to feigning weakness to lure the enemy into committing themselves before unleashing the full weight of one's power. (Sun Pin's advice in this regard, cited in our commentary to Chapter 11, merits consulting.)

Sun-tzu however offered a more simplistic approach, suggesting that significant superiority allows more direct action:

> In general, the strategy for employing the military is this: If your strength is ten times theirs, surround them; if five, then attack them; if double, then divide your forces. If you are equal in strength to the enemy, you can engage him. If fewer, you can circumvent him. If outmatched, you can avoid him. Thus a small enemy that acts inflexibly will become the captives of a large enemy.

The historical incident clearly illustrates the principle of "although capable, display incapability." Moreover, Li Mu's strategy certainly demanded great determination and patience, requiring years to resolutely create the circumstances for a single decisive battle. He even sacrificed a few thousand men to tantalize the khan, causing his cruelty to be much condemned in later historical writings. However, a comment in the *Wei Liao-tzu* should be noted:

> I have heard that in antiquity those who excelled in employing the army could bear to kill half their officers and soldiers. The next could kill thirty percent, and the lowest, ten percent. The awesomeness of one who could sacrifice half of his troops affected all within the Four Seas. The strength of one who could sacrifice thirty percent could be applied to the feudal lords. The orders of one who could sacrifice ten percent would be implemented among his officers and troops.

Many commanders in China's long military history stand out for deliberately sacrificing companies and even battalions to deceive their enemies and thereby manipulate them for fatal blows. More commonly, the ruse of apparent defeat and flight was employed to lure enemy forces into a preestablished ambush. However, in the historical illustration Li Mu deployed his forces in a extended horizontal array, one of the standard dispositions for effectively employing large numbers of troops, and then apparently succeeded in turning the khan's flanks to produce the double envelopment that allowed his massive crossbow corps to slaughter incredible numbers of the enemy, including highly mobile cavalrymen.

20 The Weak 弱

Tactical Discussion

In general, in warfare if the enemy is numerous while you are few, if the enemy is strong while you are weak, you must set out numerous flags and pennants, double the number of cookfires, and display strength to the enemy. If you make it impossible for the enemy to determine your numbers as many or few or your strategic power as strong or weak, they will certainly not lightly engage you in battle. Thus you will be able to rapidly depart, thereby preserving your army and keeping harm distant. A tactical principle from the *Art of War* states: "Strength and weakness are a matter of disposition."

Historical Illustration

During the Later Han dynasty, the Ch'iang barbarian people revolted and invaded Han territory as far as Wu-tu. Empress Dowager Teng, in control of the government, felt that Yü Hsü possessed the tactical planning skills of a commanding general and therefore dispatched him to assume the post of Grand Protector for Wu-tu. The Ch'iang then led several thousand troops forth to intercept him at the strategic pass of Yao-ku in Chen-ts'ang commandery. Yü Hsü halted his chariots, ceased his advance, and publicly announced that he had submitted a request to the central government for troops and would await their arrival before again setting out. When the Ch'iang heard about it, they divided up to plunder the nearby districts. Taking advantage of their scattering, Yü Hsü proceeded forward, traveling at double the normal pace both day and night, covering more than a hundred miles in one day. Moreover, he had his officials and officers each light two cookfires and then doubled them each succeeding day, so the Ch'iang did not dare press him. Someone asked him: "Sun Pin reduced his cookfires but you increase them. Moreover, according to the *Art of War,* an army on the march should not exceed thirty miles a day, yet today you have advanced a hundred miles. Why is this?" Yü said: "The enemy's troops are numerous while our soldiers are few. When the barbarians see our fires increasing daily, they will certainly interpret it as evidence that local troops from the commandery are joining us. Believing that our numbers are many while our speed is quick, they will hesitate to pursue us. Sun Pin manifested weakness, but I now display strength because our relative strategic power is different."

Commentary

This selection completes the strong/weak conceptual pair and ponders the problems posed by a weak force confronting a stronger, numerically superior foe, much as in Chapter 12, whose commentary should again be consulted. Expedience dictates that the weaker force must quickly resort to deceptive measures to confuse the enemy as to their actual strength and power and then take advantage of the momentary respite to either gain a local advantage and attack or effect measures to avoid the enemy. Sun-tzu himself counseled avoiding the enemy until they might be appropriately manipulated and limited victories might become possible, although slightly more than a century later Sun Pin offered suggestions for dividing the enemy's forces and one's own and then fighting fervently or exploiting ambushes. Other military writings echoed these approaches: avoidance or maneuver until locally concentrated forces might gain victory.

The historical illustration makes reference to Sun Pin's subterfuge of reducing the number of cookfires. This was a measure he implemented to lure the arrogant P'ang Chüan into overconfidently believing that his suspicions about the cowardice of Ch'i's army had been confirmed, the decreasing fires clearly indicating that desertions were reducing the number of men in camp. Thus reassured, P'ang Chüan hastily abandoned his baggage train and heavy forces to rush forward a thousand miles only to encounter Sun Pin's well-rested, deeply entrenched forces at the famous battle of Ma-ling. With a well-established killing zone, Ch'i's crossbowmen under Sun Pin easily decimated P'ang Chüan's army, killing perhaps a hundred thousand of them and ending Wei's status as a great power. (The battle of Ma-ling marks the first recorded use of crossbows in combat, even though they were already employed in massed volley fire. The crux of the battle is recounted as the historical illustration for Chapter 30, "Knowledge.")

Two statements from the *Art of War* are pivotal to understanding the historical incident. First, Sun-tzu said: "To effect a retreat that cannot be overtaken, employ unmatchable speed." Second, he decried excessive speed in advancing to battle, for it would simply deplete vital resources and exhaust the troops:

> Combat between armies is advantageous; combat between masses is dangerous. If the entire army contends for advantage, you will not arrive in time. If you reduce the army's size to contend for advantage, your baggage and heavy equipment will suffer losses.
>
> For this reason if you abandon your armor and heavy equipment to race forward day and night without encamping, covering two days normal distance at a time, marching forward a hundred miles to contend for gain, the Three Armies' generals will be captured. The strong will be first to arrive, while the exhausted will follow. With such tactics only one in ten will reach the battle site. If one contends for gain fifty miles away, it will cause the general of the Upper Army to stumble, and by following such tactics half the men will reach the objective. If you contend for gain at thirty miles, then two-thirds of the army will reach the objective.
>
> Accordingly, if the army does not have baggage and heavy equipment, it will be lost; if it does not have provisions, it will be lost; if it does not have stores, it will be lost.

Yü Hsü's critic mindlessly quoted Sun-tzu's words without attempting to understand them within an actual military context.

21 Arrogance 驕

Tactical Discussion

Whenever the enemy's forces are exceedingly strong and you cannot be certain of defeating them, you must speak humbly and cultivate obsequious behavior in order to make them arrogant. Wait until there is some political pretext that can be exploited, then with a single mobilization you can destroy them. A tactical principle from the *Art of War* states: "Be deferential to make them arrogant."

Historical Illustration

During the Three Kingdoms period, general Kuan Yü of Shu launched an attack in the north, capturing general Yü Chin of Wei and encircling Ts'ao Jen at Fan. General Lü Meng of the kingdom of Wu, who had been in command at Lu-k'ou, pleaded illness and went to Chien-yeh. Lu Sun went to see him and said: "How is it that when Kuan Yü approaches the border you journey far off and retire from your post. Will this not later be a basis for regret?" Lü Meng said: "Truly it is as you have said, but my illness is real." Lu Sun said: "Kuan Yü has always been arrogant, as well as cool and abrupt to other men. This is the first time he has realized great accomplishments and so has become even more arrogant, but also less determined. Moreover, when Kuan Yü learns that you are ill he will grow increasingly unprepared. Now if you go forth where he does not expect it, you can capture and control him. If you are going to have an audience with the emperor, it would be wise to make plans for this." Lü Meng said: "Kuan Yü's nature is courageous and fierce, and he was already a formidable enemy, but now that he occupies Ching-chou and has acted generously and established his credibility all about, coupled with his initial success, his courageous spirit is excessively robust. It will not be easy to plot against him."

Lü Meng went to the capital where the emperor, Sun Ch'üan, queried him: "Sir, since you are ill, who can replace you?" Lü Meng replied: "Lu Sun is a far-sighted and profound thinker with the talent to sustain heavy duties. I have observed his thoughts; in the end he can undertake great responsibility. Moreover, as he has not yet garnered far-reaching fame, Kuan Yü will not be troubled by his appointment. However, he will not repeat this mistake. If you employ Lu Sun you should instruct him to obscure his talents but internally investigate the army's disposition and defenses. Only then can he be victorious." Sun Ch'üan then summoned Lu Sun and appointed him as a lieutenant general and regional inspector to replace Lü Meng.

Lu Sun then proceeded to Lu-k'ou, from where he dispatched a letter to Kuan Yü that said:

> Previously, you took advantage of a political pretext to move, advanced the army in good order, and with but a little effort achieved a great conquest! When an enemy state is severely defeated, the profit extends to the victor's allies. We hope to share in some small measure in the enjoyment of your kingly achievements. Unfortunately, your servant lacks perspicacity, but ever since receiving the command to come west, I have gazed in admiration at your overwhelming majesty, constantly hoping to emulate your great achievements.

> Your capture of Yü Chin and the others has met with joyous response both near and far. Your great achievement is surely worthy of being transmitted to later generations. They even surpass the magnificent accomplishments of antiquity, including Duke Wen's victory at Ch'eng-p'u and Han Hsin's strategy to seize Chao. I have heard about Hsü Kuang's infantry and cavalry, their flags expansively arrayed, anxiously awaiting an opportunity against you. Ts'ao Ts'ao himself is a crafty brigand. When angered he pays no heed to hardship and has been secretly increasing his troop strength in order to realize his ambitions. Even though it is said that his army is weary, he still has ruthless cavalrymen. Moreover, after a great victory such as yours, there is tendency to suffer from slighting one's enemies and neglecting affairs. In antiquity, generals increased their vigilance after attaining victory. I hope you sir will plan extensively in order to achieve sole and complete conquest. Although I am but a student, lowly and unqualified to my responsibilities, I hope to exhaust my abilities to celebrate your awesome Virtue. Although they may not accord with your plans, I embrace such hopes!

When Kuan Yü read the letter with its self-deprecatory tone and apparent expression of entrusting himself to his patronage, he felt at ease and did not harbor any suspicions about him. Lu Sun then examined the strategic situation in detail and deployed in preparation for seizing the strategic positions that might be captured. Sun Ch'üan secretly advanced his army and had Lu Sun and Lü Meng act as forward units. When he arrived, they proceeded to conquer the cities of Kung-an and Nan-chün.

Commentary

Exploiting character flaws, such as tendencies to arrogance or anger, was a fundamental method for creating the requisite advantage for effective combat. Virtually all the military writers identified a whole series of such flaws and advocated ruthlessly manipulating circumstances and appearances to further nurture them, causing misperceptions and errors. A famous example was Sun Pin's actions in reducing the army's cookfires to play upon P'ang Chüan's arrogance, discussed in the preceding chapter and recounted again as the historical illustration for Chapter 30, "Knowledge." Sun-tzu himself articulated the principle noted above, and since victory tended to make men arrogant, it was a method often exploited, whether through verbal communications or battlefield ruses.

Most of the military writings pondered the talents and character traits essential to command, while many also described a number of flaws and weaknesses likely to result in disaster. A typical, balanced list appears in the *Six Secret Teachings:*

> Generals have five critical talents and ten excesses. What are referred to as the five talents are courage, wisdom, benevolence, trustworthiness, and loyalty. If he is courageous, he cannot be overwhelmed. If he is wise, he cannot be forced into turmoil. If he is benevolent, he will love his men. If he is trustworthy, he will not be deceitful. If he is loyal, he won't be of two minds.
>
> What are referred to as the ten errors are as follows: being courageous and treating death lightly; being hasty and impatient; being greedy and loving profit; being benevolent but unable to inflict suffering; being wise but afraid; being trustworthy and liking to trust others; being scrupulous and incorruptible but not loving men; being wise but indecisive; being resolute and self-reliant; and being fearful while liking to entrust responsibility to other men.
>
> One who is courageous and treats death lightly can be destroyed by violence. One who is hasty and impatient can be destroyed by persistence. One who is greedy and loves profit can be bribed. One who is benevolent but unable to inflict suffering can be worn down. One who is wise but fearful can be distressed. One who is trustworthy and likes to trust others can be deceived. One who is scrupulous and incorruptible but does not love men can be insulted. One who is wise but indecisive can be suddenly attacked. One who is resolute and self-reliant can be confounded by events. One who is fearful and likes to entrust responsibility to others can be tricked.
>
> Thus, as Sun-tzu said, "Warfare is the greatest affair of state, the Tao of survival or extinction." The fate of the state lies in the hands of the general. The general is the support of the state, a man that the former kings all valued. Thus in commissioning a general you cannot but carefully evaluate and investigate his character.

The historical incident illustrates the tangled political situation existing in the Three Kingdoms period from the perspective of Wu, which had become allied with Shu due to Liu Pei's initiatives in accord with Chu-ko Liang's strategic overview preserved in the first chapter of the *Unorthodox Strategies.* The next selection, "Alliances," discusses the same sequence of events from another perspective, drawing a rather different lesson, and should be read in conjunction with this one. Clearly, alliances were frequently matters of convenience, hardly sacred covenants carved in stone.

22 Alliances 交

Tactical Discussion

Whenever engaging an enemy in battle, if there are neighboring states off to the sides, you should speak deferentially and entangle them with generous bribes in order to gain their support. Then if you attack the enemy's front while they apply a pincer strike to the rear, the enemy's troops will certainly be defeated. A tactical principle from the *Art of War* states: "On focal terrain unite with your allies."

Historical Illustration

During the Three Kingdoms period, general Kuan Yü of Shu encircled Ts'ao Jen of Wei at Fan, so the kingdom of Wei dispatched General of the Left Yü Chin and others to rescue him. It happened that the Han River rapidly rose at this time. Kuan Yü employed boats manned by marines to capture general Yü Chin and others, some thirty thousand infantry and cavalry, and sent them back to Chiang-ling. At this time the Han emperor's capital was Hsü-ch'ang, which Ts'ao Ts'ao felt was too close to the enemy. Therefore, he wanted to shift the capital north of the Yellow River in order to avoid their front lines. Ssu-ma Yi remonstrated with him saying: "General Yü and the others were destroyed by flood waters, not through battlefield or defensive losses. It does not adversely affect the state's grand strategy, so if we shift the capital, it will display weakness to the enemy and the populace in Huai and Mien will both become unsettled. Moreover, while Sun Ch'üan and Liu Pei appear visibly close, in actuality they are estranged. Allowing Kuan Yü to realize his ambitions certainly is not something Sun Ch'üan will countenance. You can essentially order Ch'üan to mount a pincer attack on Kuan Yü's rear, thereby causing the siege at Fan to be lifted by itself." Ts'ao Ts'ao followed his advice, dispatching an emissary to form an alliance with Sun Ch'üan who subsequently dispatched Lü Meng westward to mount a sudden attack on Kung-an and Nan-chün. Lü Meng seized them and Kuan Yü indeed abandoned the siege of Fan and departed.

Commentary

Alone among the classic military writers, Sun-tzu discussed the role and importance of allies in mounting extensive military campaigns. "Focal terrain," mentioned in the quotation, is in fact defined in terms of the terrain's accessibility to other states: "Land of the feudal lords surrounded on all three sides such that whoever arrives first will gain the masses of All under Heaven is focal terrain" and "when the four sides are open to others, this is focal terrain." An army out on campaign, venturing onto focal terrain to engage an enemy, had, of necessity, to be concerned with the actions of neighboring states and undertake measures to at least ensure their neutrality—if not outright support—rather than find themselves unexpectedly enveloped by hostile forces. Accordingly, after preliminary alliance building, the army should "unite with its allies on focal terrain."

Because of their strategic value, alliances naturally comprised targets for political and military attacks. Sun-tzu said: "The highest realization of warfare is to attack the enemy's plans; next is to attack their alliances; next to attack their army; and the lowest is to attack their fortified cities." Foreknowledge, gained through spies, defectors, and generally informed travelers and officials, is essential in attempting to thwart enemy attempts to forge useful friendships: "One who does not know the plans of the feudal lords cannot forge preparatory alliances." Thereafter, through the effective application of political and military measures, the enemy can be isolated and then militarily defeated, if force proves necessary: "Now when the army of a hegemon or true king attacks a great state, their masses are unable to assemble. When it applies its awesomeness to the enemy, their alliances cannot be sustained. For this reason it does not contend with any alliances under Heaven."

The historical illustration reprises the same battle discussed in the previous chapter, "Arrogance," but from the perspective of Wu rather than Ts'ao Ts'ao's Wei dynasty. As already noted, the alliance between Liu Pei and Sun Ch'üan, characterized as being weak, was initiated by Liu Pei in accord with Chu-ko Liang's advice. In thus forming a new alliance with Ts'ao Ts'ao, Sun Ch'üan of course betrayed his covenants with Liu Pei of Shu, but only after having achieved the gains noted in the last chapter.

23 Disposition 形

Tactical Discussion

Whenever engaging an enemy in battle, if their troops are extremely numerous you should establish a vacuous form in order to cause them to segment their strategic power, for they will not dare not divide their soldiers in order to prepare for you. When the enemy's strategic power has been fragmented, their soldiers at any single point will invariably be few. Thus, if you concentrate your troops into a focused unit, they will naturally be more numerous at any chosen point. When you attack the few with the many, you will always be victorious. A tactical principle from the *Art of War* states: "Determine the enemy's disposition of force while we have no perceptible form."

Historical Illustration

In the fifth year of the Chien-an reign period (200 A.D.) at the end of the Later Han dynasty, Ts'ao Ts'ao and Yüan Shao were locked in a stalemate on opposite sides of the river at Kuan-tu. Yüan Shao dispatched his lieutenant generals Kuo T'u, Ch'un Yü-ch'iung, and Yen Liang to attack Ts'ao Ts'ao's general Liu Yen, Grand Protector for the Eastern Commandery, at the city of Pai-ma. Yüan Shao himself led his troops to Li-yang and prepared to cross the Yellow River. In the fourth month of summer (June), Ts'ao Ts'ao was about to proceed north to rescue Liu Yen at Pai-ma when Hsün Yu offered this advice: "Right now our soldiers are few and not a match for the enemy. However, if we can segment their strategic power, it will become possible. If my Lord proceeds to Yen-chin and then fords the Yellow River to move toward Yüan Shao's rear, he will certainly respond by moving west. Then your light forces can suddenly strike Pai-ma, surprising them where they are unprepared, and general Yen Liang can be captured." Ts'ao Ts'ao adopted his advice.

When Yüan Shao heard that Ts'ao's troops were about to cross the Yellow River, he divided his forces and went west in response. Ts'ao Ts'ao then led his own army on a double pace advance to race to Pai-ma. Before they had proceeded ten miles, Yen Liang, greatly startled, came forth to counterattack. Ts'ao Ts'ao deputed Chang Liao and Kuan Yü to move forward and attack them. They destroyed Yen's forces, beheaded Yen himself, and subsequently extricated the city of Pai-ma from its siege.

Commentary

The tactical discussion advocates the systematic application of a concept found in Sun-tzu's chapter entitled "Vacuity and Substance"—being formless (or having no visible disposition of forces) and thereby compelling the enemy to fragment his troops to provide an encompassing defense for his perimeter, strongpoints, and vital interests. Being formless entails concealing one's intentions, masking movements that might betray objectives:

> The location where we will engage the enemy must not become known to them. If it is not known, then the positions they must prepare to defend will be numerous. If the positions the enemy prepares to defend are numerous, then the forces we will engage will be few. Thus if they prepare to defend the front, to the rear there will be few men. If they defend the rear, in the front there will be few. If they prepare to defend the left flank, then on the right there will be few men. If they prepare to defend the right flank, then on the left there will be few men. If there is no position left undefended, then there will not be any place with more than a few. The few are the ones who prepare against others; the many are the ones who make others prepare against them.

Accordingly, Sun-tzu concluded: "The pinnacle of military deployment approaches the formless. If it is formless, then even the deepest spy cannot discern it or the wise make plans against it."

The corollary to concealing one's own disposition and intentions is fathoming the enemy's plans and deployments because localized concentrations of force can then produce decided advantages and significant victories:

> If I determine the enemy's disposition of forces while we have no perceptible form, I can concentrate my forces while the enemy is fragmented. If we are concentrated into a single force while he is fragmented into ten, then we attack him with ten times his strength. Thus we are many and the enemy is few. If we can attack his few with our many, those who we engage in battle will be severely constrained.

The historical incident chosen for this chapter only weakly illustrates the avowed principle, being instead an excellent example of manipulating an enemy, destabilizing them with a feint, and then focusing the army's main power on a hasty counterattack mounted by a secondary enemy force. Ts'ao Ts'ao's movements of course concealed his real intentions within a visible form and thus accorded with the ultimate principle of concealing the formless within an ostensible disposition. (This battle is reconsidered from a different perspective as the historical illustration for Chapter 28, "Provisions.")

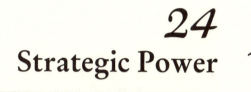

24 Strategic Power 勢

Tactical Principle

In warfare, "strategic power" refers to the exploitation of strategic advantage through power. Whenever the enemies are in a situation where they can be vanquished and destroyed, you should follow it up and press an attack on them, for then their army will certainly crumble. A tactical principle from the *Three Strategies* states: "Rely on strategic power to destroy them."

Historical Illustration

During the Wei-Chin period, Emperor Wu of the Chin dynasty had a secret plan for exterminating the Wu dynasty, but most of his court officials opposed it, with only Yang Hu, Tu Yü, and Chang Hua supporting his strategy. When Yang fell ill, he recommended Tu Yü as his replacement. When Yang then died, the emperor appointed Tu Yü as Commander-in-Chief for the Southern Suppression Forces and Military Supervisor for all of Ching-chou's military affairs. When he reached the army's encampment, he had their weapons and armor put in order, flourished their martial awesomeness, and selected the elite troops, intending to destroy Wu. Chang Cheng, Military Supervisor for Chin's Hsi-king commandery, thereupon requested the emperor to fix a date for attacking Wu, but the emperor replied that he wanted to wait for the succeeding year before undertaking a major mobilization. Tu Yü then submitted a memorial that read:

> Every affair encompasses an intermixture of both profit and loss. The prospects for profit in this effort amount to eight or nine out of ten, while the possibilities for loss are merely one or two in ten. By stopping now, we will simply fail to realize any gains at all. Your court ministers claim that we cannot achieve our objective of destroying the enemy only because they did not advance the plan themselves and the credit will not devolve to them. Being ashamed of their former errors, they all cling to this position.
>
> Formerly Emperor Hsüan of the Han, after discussing military problems along the border raised in a memorial by general Chao Ch'ung-kuo, upbraided the discussants, who then bowed their heads apologetically for having obstructed dissenting opinions. Ever since autumn our preparations for eradicating these brigands have become obvious. Even if we suspend them now, Sun Hao has become frightened and will formulate his own tactics, perhaps shifting his capital to Wu-chang or augmenting and repairing various cities south of the Yellow River. This will move his populace further away; his cities will not be attackable; the fields will not have anything to forage; and if we must assemble large boats at Hsia-k'ou to cross the river, we may be unable to implement our plans even next year.

The emperor was playing chess with Chang Hua just when Tu Yü's memorial arrived. Chang Hua pushed the chess board forward, folded his hands together and said: "Your Majesty possesses the enlightenment of a Sage and the martial understanding of the spirits. The state is rich and the army strong, while the king of Wu is dissolute and brutal, killing and executing the worthy and talented. If you now launch a punitive campaign against him, the matter can be settled with little effort." The emperor then assented.

Tu Yü deployed his troops at Chiang-ling and dispatched Chou Chih and Wu Ch'ao, with others, one night to lead their troops in crossing the river in sailing vessels in order to suddenly strike Yüeh-hsiang. When launching the assault they multiplied their flags and pennants, raised fires as high as Mount Pa, and sallied forth at strategic points in order to seize the enemy's mind. Subsequently they captured Sun Hsin, Wu's Military Supervisor. Having secured the upper reaches of the Yellow River, Wu's provinces and commanderies from Hsiang-chiang south as far as Chiao-chou and Kuang-chou, bending with the wind, returned their allegiance to Chin, and Tu Yü pacified the area in the emperor's name.

When Chin's generals next convened someone said: "The men of Wu have been brigands for a hundred years and cannot be easily conquered. Now is the height of the summer heat so the water level is about to drop and epidemics will soon arise. It would be best to wait for winter before mounting another expedition." Tu Yü said: "In antiquity Yüeh Yi availed himself of a single battle in the west of Ch'i to seize all of the strong state of Ch'i. Now our army's awesomeness already shakes the realm. This might be compared to destroying bamboo—after several sections the remaining ones easily meet the blade and split; there is no need to apply great effort again." Subsequently he directed his commanders to advance directly to Mo-ling. Every city they passed submitted without resistance and eventually they subjugated Sun Hao.

Commentary

The concept of strategic power—military power coupled with and multiplied by positional strategic advantage—was fundamental to Chinese military thought, having been first articulated by Sun-tzu in the *Art of War,* where it is already a highly sophisticated concept. In essence, Sun-tzu graphically stressed that strategic power properly exploited would invariably overwhelm the enemy:

> The strategic configuration of power is visible in the onrush of pent-up water tumbling stones along. The effect of constraints is visible in the onrush of a bird of prey breaking the bones of its target. Thus the strategic configuration of power of those that excel in warfare is sharply focused; their constraints are precise. Their strategic configuration of power is like a fully drawn crossbow; their constraints like the release of the trigger.

A knowledgeable commander seeking to exploit his power need only focus upon formulating the tactics necessary to gain a positional advantage and thereby create the appropriate circumstances for victory.

The tactical discussion raises another of Sun-tzu's admonitions—never fail to exploit a victory: "Now if someone is victorious in battle and succeeds in attack but does not exploit the achievement, it is disastrous, and his fate should be termed 'wasteful and tarrying.'" This lesson is also embodied in the historical illustration, expressive of Sun-tzu's underlying feeling that "warfare is the greatest affair of state"—expensive to mount, debilitating to the state, and of necessity to be kept short: "In military campaigns I have heard of awkward speed but have never seen any skill in lengthy campaigns. No country has ever profited from protracted warfare." Virtually all the Chinese military theorists agreed, with Sun Pin and some others even asserting that the more numerous the victories, the greater the damage.

Night battles were not common in antiquity because the defenders, entrenched on familiar terrain, enjoyed almost insurmountable advantages.

However, when launched by a well-disciplined force against an unprepared foe, surprise coupled with laxity could produce dramatic results for aggressors. The state of Yüeh employed a night attack coupled with a river crossing, much as in the historical illustration, at the famous battle of Li-che River just after the end of the Spring and Autumn period and essentially destroyed Wu's army. (This battle is recounted in the introduction to our translation of the *Art of War* and also briefly presented as the historical illustration for Chapter 26, "Night.") In directing their strategy, Tu Yü—not surprisingly because he was one of the earliest and foremost commentators on the *Art of War*—employed several of Sun-tzu's concepts, including multiple measures in night battles, to create the effects necessary to overwhelm the enemy's mind and spirit. As Sun-tzu said: "The spirit (*ch'i*) of the Three Armies can be snatched away; the commanding general's mind can be seized." This would be particularly true when an entrenched army, assuming a nearby river that constituted a formidable barrier during daylight hours would certainly be impossible to attempt at night, would not—as the T'ai Kung predicted—mount a strong defense.

Tu Yü's memorial also provides tangential evidence of the analytical methods employed before undertaking a campaign, assuming he did not simply fabricate the high probability for success as a persuasive device. His words exemplify Sun-tzu's statement: "The wise must contemplate the intermixture of gain and loss. If they discern advantage in difficult situations, their efforts can be trusted. If they discern harm in prospective advantage, difficulties can be resolved."

25 Daylight 晝

Tactical Discussion

Whenever engaging an enemy in battle during daylight, you must set out numerous flags and pennants to cause uncertainty about your forces. When you prevent the enemy from determining your troop strength, you will be victorious. A tactical principle from the *Art of War* states: "In daylight battles make the flags and pennants numerous."

Historical Illustration

During the Spring and Autumn period, when the lord of Chin was advancing to attack the state of Ch'i, the lord of Ch'i ascended a mountain to observe Chin's army. Chin's forces had established outposts throughout the strategic mountain and marsh areas and had invariably set out flags even where the army would not venture, indicating an expansive deployment. Moreover, they had real men drive their chariots but dummies manned the right side of each vehicle. Behind the flags flying on each chariot they affixed brushwood that dragged in the dust. When the lord of Ch'i saw this he was afraid of their large numbers and quickly fled.

Commentary

The ancients practiced innumerable ruses and deceptions to prevent their enemies from gathering accurate military intelligence. If spies and reconnaissance patrols could be prevented from penetrating the army, whatever measures might confuse distant observers relying upon naked sight alone might be turned to advantage. The arsenal of tricks to increase apparent force size included soldiers and vehicles dragging brush; the building of numerous cookfires; augmenting the number of supply wagons; placing straw men in trenches or vehicles; recirculating companies by having them visibly enter, secretly depart, then reenter; and multiplying the number of unit pennants and command flags, as well as the number of drums. Conversely, when attempting to create the opposite impression—fewer forces than actually present—every method that would conceal troop strength had to be employed, such as encamping them in heavy forests, deep valleys, heavy vegetation, or high in the mountains; keeping the number of cookfires sparse; restricting rations to immediate needs, thereby reducing the supply train; packing men closely and delaying their deployment into segmented formations; and spreading rumors or employing double agents to suggest a limited force size.

As cited in the tactical discussion, the quotation would seem to imply that Sun-tzu advocated using numerous flags (and fires at night, as will be discussed in the next selection) to confuse the enemy. However, the original context is somewhat different, for the sentence actually concludes a short discussion that began with an extract from an ancient work addressing the problem of battlefield communication:

> The Military Administration states: "Because they could not hear each other they made gongs and drums; because they could not see each other they made pennants and flags." Gongs, drums, pennants, and flags are the means to unify the men's ears and eyes. When the men have been unified, the courageous will not be able to advance alone and the fearful will not be able to retreat alone. This is the method for employing large numbers.
>
> Thus in night battles make the fires and drums numerous, and in daylight battles make the flags and pennants numerous in order to change the men's ears and eyes.

In this matter most of the military writers were in agreement, often paraphrasing or quoting these arguments. For example, Wu Ch'i said:

> Now the different drums, gongs, and bells are the means to awe the ear; flags and banners, pennants and standards the means to awe the eye; and prohibitions, orders, punishments, and fines the means to awe the mind. When the ear has been awestruck by sound, it cannot but be clear. When the eye has been awestruck by color, it cannot but be discriminating. When the mind has been awestruck by penalties, it cannot but be strict. If these three are not established, even though you have the support of the state you will invariably be defeated by the enemy. Thus it is said that wherever the general's banners are everyone will go, and wherever the general points everyone will move forward, even unto death.

Accordingly, visible means are employed during daytime, auditory signals at night: "In general it is a rule of battle that during daylight hours the flags, banners, pennants, and standards provide the measure, while at night the gongs, drums, pipes, and whistles provide the constraints. When left is signaled, they should go left; when right, then right. When the drum is beaten they should advance; when the gongs sound they should halt." As a result, by the late Spring and Autumn period Chinese military forces were capable of articulated maneuver, of being commanded rather than led by their generals, and could execute complex, changing tactics prompted by the evolving battlefield situation. At the same time other tacticians, such as the T'ai Kung, resorted to multiplying the flags when the army was in difficulty or when it was desirable to amplify force impression, as Sun Pin does in his chapter entitled "Ten Deployments." A similar application has already been witnessed in Chapter 20, "The Weak," and will be seen again in Chapter 91, "Doubt."

26 Night 夜

Tactical Discussion

Whenever engaging an enemy in a night battle, you must employ numerous fires and drums to change and confuse their eyes and ears. If you befuddle the enemy so that they cannot make preparations against your tactics, you will be victorious. One who has caused the enemy not to know where to prepare for his tactics will be victorious. A tactical principle from the *Art of War* states: "In night battles make the fires and drums numerous."

Historical Illustration

During the Spring and Autumn period, the state of Yüeh attacked the state of Wu. Wu's forces mounted a defense at the Li-che River, so both sides deployed hard along the river. Yüeh had the armies arrayed on the left and right flanks alternately beat their drums, set up a great clamor, and advance across the river. When Wu divided its forces to resist them, Yüeh's central army secretly forded the river, confronted Wu's central force, and only then beat their drums. Wu's forces were thrown into chaos, and Yüeh went on to destroy them.

Commentary

Whereas the previous selection discussed measures to startle and confuse the enemy during daylight engagements, this one considers techniques to achieve similar results in the infrequent night battles. Sun-tzu's quotation is again somewhat misapplied because it originally addressed problems of communication (as discussed in the commentary to the previous selection), although other writers recommended exploiting the combined effect of noise and fire to disorient the enemy. However, the Battle of Li-che River sketched in the historical illustration turned on surprise rather than numerous drums, for Yüeh managed to throw Wu's forces into chaos by making a deliberately noisy, nighttime river crossing to suddenly threaten Wu's relatively unguarded flanks with a double envelopment, compelling their troops to rush to the perimeter. Once they responded it was easy to attack when and where unexpected, striking their now destabilized troops to exploit their chaos and wrest an easy victory. (The Battle of Li-che River also appears as the historical incident for Chapter 64, "The Nearby," where it illustrates the principles of distraction and division.)

An example of a brilliant Western night attack was Scipio Africanus' stunning victory over the mixed Carthaginian forces of Syphax and Habsdrubal near Utica in 204 B.C. Again the attack consisted of two stages, designed to evoke a reaction and then exploit it. A secondary force quietly set fire to Syphax's camp, taking the defenders unaware. The troops in Habsdrubal's fortress, spotting the conflagration about a mile off, rushed to aid the firefighting efforts, unaware that Scipio's forces had advanced to positions just outside their own encampment. Their hasty actions provided Scipio with an opportunity to penetrate the fortress gates and again employ incendiary weapons. Amid the flames that also illuminated the interior of the fortress, the Romans easily destroyed many of the entrapped forces. Estimates of total losses from these coordinated twin attacks ran as high as forty thousand men, providing evidence of Scipio's tactical ability in overcoming superior forces on their own terrain and his courage in risking a difficult night attack.

27 Preparation 備

Tactical Discussion

Whenever you send the army forth on a punitive campaign to exterminate an enemy, on the march you must be prepared against being intercepted; when halting, be prepared for surprise attacks; when encamped, take precautions against thieves; and in windy conditions, be prepared for incendiary attacks. If you make such preparations, you will always be victorious and never be defeated. A tactical principle from the *Tso Chuan* states: "One who is prepared will not be defeated."

Historical Illustration

During the Three Kingdoms period Wu Lin, Wei's commander-in-chief, went south on a punitive campaign. When the army reached Ching Lake, the forward army commanded by General Man Ch'ung deployed directly across the lake from the enemy. General Man Ch'ung addressed his subordinates: "The wind is extremely fierce tonight, so the enemy will certainly approach to set fire to our encampment. It would be best to prepare for them." His generals were all startled. In the middle of the night the enemy indeed dispatched ten companies to advance and ignite the encampment, but Man Ch'ung intercepted them with a surprise attack and destroyed them.

Commentary

Given that the most widely recognized tactical principle was "attack where unexpected," commanders should have been paranoiac about maintaining constant vigilance, particularly when in exposed situations. However, the realities of warfare, with men overfatigued and highly confident in the unlikeliness of an attack, invariably led to negligence and laxity. Thus Sun-tzu said: "Do not rely upon their not coming, but depend upon having the means to await them. Do not rely on their not attacking, but depend upon having an unassailable position."

The historical incident illustrates the dangers posed by encamping downwind of an opposing army, for any substantial wind, coupled with abundant grass, woods, or other dry matter, would immediately provide the enemy with an opportunity to create a firestorm. Only three of the classic writers discussed incendiary warfare: Sun-tzu, who devoted a chapter to it; Sun Pin; and the T'ai Kung, who focused on defending against them. His defensive methods are largely preserved in a chapter appropriately entitled "Incendiary Warfare" in the *Six Secret Teachings:*

> King Wu asked the T'ai Kung: "Suppose we have led our troops deep into the territory of the feudal lords where we encounter deep grass and heavy growth that surround our army on all sides. The Three Armies have traveled several hundred miles; the men and horses are exhausted and have halted to rest. Taking advantage of the extremely dry weather and a strong wind, the enemy ignites

> fires upwind from us. Their chariots, cavalry, and elite forces are firmly concealed in ambush to our rear. The Three Armies become terrified, scatter in confusion, and run off. What can be done?"
>
> The T'ai Kung said: "Under such circumstances use the cloud ladders and flying towers to look far out to the left and right, to carefully investigate front and rear. When you see the fires arise, then set fires in front of our own forces, spreading them out over the area. Also set fires to the rear. If the enemy comes, withdraw the army and take up entrenched positions on the blackened earth to await their assault. In the same way, if you see flames arise to the rear, you must move far away. If we occupy the blackened ground with our strong crossbowmen and skilled soldiers protecting the left and right flanks, we can also set fires to the front and rear. In this way the enemy will not be able to harm us."
>
> King Wu asked: "Suppose the enemy has set fires to the left and right, and also to the front and rear. Smoke covers our army, while his main force appears from over the blackened ground. What should we do?"
>
> The T'ai Kung said: "In this case (assuming you have prepared a burnt section of ground), disperse the Martial Attack chariots to form a fighting barrier on all four sides and have strong crossbowmen cover the flanks. This method will not bring victory but will also not end in defeat."

The existence of this textual material, probably compiled in the middle Warring States period from even earlier materials, indicates that commanders frequently took advantage of dry, windy circumstances to launch incendiary attacks. The techniques for mounting such attacks, as advanced by Sun-tzu and Sun Pin, will be analyzed in Chapter 66 on "Incendiary Strategies."

28 Provisions 糧

Tactical Discussion

Now when your forces and the enemy are maintaining fortified positions in a standoff, with victory and defeat still undecided, whoever has provisions will be victorious. Accordingly, you must vigorously augment the protective measures for our own supply lines, fearing the enemy's troops might seize your provisions. Moreover, you should dispatch elite troops to sever the enemy's supply routes. Then, since the enemy lacks provisions, his troops must withdraw and an assault on them will produce victory. A tactical principle from the *Art of War* states: "An army without provisions and foodstuffs is lost."

Historical Illustration

At the end of the Later Han dynasty, Ts'ao Ts'ao and Yüan Shao were locked in a stalemate on opposite sides of the river at Kuan-tu. When Yüan Shao wanted to dispatch provisions to his army he had Ch'un Yü-ch'iung and four others, in command of more than ten thousand troops, escort them. They encamped about forty miles north of Shao's position. Hsü Yu, Shao's chief-of-staff, was covetous and greedy. As Yüan Shao did not employ him in a way that satisfied him, he fled to join Ts'ao Ts'ao and then encouraged Ts'ao to take action: "Right now Yüan Shao has more than ten thousand provision wagons nearby, but they lack strong defensive preparations. If you should suddenly strike them with light troops and incinerate their accumulated supplies, in less than three days Yüan Shao will have defeated himself."

Ordering Ts'ao Hung to remain behind to guard their encampment, Ts'ao Ts'ao then personally took command of more than five thousand infantry and cavalry. They all carried the flags and pennants of Shao's army, and even gagged the soldiers' and horses' mouths, and went forth at night along back roads. Someone carrying a bundle of firewood they passed along the way queried them, to which Ts'ao Ts'ao replied: "Duke Shao, being afraid Ts'ao Ts'ao might plunder our rear army, has dispatched these troops to augment their preparedness." The wood carrier believed it to be true. In this fashion they arrived at their destination without incident, surrounded the encampment, and set extensive fires. The soldiers in the camp were frightened and confused, and Ts'ao Ts'ao inflicted a severe defeat. Yüan Shao then abandoned his armor and fled.

Commentary

The basic tactical principle stems from Sun-tzu's *Art of War*, where it is the conclusion to his analysis of the inappropriateness of racing too far to engage in battle and thereby losing men, equipment, and essential stores. The actual sentence is somewhat different: "If the army does not have baggage and heavy equipment it will be lost; if it does not have provisions it will be lost; if it does not have stores it will be lost."

In antiquity, in the absence of mechanized transport and adequate roads, supplying and provisioning a typical hundred-thousand-man force required Herculean efforts and thousands of ponderous, usually ox-drawn supply wagons. Thus Sun-tzu cautioned against wantonly engaging in warfare and advocated, as did several other military writers, foraging and plundering once beyond the state's borders. Such aggressive measures characterized ancient armies in Greece and Rome as well, but their potential success depended upon the availability of warehoused goods, herds of animals, and even ripe crops standing in the fields. Conversely, severing an enemy's supply routes would quickly reduce them to starvation and make their conquest an easy matter.

The historical anecdote encompasses four additional fundamental principles, all extensively discussed by the classic military writers: exploit intelligence; be deceptive, such as by using disguises; move swiftly; and strike when least expected, where the enemy remains unprepared. It would only be through exploiting such opportunities that weaker forces, such as Ts'ao Ts'ao's, could successfully attack and vanquish stronger foes, such as Yüan Shao, as may be seen in many of the book's historical illustrations. (This battle previously appeared as the historical illustration for Chapter 23, "Disposition." The effectiveness of nighttime incendiary attacks should again be noted.)

29 Local Guides 導

Tactical Discussion

Whenever engaging an enemy in battle—whether on level or precipitous terrain, whether the road is circuitous or straight—you must employ local people to guide the army. Only then will you know the advantages of terrain and be victorious in combat. A tactical principle from the *Art of War* states: "One who does not employ local guides will not be able to secure advantages of terrain."

Historical Illustration

During the reign of Emperor Wu in the Former Han dynasty, the Hsiung-nu mounted yearly border incursions, killing many and plundering extensively. In the spring of the fifth year of the Yüan-shuo reign period (124 B.C.), the emperor ordered General Wei Ching to assume command of thirty thousand cavalrymen and go out beyond the border. Even when informed of General Wei's approach, one of the Hsiung-nu leaders, the Worthy King of the Right, believing the army could not reach them, got drunk and fell asleep in his tent. That night the Han forces arrived and surrounded the king's encampment. The Hsiung-nu were greatly surprised, and the king barely managed to escape with just his beloved concubine and few hundred cavalry, breaking through the encirclement and fleeing north into the night.

General Wei Ching deputed Kuo Ch'eng, Colonel of the Light Cavalry, to pursue him. Although they raced more than four hundred miles, Kuo failed to catch him. However, at the encampment Wei Ching's forces killed and captured more than a hundred officers, five thousand men and women, and several million head of livestock. Thereupon Wei Ching led his forces back to the border. An emissary from the emperor, bearing the seal of a general-in-chief, appointed Wei Ching in the encampment as general-in-chief, while his subordinates, with appropriate new designations, returned with their troops and were appointed as colonels. This victory resulted from employing Chang Ch'ien, who had frequently acted as an ambassador to the Ta-Hsia and thus lingered long among the Hsiung-nu, to guide the army. Because he knew the location of water and grass, the army was able to avoid hunger and thirst.

Commentary

Sun-tzu's *Art of War* contains the first descriptions of basic configurations of terrain with appropriate tactical suggestions. For Sun-tzu and the strategists who followed him, knowledge of terrain was one of the five critical factors in warfare, essential to every aspect of military activity, from campaign movement through exploiting the natural advantages offered by battle sites. In his very first chapter Sun-tzu states: "Earth encompasses far or near, difficult or easy, expansive or confined, fatal or tenable terrain." Accordingly, extraordinary efforts had to be made to acquire accurate information about the terrain's configuration before initiating the decisionmaking process. An aspect of such intelligence was both general and detailed information about potential routes of march, as the expanded passage for the quotation cited in the tactical discussion states: "Someone unfamiliar with the mountains and forests, gorges and defiles, the shape of marshes and wetlands, cannot advance the army. One who does not employ local guides cannot gain advantages of terrain." Of course, the reliability of the guide's information would have to be otherwise verified before risking the army!

The historical illustration reflects one episode in the ongoing conflict between the nomadic steppe peoples generally living outside the rainfall line, where the Great Wall was eventually constructed, and those dwelling within the Han empire itself. Wei Ching's name is preserved because he commanded essentially the earliest imperial campaign into nomadic territory, although during the Warring States period certain individual border states had also achieved temporary victories with expeditionary armies. As the incident recounts, Wei Ching's success stemmed from advance knowledge of the terrain, the enemy's location, and feasible routes of march. The element of surprise loomed large, the king's negligence in making essential preparations, in underestimating his enemy and thus not having good perimeter defenses or even viable lookout posts, obviously fating him to defeat. (Another interesting example of the importance of employing local guides is provided by the Spring and Autumn period battle of Po-chü where Wu successfully invaded Ch'u because disaffected officials from a minor Ch'u state provided guides and information on routes through the T'ai-hang mountains. It is recounted and analyzed in the introduction to our *Art of War* translation.)

30 Knowledge 知

Tactical Discussion

Whenever mobilizing the army to attack an enemy, you must know where the battle will occur. On the day the army arrives, if you can compel the enemy's forces to advance at the right moment, when you engage in battle you will be victorious. When you know the day for battle, your preparations will be unified and your defenses solid. A tactical principle from the *Art of War* states: "If one knows the field of battle and knows the day of battle, he can traverse a thousand miles and assemble to engage in combat."

Historical Illustration

During the Warring States period, Wei and Chao attacked the state of Han. Han reported the extremity of its situation to Ch'i. Ch'i then commissioned T'ien Chi to take command and go forth, proceeding straight to Wei's capital of Ta-liang. When general P'ang Chüan of Wei heard about it, he abandoned his attack on Han and embarked on his return. Ch'i's army had already passed by and was proceeding to the west. Sun Pin said to T'ien Chi, "Wei's soldiers are coarse, fearless and courageous, and regard Ch'i lightly. Ch'i has been termed cowardly. One who excels in warfare relies upon his strategic power and realizes advantages from leading the enemy where he wants. As the *Art of War* notes, 'One who races a hundred miles in pursuit of profit will suffer the destruction of his foremost general; one who races fifty miles in pursuit of profit will arrive with only half his army.' Have our army of Ch'i, upon entering Wei's borders, light one hundred thousand cooking fires. Tomorrow make fifty thousand, and again the day after tomorrow start thirty thousand cooking fires."

P'ang Chüan, after advancing three days, greatly elated, said: "Now I truly know that Ch'i's army is terrified. They have been within our borders only three days but the number of officers and soldiers that have deserted exceeds half." Thereupon he abandoned his infantry and covered double the normal day's distance with only light, elite units in pursuit of them. Sun Pin, estimating his speed, determined that he would arrive at Ma-ling at dusk.

The road through Ma-ling was narrow, and to the sides there were numerous gullies and ravines where troops could be set in ambush. There Sun Pin chopped away the bark on a large tree until it showed white and wrote on it, "P'ang Chüan will die beneath this tree."

Then he ordered ten thousand skilled crossbowmen to wait in ambush on both sides, instructing them, "At dusk, when you see a fire, arise and shoot together." In the evening P'ang Chüan indeed arrived beneath the debarked tree. He saw the white trunk with the writing, struck a flint, and lit a torch. He had not finished reading the message when ten thousand crossbowmen fired en masse. Wei's army fell into chaos and mutual disorder. P'ang Chüan knew his wisdom was exhausted and his army defeated, so he cut his own throat.

Commentary

The tactical discussion reflects the classic concern with seizing the initiative, determining advantageous sites for engaging in battle, and then compelling the enemy to race there after having already assumed and improved the position. By controlling the sequence of movements, one's own forces will be both prepared and rested while the enemy will be fatigued and disordered. Accordingly, Sun-tzu said: "In general, whoever occupies the battleground first and awaits the enemy will be at ease; whoever occupies the battleground afterward and must race to the conflict will be fatigued. Thus one who excels at warfare compels men and is not compelled by other men." Wu Ch'i, who stressed the importance of constraining the army's expenditure of strength while in movement so as to avoid becoming overly fatigued and thereby offering an easy target, observed that the optimum moment to attack thus arose when confronting a weary foe:

> In employing the army you must ascertain the enemy's voids and strengths and then race to take advantage of his endangered points. When the enemy has just arrived from afar and their battle formations are not yet properly deployed, they can be attacked. If they have eaten but not yet established their encampment, they can be attacked. If they are running about wildly, they can be attacked. If they have labored hard, they can be attacked. If they haven't yet taken advantage of the terrain, they can be attacked. When they have lost the critical moment and not followed up opportunities, they can be attacked. When they have traversed a great distance and the rear guard hasn't had time to rest yet, they can be attacked. When fording rivers and only half of them have crossed, they can be attacked. In narrow and confined roads, they can be attacked. When their flags and banners move about chaotically, they can be attacked. When their formations frequently move about, they can be attacked. When a general is separated from his soldiers, they can be attacked. When they are afraid, they can be attacked. In general in circumstances such as these select crack troops to rush upon them, divide your remaining troops, and continue the assault, pressing the attack swiftly and decisively.

The tactical discussion in this selection seems, however, somewhat askew, envisioning an extremely close timing. This may have reflected Sung dynasty realities but was certainly not the ideal, for little time would be allowed for entrenching forces, building palisades, setting up shooting zones (such as by clearing obstructive vegetation), or just generally organizing the deployment and resting the troops for at least a few hours or a day. In contrast, the battle of Ma-ling, briefly recounted in the historical illustration (and extensively discussed in the introduction to our translation of Sun Pin's *Military Methods*), exemplifies the careful selection of terrain—a constricted valley—for maximum confinement of an onrushing enemy coupled with natural cover, height advantages to exploit the power of missile weapons, and adequate time to rest and prepare. Moreover, throughout Chinese history it has been cited to illustrate the effective exploitation of arrogance, a fatal flaw in commanders, as previously mentioned.

31 Observers 斥

Tactical Discussion

Among the methods for directing an army on campaign, establishing forward observers is foremost. On level, easy ground employ cavalry; on precipitous and obstructed terrain employ infantry. Five men should compose a squad, and each man should carry a white flag. When the army ventures out far, at the front and rear, left and right establish connected observation posts and lookouts. If they see enemy cavalry coming, they should successively transmit the signal and a white flag should be reported. The commanding general should then assemble the troops and make preparations against the attack. A tactical principle from the *Art of War* states: "One who, fully prepared, awaits the unprepared will be victorious."

Historical Illustration

During the reign of Emperor Hsüan of the Former Han dynasty, the Hsien-ling Ch'iang revolted, crossed the border, entered the pass, attacked cities, and killed the chief officials. Thereafter the emperor sent an emissary to Chao Ch'ung-kuo, an aged general of more than seventy years whom he now regarded as too old, to inquire who could command a mission against the barbarians. General Chao replied: "A hundred reports are not as good as one look. Military affairs are difficult to determine in advance. I am willing to race to Chin-ch'eng and develop tactical plans for your majesty. These Ch'iang are a minor barbarian group that has turned against Heaven in revolt. Their extermination will not require long. I request your August Majesty entrust it to your aged servant. You will not have any cause for regret." The emperor laughed and assented.

When general Chao reached Chin-ch'eng, the entire force he required of ten thousand cavalry wanted to cross the river, but he was afraid they might be unexpectedly overwhelmed by the barbarians. Accordingly, that night he dispatched three colonels with their troops to silently ford the river and immediately establish the camp's deployment. The next day all the troops crossed over and assembled there.

Groups of a few hundred barbarian cavalry came up and skirmished with their perimeter forces. General Chao said: "Our soldiers and horses have just arrived, so they are exhausted and cannot pursue cavalry. The enemy's horsemen are strong and skilled, difficult to master. Moreover, I fear they may be baiting our army. We should attack the barbarians only when we can exterminate them. This sort of small profit is not worth coveting." He ordered his soldiers not to attack them.

General Chao dispatched scouts to observe the situation within Ssu-wang-hsia gorge, and they reported no barbarians present. By the middle of the night they were able to proceed to Luo-tu where General Chao summoned his colonels and addressed them: "I knew the Ch'iang barbarians were incompetent! If they had sent out a few thousand men to occupy Ssu-wang-hsia gorge, how would our large mass of soldiers been able to enter barbarian territory?"

General Chao always emphasized the dispatch of distant scouts and observers. Therefore, on the march they would invariably be prepared for battle, and when they halted solid fortifications were erected about the encampment. Moreover, he was highly regarded, loved his officers and troops, and always made plans before engaging in battle. Eventually he pacified the Hsien-ling Ch'iang.

Commentary

The importance of reconnaissance patrols, guard posts, lookouts, and roving scouts for any campaign army or force unit was generally assumed but little discussed in the classic military writings. For example, the T'ai Kung briefly stated: "Now the rule for commanding the army is always to first dispatch scouts far forward so that when you are two hundred miles from the enemy, you will already know their location." Sun Pin also addressed the practices for perimeter security in his *Military Methods:* "Five miles from your defenses establish lookout posts, ordering that they be within sight of each other. If encamped on high ground, deploy them in a square array; if encamped on low ground, deploy them in a circular perimeter. At night beat the drums; in the daytime raise flags."

The need for permanent observation posts along the borders and out into disputed territories was particularly felt once the empire was settled by the Han dynasty and the main military threats—except during dynastic convulsions—were the various peoples emerging from the steppes. Signal flags hoisted by counterbalanced long shafts could be quickly raised and would be visible for several miles over open terrain, especially in favorable winds that ruffled the flags or where the signal post exploited a relative height advantage. Drums were less reliable, their cadence being easily muffled or inopportunely blown away by frequent steppe winds, while lighting the individual signal fires that would be highly visible during clear night conditions required more time even though properly piled, easily combustible material was maintained in a constant state of readiness. (The campaign described in the historical illustration reappears in Chapter 92, "The Impoverished," where further tactical information will be presented.)

32 Marshes 澤

Tactical Discussion

Whenever you mobilize the army and send it forth on campaign, if they encounter wetlands and marshes, or terrain where the levies are ruined, you should employ a double pace and extended marches to quickly pass through. You must not remain in them. If there is no alternative, if you are unable to get out at once—perhaps because the road is long and the sun setting—and you must pass the night in them, you should move to terrain shaped like a turtle's back. In every case you should then establish a circular encampment on high ground where the terrain slopes away on all four sides so as to be able to withstand enemy attacks from every direction. This will prevent being endangered by floodwaters, and you will also be prepared against being encircled by enemy raiders. A tactical principle from the *Ssu-ma Fa* states: "Pass through wetlands, cross over damaged roads, and select ground for encamping configured like a turtle's back."

Historical Illustration

In the first year of the T'iao-lu reign period of the T'ang Dynasty (679 A.D.), it was reported that the nomadic Turkish leader A-shih-te-wen had revolted. The emperor summoned the Minister of Personnel, concurrently General-in-Chief of the Right Imperial Guards, P'ei Hsing-chien to be the commander-in-chief for the campaign army of Ting-hsiang region. When the army arrived at the khan's border the sun had already set, so they established their camp and dug protective moats and ditches all around. However, general P'ei then ordered that they move the encampment to a high mound. His adjutant said: "The officers and soldiers are already settled in camp, they cannot be troubled." General P'ei refused to listen and moved them. That night fierce winds, torrential rains, and thunder and lightening explosively descended, resulting in more than six feet of water at their former encampment. Everyone was startled and asked how the general knew there would be wind and rain. General P'ei smiled and replied: "From now on just rely upon my constraints and measures, do not ask how I know such things."

Commentary

Water in all its forms presented ancient armies with almost insurmountable obstacles. Lakes and ponds required boats if long marches along the circumference were to be avoided; on swiftly flowing rivers, especially during the rainy season, the current might preclude any crossing at all. Temporary pontoon bridges were known and employed, already recorded in the *Six Secret Teachings,* but such equipment would hopelessly burden a campaign army proceeding across anything but the smoothest open terrain. Marshes and wetlands, whether standing or formed during seasonal flooding, simply stopped wheeled transport, as did the heavy rains that turned most roads into quagmires. Such difficulties prompted Sun Pin to assert: "What causes trouble for the army is the terrain. Thus it is said that three miles of wetlands will cause trouble for the army; crossing through such wetlands will result in leaving the main force behind."

Thus the general principle for chariot-based armies, and later even cavalry forces, was to simply avoid the wetlands and enmiring terrain that not only made movement difficult but also turned the forces into easy targets for enemy crossbowmen. For example, Wu Ch'i said: "In general, desist from employing chariots when the weather is rainy and the land wet but mobilize them when it is hot and dry. Value high terrain; disdain low ground. When racing your strong chariots, whether advancing or halting, you must adhere to the road. If the enemy arises, be sure to follow their tracks."

However, finding oneself on enmiring terrain, the general principle was to somehow determine and occupy tenable, higher ground, as this dialogue indicates:

> Marquis Wu asked: "If we encounter the enemy in a vast, watery marsh where the chariot wheels sink down to the point that the shafts are under water, both our chariots and cavalry are floundering, and we haven't prepared any boats or oars, so cannot advance or retreat—what should we do?"
>
> Wu Ch'i replied: "This is referred to as water warfare. Do not employ chariots or cavalry but have them remain on the side. Mount some nearby height and look all about. You must ascertain the water's condition, know its expanse, and fathom its depth. Then you can conceive an unorthodox stratagem for victory. If the enemy begins crossing the water, press them when half have crossed."

Apart from the problems of mobility, there was also the danger of flooding—whether through sudden inundations or deliberate actions by the enemy to break dams, divert streams, or temporarily stem a river's flow until a sufficient volume of water had accumulated to sweep away an enemy. All the writers warned against occupying low-lying positions—even dry ones—susceptible to such attacks, and virtually everyone subscribed to Sun-tzu's dictums: "When you cross salt marshes and wetlands, concentrate upon quickly getting away from them. Do not remain. If you engage in battle in marshes or wetlands, you must stay in areas with marsh grass and keep groves of trees at your back. This is the Way to deploy the army in marshes and wetlands."

33 Contentious Terrain 爭

Tactical Discussion

Whenever engaging an enemy in battle, if a conducive location offers strategic advantages, you should contend with the enemy to be first to occupy it, for then you will be victorious in combat. Should the enemy's forces arrive first, do not attack them; it will be more advantageous to await some change in their situation and then suddenly strike. A tactical principles from the *Art of War* states: "Do not attack on contentious terrain."

Historical Illustration

During the Three Kingdoms period, in the second year of the Ch'ing-lung reign period (234 A.D.) of the Wei dynasty, General Chu-ko Liang of the kingdom of Shu came forth through Hsieh-ku valley. At this time General Ssu-ma Yi of Wei was encamped south of the Wei River. General Kuo Huai of Wei calculated that Chu-ko Liang would certainly contend with them to reach the northern plains, so they should occupy them first, but the other discussants contradicted him. Huai said: "If Chu-ko Liang crosses the Wei River and ascends the plains, stretches his troops across the northern mountains, severs the imperial roads, and causes panic among the people, this will not be to the state's advantage."

Ssu-ma Yi seconded his estimation and had Huai subsequently encamp on the northern plains. Before his moats and fortifications were complete, Shu's army appeared. Huai quickly launched a counterattack against them. Several days later, with a great flourish of his army, Chu-ko Liang moved west, so Huai's generals all interpreted it as preparatory to mounting an attack in the west. Huai alone felt that Chu-ko Liang was simply manifesting an appearance of moving west in order to precipitate a response from Wei's numerous troops and that he would certainly mount an attack in the east. That night Chu-ko Liang indeed attacked Yang-tui, but as they were prepared they were not defeated.

Commentary

The concept of "contentious terrain" was first elaborated by Sun-tzu in "Nine Terrains" as follows: "If when we occupy it, it will be advantageous to us, while if they occupy it, it will be advantageous to them, it is 'contentious terrain.'" His tactics for contentious terrain were simple: "On contentious terrain do not attack" and "On contentious terrain I race our rear elements forward." However, in a series of passages attributed to Sun-tzu preserved in the eighth-century *T'ung Tien,* a more detailed explication appears:

> The king of Wu asked Sun-tzu: "On contentious terrain, suppose the enemy arrives first, occupies the strategic positions and holds the advantageous ones with selected troops and well-trained soldiers. Some of them go forth, others assume defensive positions, thereby being prepared against our unorthodox tactics. What should we do?"
>
> Sun-tzu replied: "The rule for fighting on contentious terrain is that one who yields will gain, while one who fights will lose. If the enemy has gained a position, then be careful not to attack it. Draw him away by pretending to go off. Set up flags, beat the drums, and move swiftly toward what he loves. Drag wood to raise clouds of dust, befuddle his ears and eyes. Divide up our superior troops, secretly placing them in ambush. The enemy will certainly come forth to rescue the endangered target. What others want we will give them; what they abandon we will take. That is the Tao for fighting for land they occupy first.
>
> If we arrive first and the enemy uses this strategy, then select fierce troops to solidly defend our position. Have our light troops pursue the enemy's feigned departure, splitting some off to set up ambushes in the ravines and defiles. If the enemy turns about to fight, the troops in ambush on the flanks should rise up. This is the Tao for achieving complete victory."

34 Advantageous Terrain 地

Tactical Discussion

Whenever you engage an enemy in battle, the Three Armies absolutely must secure advantageous terrain; only then can the few contend with the many and the weak attain victory over the strong. Sun-tzu said that "knowing that the enemy can be attacked and that our troops can mount an attack, without knowing the advantages of terrain, is only half of victory." This asserts that when one already knows the other, and moreover knows himself, but fails to gain the assistance of advantageous terrain, the victory will not be complete. It is a tactical principle that "the seasons of Heaven are not as good as advantages of Earth."

Historical Illustration

During the Northern and Southern Dynasties period, when Emperor Wu of the Chin dynasty mounted a punitive expedition to extirpate the kingdom of Southern Yen, King Mu-jung Ch'ao of Southern Yen summoned his ministers to discuss how to repel Chin's army. Kung-sun Wu-lou said: "Chin's forces are strong and determined, qualities that are advantageous in rapid engagements. At the outset their front, being courageous and fierce, should not be attacked. It would be best to occupy the T'ai-hsien mountain area to prevent them from entering our borders. We should force them to waste days and dissipate hours, thereby frustrating their fervent spirit. You can leisurely select two thousand elite cavalrymen to secretly go south along the sea to severe their supply lines. Separately depute Tuan Hui to lead an army assembled from our prefectures to edge around the mountain and down to the east to suddenly attack them from both front and rear. This would be a superior plan.

Or, in every case order your defensive commanders to rely upon strategic defiles for their solidity. Apart from essential provisions, burn everything and cut down the grain and corn in the fields in order to ensure that when the enemy comes forth there will be nothing left for them to rely upon. Then await their aggression with solid walls and emptied fields, which would be a mediocre plan.

Or again, allow the villains to enter the mountain region and then go forth from our cities to counter them in battle, which would be the poorest plan."

Mu-jung Ch'ao replied: "The metropolitan prefecture is rich and flourishing; the population many and numerous. It is impossible to go in and defend it in just a short time. The green crops spread throughout our fields cannot be suddenly cut down. I am not capable of destroying the crops and defending the city just to preserve our lives. If we rely upon the strength of our five prefectures, integrating the fastness of our mountains and rivers together with our ten thousand chariots and tens of thousands of elite cavalrymen, we can allow them to pass through the T'ai-hsien mountain area out onto the level plains and then leisurely employ our elite troops to control them. They will certainly be captured."

Mu-jung Chen said: "If we follow your enlightened direction, we should certainly deploy our army about ten miles out onto the plains. Once the army's fortifications have been erected we can employ our cavalry advantageously. When we thus go forth from the T'ai-hsien mountain area to counter the enemy in battle, if we are not victorious we can still retreat to a defensive position in the mountains. It would be inappropriate to allow the enemy to invade the T'ai-hsien mountain area, thereby voluntarily giving them the means to oppress us. Anciently, the Lord of Ch'eng-an did not defend the precipitous terrain at Ching-hsing and ended up being subjugated by Han Hsin. Chu-ko Chan failed to defend the ravines at Chien-ko and was suddenly captured by Teng Ai. I believe that the seasons of Heaven are not as good as advantages of Earth. Accordingly, stopping up and defending the T'ai-hsien mountain area is the best strategy."

Again Mu-jung Ch'ao did not follow his tactical advice, but instead ordered the two border prefectures of Sheh-lü and Liang-fu to repair their walls and defensive ditches, select warriors and horses, and nurture an elite spirit to await the enemy. That summer Chin's forces conquered the east, so Mu-jung Ch'ao dispatched the fifty thousand infantrymen and cavalrymen in the Army of the Left commanded by Tuan Hui and others to enter and occupy Lin-ch'ü. Shortly thereafter Chin's army crossed through the T'ai-hsien mountain area and Mu-jung Ch'ao, becoming fearful, led his remaining forty thousand troops to join with Tuan Hui at Lin-ch'ü. Then they engaged Chin's forces but were defeated. Mu-jung Ch'ao fled to Kuang-ku, which was itself taken several days later. Southern Yen's territory was thus pacified.

Commentary

The tactical principle cited in the discussion appears in several early writings, including the *Wei Liao-tzu,* where it is quoted in support of the principle that human effort, rather than prayer or other appeals to Heaven and the spirits, is paramount: "The seasons of Heaven are not as good as the advantages of Earth. Advantages of Earth are not as good as harmony among men. What Sages esteem is human effort, that is all." Most of the military writers subscribed to Sun-tzu's definition of Earth in this context—"Earth encompasses far or near, difficult or easy, expansive or confined, fatal or tenable terrain"—and continued to expand his definition over the centuries. However, Heaven continued to be critical, defined not only in terms of spirits and portents, weather, and natural phenomena, but also in terms of the behavior of men, as will be discussed in Chapters 85 and 86, "The Heavens" and "The Human" respectively.

The necessity for occupying advantageous terrain, "good ground," was widely recognized and emphasized in the Warring States period, just as in the West during the age of Napoleon and on into the Civil War, falling somewhat into disfavor thereafter. During the Warring States period configurations of terrain became highly particularized, basically evolving from Sun-tzu's initial categories. Accordingly, even the most ignorant general would be expected to focus his efforts upon gaining the tactical advantages ensured by superior positions and implement tactics designed to exploit them with whatever troops and firepower might be available. Outnumbered forces were particularly counseled to deploy in terrain constricted enough to constrain the enemy's mobility and allow the establishment of a killing zone, such as witnessed at the famous battle of Ma-ling where Sun Pin defeated the headstrong P'ang Chüan and Wei's elite forces. To voluntarily abandon a natural line of defense, particularly one exploiting the impregnability of mountains and ravines, as Mu-jung Ch'ao did just at the beginning of the fifth century A.D. and thereby lost both his life and kingdom, verged upon lunacy and perhaps resulted from his many years of licentious dissipation.

The famous battles discussed in Mu-jung Chen's persuasion are briefly recounted by the historical illustrations found in Chapters 18, "The Guest" (for Han Hsin) and 41, "The Unorthodox" (for Teng Ai). The frequent use of historical precedent in such persuasions provides evidence of the textually based nature of Chinese military studies and the attention paid to actual battlefield lessons.

35 Mountains 山

Tactical Discussion

Whenever engaging an enemy in battle, whether in mountain forests or on level terrain, you must occupy high ground and rely upon strategic configurations of terrain that are conducive to attacks and probes and will facilitate racing forward to assault the enemy, for then you will be victorious in combat. A tactical principle states: "In mountain combat, do not go counter to heights."

Historical Illustration

During the Warring States period, Ch'in attacked Han, and Han in turn beseeched Chao to rescue it. The king of Chao summoned Lien P'o and asked him: "Can we rescue them or not?" Lien P'o replied: "The march would be long and the road narrow, so it would be difficult to rescue them." The king also summoned Yüeh Ch'eng and asked: "Can we rescue Han or not?" Yüeh Ch'eng replied similarly to Lien P'o. The king further summoned Chao She and raised the same question, but Chao She replied: "The march would be long and the road narrow. It might be compared with two rats fighting in a hole. The more courageous general will win." The king then ordered Chao She to assume command of the army and rescue Han.

When the army had proceeded about thirty miles from Chao's capital of Han-tan, Chao She had them halt and construct solid fortifications, after which he circulated an edict stating that "anyone who dares to remonstrate on military matters will be executed." When Ch'in's army reached Wu-an, one man in Chao She's camp criticized the general's inaction and was immediately executed. Chao She further solidified the walls, remained for twenty-eight days without advancing, and then again increased their fortifications. Spies from Ch'in came; Chao She fed them well and sent them back. When these spies reported, Ch'in's commanding general elatedly said: "They are only thirty miles outside their borders but instead of advancing merely augment their fortifications. Chao She will certainly not venture this far." However, immediately after dispatching Ch'in's spies, Chao She ordered his forces to roll up their armor and race after them, so they arrived at Ch'in's encampment in only a day and a night. When Ch'in's forces learned of it, they all donned their armor and came forth.

Hsü Li, one of his officers, requested permission to go in and remonstrate with Chao She. General Chao admitted him and Hsü Li said: "Ch'in did not expect our army to reach here. They have come forth full of spirit, so you, general, should deploy in a dense formation to await them. Otherwise, we will certainly be defeated." Chao She said: "I would like to receive your instructions." Hsü Li said: "I ask to be punished." Chao She said: "You must wait until after we order the return to Han-tan." Hsü Li then advised: "Whoever first occupies the mountain to the north will be victorious; whoever arrives later will be defeated." Chao She agreed and therefore dispatched ten thousand men to race there. Ch'in's forces subsequently arrived and fought to ascend the mountain but could not. Chao She released his soldiers to attack them, severely destroying Ch'in's army and thereby forcing them to release the siege of Han.

Commentary

This selection and the next, nominally focused on valley warfare, address the tactical concerns of mountain engagements and, as in the illustration, the importance of gaining and exploiting the high ground. As the T'ai Kung said: "Occupying high ground is the means by which to be alert and assume a defensive posture." However, the issue was not simple because mountain forces could become isolated, cut off from supplies and external support, as the historical illustration of the next selection well illustrates.

While there was a general tendency to advise deploying on the *yang* (or south-facing) side of a mountain—no doubt due to better exposure to sunlight from the south, thereby avoiding dampness and the problems it might entail—the principle was not absolute. The *Six Secret Teachings* preserves a typical situational analysis:

> King Wu asked the T'ai Kung: "Suppose we have led the army deep into the territory of the feudal lords where we encounter high mountains with large flat rock outcroppings, on top of which are numerous peaks, all devoid of grass and

trees. We are surrounded on all four sides by the enemy. Our Three Armies are afraid, the officers and troops confused. I want to be solid if we choose to defend our position, and victorious if we fight. What should we do?"

The T'ai Kung said: "Whenever the Three Armies occupy the heights of a mountain they are trapped on high by the enemy. When they hold the land below the mountain they are imprisoned by the forces above them. If you have already occupied the top of the mountain, you must prepare the Crow and Cloud Formation. The Crow and Cloud Formation should be prepared on both the *yin* and *yang* sides of the mountain. Some will encamp on the *yin* side; others will encamp on the *yang* side. Those that occupy the *yang* side must prepare against attacks from the *yin* side. Those occupying the *yin* side must prepare against attacks from the *yang* side. Those occupying the left side of the mountain must prepare against the right side. Those on the right, against the left. Wherever the enemy can ascend the mountain, your troops should establish external lines. If there are roads passing through the valley, sever them with your war chariots. Set your flags and pennants up high. Be cautious in commanding the Three Armies; do not allow the enemy to know your true situation. This is referred to as a 'mountain wall.'

After your lines have been set, your officers and troops deployed, rules and orders already issued, and tactics, both orthodox and unorthodox, already planned, deploy your assault formation at the outer perimeter of the mountain and have them improve the positions they occupy. Thereafter divide your chariots and cavalry into the Crow and Cloud Formation. When your Three Armies urgently attack the enemy, even though the latter are numerous, their general can be captured."

In the historical illustration, Ch'in's commanding general probably interpreted Chao She's fixed deployment as part of a preemptive strategy designed to preposition forces outside Chao's border and thereby prevent an invasion of Chao itself. This interpretation, no doubt deliberately fostered by Chao She, was likely because the ostensible siege of Han could well have been a ruse to conceal Ch'in's larger objectives, as many similar incidents in the Warring States period painfully showed.

36 Valleys 谷

Tactical Discussion

Whenever moving an army over mountains and through ravines, if you want to deploy, it should certainly be done by relying upon the valleys. This will allow taking advantage of grass and water, and you will also have solid defensive positions available in the nearby ravines. If you then engage in battle, you will be victorious. A tactical principle from the *Art of War* states: "To cross mountains, follow the valleys."

Historical Illustration

During the Later Han dynasty when general Ma Yüan was serving as Grand Protector for Lung-hsi, the Ts'an-lang Ch'iang, together with other peoples from outside the pass, made raids upon the area, killing local senior officials. Ma Yüan, in command of more than four thousand soldiers, went out to attack them and eventually reached the Ti-tao district. The Ch'iang occupied the mountain heights so Ma had his army occupy tenable terrain below, where they seized the water and grass but did not engage the enemy. After some time the Ch'iang became extremely distressed. Several hundred thousand soldiers fled out beyond the pass, while their generals and more than ten thousand other men all surrendered. The Ch'iang failed to understand the advantages of relying upon valleys and thus brought about their own defeat.

Commentary

This selection, which complements the previous one on mountain warfare, points out the difficulties that might arise from occupying mountains because the latter, while providing advantages of height and cover, often lack other important resources. Moreover, when encamped on precipitous terrain, even with extensive supply lines, provisioning the army invariably proves much more difficult. Thus the advantages suggested in the previous selection can be secured only with foresight, or should be temporarily exploited when under severe duress, such as finding oneself badly outnumbered, and extreme measures are dictated.

Although the tactical discussion raises the general question of valley warfare, the historical incident—which recounts an excellent example of Sun-tzu's ideal of winning without actually engaging in combat—illustrates it in a negative sense. In general, good strategists sought to funnel enemy forces into well-defended valleys to maximize their firepower with minimum risk. However, more common situations were finding a valley already defended or suddenly confronting an enemy within a large valley. In the former case, in "Ten Questions" Sun Pin advised that the enemy should be lured out, while Wu Ch'i provided some methods for the latter encounter:

> Marquis Wu asked: "If I encounter the enemy in a deep valley, where gorges and defiles abound to the sides, while his troops are numerous and ours few, what should I do?"
>
> Wu Ch'i replied: "Traverse hilly regions, forests, valleys, deep mountains, and vast wetlands quickly, departing from them posthaste. Do not be dilatory. If in high mountains or a deep valley the armies should suddenly encounter each other, you should first beat the drums and set up a clamor, taking advantage of it to advance your archers and crossbowmen, both shooting the enemy and taking prisoners. Carefully investigate their degree of control; if they are confused then attack without doubt."
>
> Marquis Wu asked: "On the left and right are high mountains, while the land is extremely narrow and confined. If when we meet the enemy we dare not attack them, yet cannot escape, what should we do?"
>
> Wu Ch'i replied: "This is referred to as valley warfare. Even if your troops are numerous they are useless. Summon your talented warriors to confront the enemy, the nimble footed and sharpest weapons to be at the forefront. Divide your chariots and array your cavalry, concealing them on all four sides several miles apart, so that they will not show their weapons. The enemy will certainly assume a solid defensive formation, not daring to either advance or retreat. Thereupon display your flags and array your banners, withdraw outside the mountains, and encamp. The enemy will invariably be frightened, and your chariots and cavalry should then harass them, not permitting them any rest. This is the Tao for valley warfare."

37 Offense 攻

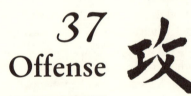

Tactical Discussion

In general, in warfare what is referred to as an "attack" means knowing the enemy. When you know the enemy has some aspect that can be destroyed and you send the army forth to attack it, you will always be victorious. A tactical principle from the *Art of War* states: "One who can be victorious attacks."

Historical Illustration

During the Three Kingdoms period, Ts'ao Ts'ao of Wei dispatched Chu Kuang as Grand Protector for Lu-chiang, with an encampment at Wan. He also embarked on an extensive program to bring fallow lands under cultivation and moreover ordered his spies to entice forces previously defeated by the kingdom of Wu now dwelling in P'o-yang to mount an internal uprising.

General Lü Meng of Wu said to the king: "Their fields and wilds in Lu-chiang are fertile. If they achieve a single harvest, their numbers will certainly increase. A few years like this and it will be difficult to control Ts'ao Ts'ao. It would be best to expel him early on." He then proceeded to outline the military situation in detail. Subsequently, Sun Ch'üan, king of Wu, personally led their forces to attack Chu Kuang, reaching Wan in just a day and night. When the king queried his generals about appropriate tactics, they all encouraged him to erect siege structures around the city. Lü Meng said: "Erecting siege structures would require several days to complete, while their fortifications and preparations are already well undertaken. A rescue by external forces is certain to occur, and so a siege cannot be planned. Moreover, if we take advantage of the rains to invade the city, should we linger for a few days, we will be forced to completely withdraw. Our withdrawal route will then be extremely difficult, so we will certainly be endangered. However, I have observed that their city walls are not very solid. If we attack them from all four sides with our Three Armies at fever-pitch, in no time at all they can be taken. Returning to our home base before the seasonal flood waters rise would be the strategy for preserving victory." Sun Ch'üan, king of Wu, agreed with him.

Lü Meng then recommended Kan Ning, Supervisor of the Siege Walls, to command the assault on Wei's forward position, while he himself would follow up with their elite troops. When they advanced to attack at first light, Lü Meng personally wielded the drumsticks to beat the drums. The officers and troops leapt forward and ascended the walls by themselves, and within the space of a meal they had destroyed the city of Wan. After it was over Chang Liao, with a Wei rescue force, reached Chia-shih, but when he heard that the city had already fallen, he withdrew. Sun Ch'üan congratulated Lü Meng on his victory and appointed him as Grand Protector for Lu-chiang commandery.

Commentary

This selection and the next, entitled "Defense" comprise another tactical pair derived from the *Art of War.* Until recently, Sun-tzu's doctrine of interrelated offense and defense contained puzzling aspects that had troubled commentators for roughly 2,500 years. However, the discovery of the so-called Tomb Text some two decades ago resolved the difficulties, as discussed in the notes to our Sun-tzu translation. The critical passages appear in the chapter entitled "Military Disposition":

> In antiquity those that excelled in warfare first made themselves unconquerable in order to await the moment when the enemy could be conquered. Being unconquerable lies with yourself; being conquerable lies with the enemy. Thus one who excels in warfare is able to make himself unconquerable, but cannot necessarily cause the enemy to be conquerable. Thus it is said a strategy for conquering the enemy can be known but yet not possible to implement.
>
> One who cannot be victorious assumes a defensive posture; one who can be victorious attacks. In these circumstances by assuming a defensive posture, strength will be more than adequate, whereas in offensive actions it would be inadequate.

As immediately evident, the quotations cited in the tactical discussions for this and the following selection are slight variants of the passage's concluding paragraph.

The *Questions and Replies* provides another perspective on Sun-tzu's concept, explicating it in terms of implementation:

The T'ai-tsung said: "Are the two affairs of attacking and defending in reality one method? Sun-tzu said, 'When one excels at attacking, the enemy does not know where to mount his defense. When one excels at defense, the enemy does not know where to attack.' He did not speak about the enemy coming forth to attack me, and I also attacking the enemy. If we assume a defensive posture, and the enemy also takes up a defensive position, if in attacking and defense our strengths are equal, what tactic should be employed?"

Li Ching said: "Cases like this of mutual attack and mutual defense were, in previous ages, numerous. They all said, 'One defends when strength is insufficient; one attacks when strength is more than sufficient.' Thus they referred to insufficiency as being weakness and having an excess as strength. Apparently they didn't understand the methods for attack and defense. I recall Sun-tzu said, 'One who cannot be victorious assumes a defensive posture; one who can be victorious attacks.' This indicates that when the enemy cannot yet be conquered I must temporarily defend myself. We wait until the point when the enemy can be conquered, then we attack him. It is not a statement about strength and weakness. Later generations did not understand his meaning, so when they should attack they defend, and when they should defend they attack. The two stages are distinct, so the method cannot be a single one."

The T'ai-tsung said: "I can see that the concepts of surplus and insufficiency caused later generations to be confused about strength and weakness. They probably didn't know that the essence of defensive strategy is to show the enemy an inadequacy. The essence of aggressive strategy lies in showing the enemy that you have a surplus. If you show the enemy an insufficiency, then they will certainly advance and attack. In this case 'the enemy does not know where to attack.' If you show the enemy a surplus then they will certainly take up defensive positions. In this case 'the enemy does not know where to mount his defense.' Attacking and defending are one method, but the enemy and I divide it into two matters. If I succeed in this matter, the enemy's affairs will be defeated. If the enemy is successful, then my aims will be defeated. Gaining and losing, success or failure, our aims and the enemy's are at odds, but attacking and defending are one! If you understand that they are one, then in a hundred battles you will be victorious a hundred times. Thus it is said, 'If you know yourself and you know the enemy, in a hundred battles you will not be endangered.' This refers to the knowledge of this unity, doesn't it?"

Li Ching bowed twice and said: "Perfect indeed are the Sage's methods! Attacking is the pivotal point of defense; defending is the strategy for attack. They are both directed toward victory, that's all. If in attacking you do not understand defending, and in defending you do not understand attacking, but instead not only make them into two separate affairs but also assign responsibility for them to separate offices, then even though the mouth recites the words of Sun-tzu and

Wu-tzu, the mind has not thought about the mysterious subtleties of the discussion of the equality of attack and defense. How can the reality then be known?"

38 Defense 守

Tactical Discussion

In general, in warfare what is meant by "defense" refers to knowing oneself. When you know that you do not yet have the strategic power to forge victory, you should solidify your defenses and await the moment when the enemy can be destroyed. If you then send the army forth to assault the enemy, you will always be victorious. A tactical principle from the *Art of War* states: "One who knows he cannot be victorious assumes a defensive posture."

Historical Illustration

During the reign of Emperor Ching in the Former Han dynasty, seven states, including Wu and Ch'u, revolted against imperial authority. The emperor appointed Chou Ya-fu as Defender-in-Chief and entrusted him with the mission of going east to attack Wu, Ch'u, and the other states. Thereupon Chou personally made a request to the emperor: "Ch'u's soldiers are nimble and light, so it is difficult to engage their front in battle. I would like to employ the minor state of Liang as a lynch pin. If we then sever the enemy's supply lines, we can gain control over them." The emperor assented, so Chou Ya-fu proceeded to the assembly point for his forces at Jung-yang. Wu had just mounted an attack against Liang, so the king of Liang requested that Chou Ya-fu rescue them. Chou led his forces to the northeast, rushing to Ch'ang-yi where he then established solid fortifications and set up his defenses. The king of Liang dispatched an emissary to request Chou to take action, but Chou simply maintained his defenses and made appropriate improvements and did not go out to rescue them.

The king of Liang then submitted a memorial to Emperor Ching, and the emperor directed Chou to rescue Liang. Chou did not obey the mandate but instead strengthened his walls without going forth. However, he did order the marquis of Kung-kao and others, in command of light cavalry, to sever the supply routes behind Wu and Ch'u's forces. Soon the armies of Wu and Ch'u lacked provisions, became hungry, and wanted to withdraw. Several times they tried to provoke battles with Chou's forces, but he always refused to be drawn into an engagement. That night the soldiers within his army were frightened and disordered, fighting with each other outside his tent. As Chou was sleeping soundly he did not get up, and the disorder shortly settled down by itself.

Wu's forces raced to the southeast corner of the walls, but Chou ordered his troops to prepare in the northwest. When they had finished, Wu's soldiers indeed raced to the northwest but failed to gain entrance. Wu and Ch'u's armies were famished so they withdrew their soldiers and retreated. Thereupon Chou Ya-fu dispatched his elite units to pursue and attack them, extensively destroying them. The king of Wu suddenly abandoned his army and fled with several thousand stalwart soldiers to ensconce himself at Tan-t'u south of the Yangtze River. The Han forces, continuing to exploit their victory, pursued and attacked them, in the end capturing or killing them all but the king, forcing their provinces and commanderies to surrender. Chou Ya-fu issued an edict that stated: "Whoever obtains the head of the king of Wu shall be rewarded with a thousand catties of gold." In slightly more than a month a native of Yüeh beheaded him and reported it. In all, their defense and attacks lasted seven months, but then Wu and Ch'u were completely pacified.

Commentary

This selection reprises the second half of Sun-tzu's critical concept of the interrelatedness of offense and defense and should be read in conjunction with the preceding selection and its extended commentary as well as the tactical discussion for Chapter 77, "Refusing Battle." The measures employed in the historical incident are of course similar to those witnessed in previous illustrations, although emphasizing the aggressive nature of a defensive posture. As before, refusing to give battle allows harboring strength and when coupled with effective thrusts against the enemy's supply lines, precipitates hasty action by enemy commanders desperate to wrest victory before their dwindling provisions are exhausted. These incidents also reveal an interesting command problem—coping with the frustration of inaction, defusing the tensions that arise in camp when the soldiers are prevented from engaging in combat even though it might be what they fear most.

39 Initiative 先

Tactical Discussion

Whenever engaging an enemy in battle, if after arriving they have not yet decisively deployed their power or put their formations in order, should you be the first to urgently mount a sudden attack, you will be victorious. It is a stated principle that "one who precedes others seizes their minds."

Historical Illustration

During the Spring and Autumn period Duke Hsiang of Sung was about to engage Ch'u's forces in battle at the Hung River. Sung's forces had already formed their lines, but Ch'u's soldiers had not yet finished crossing the river. Ssu-ma Tzu-yü said to Duke Hsiang: "They are numerous while we are few. Before they have finished fording the river I suggest that we suddenly strike them." Duke Hsiang did not grant permission. When Ch'u's forces had nearly completed fording the river but had not yet formed their lines, Tzu-yü repeated his request, but the Duke again denied it. After Ch'u assumed formation the battle commenced and Sung's army was severely defeated.

Commentary

The tactical principle cited in the discussion originally appears in the *Art of War* as follows: "The spirit of the Three Armies can be snatched away; the commanding general's mind can be seized." However, a similar but somewhat more complex analysis is preserved in the *Wei Liao-tzu:* "Now the means by which the general fights is the people; the means by which the people fight is their spirit. When their spirit is substantial they will fight; when their spirit has been snatched away they will run off. One who excels at employing the army is able to seize men and not be seized by others. This seizing is a technique of mind." Accordingly, methods for seizing the initiative and thereby undermining the enemy's spirit were much discussed by the tactical writers, as will be evident from Chapter 74, "Spirit."

The famous battle of 638 B.C. described in the historical illustration was anachronistic even in the Western Chou, for the Spring and Autumn period had already witnessed a sudden expansion in the scope and severity of warfare. Formalistic combat between chariot-based individual warriors or select groups had long yielded to infantry tactics and hierarchical organization, yet Duke Hsiang, although outnumbered, remained a fervent believer in the duties nominally imposed by the *lii*, the forms of behavior incumbent upon the nobility. His famous chivalry resulted in his death as well as an undying reputation for foolishly flying in the face of reality, rather than glory for heroically upholding the values of a more righteous age. Thereafter only a single commander—in the T'ang dynasty—ever repeated his folly. Seizing the initiative, attacking when the enemy is unprepared and exposed—such as when crossing rivers—became the method of the day.

40 Response 後

Tactical Discussion

In general, in warfare if the enemy's forces are deployed in good order and their spirits are sharp, you should not yet engage them in battle. Rather, it would be better to solidify your fortifications and outlast them, waiting for their spirits to decline as their deployment becomes prolonged. If you then arise and strike them, you will always be victorious. A tactical principle states: "Move after others in order to await their decline."

Historical Illustration

In the middle of the T'ang dynasty's initial reign period, Li Shih-min, the future emperor, besieged Wang Shih-ch'ung at the Eastern Capital of Loyang. Tou Chien-te, with all his troops, came forth to rescue Wang Shih-ch'ung, so Li Shih-min established his defenses at Wu-lao to resist him. Tou Chien-te deployed east of Fan River, his troops stretching and winding for several miles. Li's generals all blanched with fear.

Li Shih-min, in command of several cavalry, ascended a nearby height in order to observe them, then addressed his subordinates: "These brigands come from east of the mountains, so they have never seen a major enemy before. When they crossed the ravines they were noisily disordered, which means the army lacks administrative discipline. They deployed close to our city walls, indicating that they view our forces with contempt. If we restrain our troops and do not move but instead wait for their spirits to decline and the soldiers to become hungry from maintaining a prolonged deployment, they will certainly withdraw of their own accord. If we strike them as they are withdrawing, how can we go forth and not be victorious?"

Tou Chien-te's soldiers stood arrayed in formation from early morning until somewhat after noon. His troops grew hungry and tired; many eventually sat down while others fought over drinking water. Li Shih-min had Yuwen Shih-chi lead three hundred cavalrymen past the brigands on their west and then race toward the south, cautioning him: "If the brigands do not move then just withdraw and return. If you perceive movement, you should lead them to the east." When Shih-chi had just passed the west side, the brigand's troops indeed stirred. Li Shih-min said: "They can be attacked" and then ordered his cavalry generals to set out their flags and array their formations, and proceed from Wu-lao, taking advantage of the heights to enter the southern mountains, finally following the valleys to the east in order to envelope the brigands from the rear. Thereupon, Tou Chien-te hurriedly led his forces to withdraw, halting at Tung-yüan. They had not yet deployed into orderly formations when Li Shih-min's light cavalry suddenly struck, laying waste wherever they turned. Ch'eng Yao-chin and the other commanders, leading their cavalry with flags affixed and unfurled, entered the enemy's position and directly punched through to the brigand's rear. With their flags still well ordered and the interior and exterior both fervently pressing the attack, the enemy's troops were fatally shattered and Tou Chien-te was even captured alive.

Commentary

The tactical discussion summarizes the advantages of outwaiting an enemy bent upon combat, harboring one's energy until their spirits flag and they become exasperated. Innumerable battles—including several recounted in the *Unorthodox Strategies*—employed such tactics, often on a massive scale, and thus turned disadvantageous situations into easy victories. However, in general it was felt that commanders should take the initiative, manipulate the enemy, and compel their opponents into responding. This might require choosing a defensive posture as advocated in Chapter 77, "Refusing Battle," but might equally dictate a sudden, pell-mell thrust at an early moment. The psychological dimension was just as important as force strength and disposition, as will be discussed in Chapter 74, "Spirit." However, one critical aspect was the danger of delaying too long—the counterpart of moving too soon—and possibly allowing doubt and hesitation to doom the army to defeat. The early *Ssu-ma Fa,* whose authors pondered the issue, said: "In general, in warfare if you move first it will be easy to become exhausted. If you move after the enemy, the men may become afraid. If you rest, the men may become lax; if you do not rest, they also may become exhausted. Yet if you rest very long, on the contrary, they also may become afraid." Command thus required carefully wrought choices between extremes and an expert eye ever focused on both the tactical situation and the spirit (or *ch'i*) of the men.

41 The Unorthodox 奇

Tactical Discussion

In general, in warfare what is referred to as the "unorthodox" means attacking where the enemy is not prepared and going forth when they do not expect it. When engaging an enemy, frighten them in the front and overwhelm them in the rear, penetrate the east and strike in the west, causing them never to know where to mount defensive preparations. In this fashion you will be victorious. A tactical principle from the *Questions and Replies* states: "When the enemy is vacuous, then I must be unorthodox."

Historical Illustration

In the fourth year of the Ching-yüan era (263 A.D.) in the Three Kingdoms period, the emperor of Wei summoned his generals to undertake a punitive campaign against the kingdom of Shu. The Grand General of the Army Ssu-ma Hsüan Wang, who had been designated as Regional Inspector with responsibility for overall command, dispatched general Teng Ai to thoroughly entangle the forces of Shu's general Chiang Wei in Yung-chou while Inspector Chu-ko Hsü cut across behind Chiang Wei so that the latter's forces would be unable to return home. General Teng Ai then dispatched Wang Ch'i, Protector General for T'ien-shui, with others to directly assault Chiang Wei's encampment; Ch'ien Hong, the Protector General for Long-hsi, to press his forward positions; and Yang Hsin, Protector General for Chin-ch'eng, to go to Kan-sung. Chiang Wei learned that the armies under Wei's general Chung Hui had already entered Han-chung commandery, so he retreated. Wang Ch'i's forces from Wei ascended through the mountain pass and badly defeated Chiang Wei, who then fled with his forces. Chiang Wei subsequently heard that the Regional Inspector for Yung-chou, Chu-ko Hsü, had already blocked the roads and encamped at Ch'iao-t'ou, so he entered the road to the north through K'ung-han valley seeking to come out behind Yung-chou commandery. Chu-ko Hsü learned of it and so withdrew about thirty miles. When Chiang Wei himself had advanced on the northern road about thirty miles, he in turn learned of Chu-ko Hsü's withdrawal and passed through Ch'iao-t'ou. Chu-ko Hsü raced across to intercept him but spent the day without making contact.

Chiang Wei subsequently retreated to the east and took up a defensive position at Chien-ko, where he was attacked by Chung Hui, who proved unable to defeat him. Grand General Teng Ai submitted a memorial to the emperor stating: "Now that the enemy brigands have been pushed to the breaking point, it would be appropriate to go from Yin-p'ing by way of the wretched roads passing through Te-yang-t'ing in Han-chung district to race to Fu district, venturing west a hundred miles from Chien-ko and more than three hundred miles from Ch'eng-tu, so that our unorthodox forces can penetrate their very heart. The defenders at Chien-ko must certainly go back to Fu, and our forces at Chien-ko can then follow in their tracks and advance. If Shu's army at Chien-ko does not return to Fu, there will be few troops deployed in Fu to respond to our unorthodox attack. The *Military Pronouncements* states: 'Attack where they are not prepared, go forth where they do not expect it.' Now if we can overwhelm their voids and vacuities, we will certainly destroy them."

General Teng Ai then advanced from Yin-p'ing through deserted territory for more than seven hundred miles, hacking out a passage through the mountains, building bridges and timber roadways. The mountains were high and the valleys deep, the going extremely arduous. Their supply train was almost exhausted; they were frequently endangered and threatened. Teng Ai, wrapping himself in a coarse blanket, pushed and shoved his way forward.

His officers and warriors, climbing among the trees and scrambling along the cliffs, negotiated the mountain trail one after another.

When they reached Chiang-yu, the general in charge of Shu's defense, Ma Miao, surrendered. Shu's imperial guard commander, Chu-ko Chan, returned to Fu through Mien-chu and arrayed his troops to await Teng Ai. Teng Ai dispatched his son Teng Chung to go forth on the right and Ssu-ma Shih-ch'i on the left. Both Chung and Ch'i engaged the enemy unsuccessfully and withdrew, saying: "The brigands cannot yet be conquered." Teng Ai, enraged, said: "The difference between survival and extinction lies in this battle. How can they not be defeated?" He cursed them and the others and was about to have both of them beheaded. However, Chung and Ch'i galloped back and courageously reengaged the enemy in fervent combat, inflicting a severe defeat. They slew Chu-ko Chan and advanced the army to Cheng-tu. Liu Shan of Shu dispatched an emissary with an offer of surrender, and the kingdom of Shu was thus extinguished.

Commentary

The concepts of the unorthodox and orthodox, found in this and the following selection, probably originated with Sun-tzu and were fundamental to his overall vision and understanding of the battlefield. Briefly summarized, "orthodox" tactics employ troops in conventional ways, such as massive frontal assaults, while stressing order and deliberate movement. In contrast, "unorthodox" tactics are primarily realized through employing forces, especially flexible ones, in imaginative, unconventional, and unexpected ways. Therefore, instead of direct chariot attacks, unorthodox tactics would mount circular or flanking thrusts. Instead of frontal assaults, they would follow indirect routes to stage behind-the-lines forays, particularly after the enemy has been manipulated and misled, resulting in voids and vacuities. Their definition is of course dependent upon normal expectation within a particular battlefield context, as well as the enemy's actual anticipations, and therefore they are mutually defining, mutually transforming, and circular in essence, as Sun Pin's summary of the entire conceptualization, found in the commentary for the next selection on "The Orthodox," will explicate.

The *Art of War* preserves one succinct passage that defines the parameters of the unorthodox and orthodox:

> What enable the masses of the Three Armies invariably to withstand the enemy without being defeated are the unorthodox and orthodox. If wherever the army attacks it is like a whetstone thrown against an egg, it is due to the vacuous and

> substantial. In general, in battle one engages with the orthodox and gains victory through the unorthodox. Thus one who excels at sending forth the unorthodox is as inexhaustible as Heaven, as unlimited as the Yangtze and Yellow rivers. In warfare the strategic configurations of power do not exceed the unorthodox and orthodox, but the changes of the unorthodox and orthodox can never be completely exhausted. The unorthodox and orthodox mutually produce each other, just like an endless cycle. Who can exhaust them?

Thus, as explicitly discussed by other military writings, the orthodox may be used in unorthodox ways, while an orthodox attack may be unorthodox when unexpected precisely because it is orthodox; a flanking or indirect assault would thereby be considered normal and therefore orthodox. A frontal feint by a large force, designed to distract or lure an enemy, would also be unorthodox. The concept lends itself to extreme complexities of thought and has often been misunderstood throughout Chinese history, or even dismissed as simplistic, when it is quite the opposite. However, in essence it remains a descriptive tool for tactical conceptualization, for characterizing and manipulating forces within—and by exploiting—an enemy's matrix of expectations rather than a transformational mode to be actualized in the concrete reality of men and weapons the way a military formation is deployed.

Tacticians over the ages have extensively contemplated the unorthodox and orthodox and how they might be applied in actual battles. Some, such as Wei Liao-tzu, adopted a simplistic approach: "Those who excel at repulsing the enemy first join battle with orthodox troops, then use unorthodox ones to control them. This is the technique for certain victory." The famous T'ang general Li Ching also noted that the historical practice in warfare had been to implement the orthodox first: "I have examined the art of war as practiced from the Yellow Emperor on down. First be orthodox, and afterward unorthodox; first be benevolent and righteous, and afterward employ the balance of power and craftiness. In general, when troops advance to the front it is orthodox; when they deliberately retreat to the rear it's unorthodox. The *Art of War* states, 'Display profits to entice them, create disorder in their forces and take them.'" However, Li Ching also asserted that "for those who excel at employing troops there are none that are not orthodox, none that are not unorthodox, so they cause the enemy never to be able to fathom them. Thus with the orthodox they are victorious, with the unorthodox they are also victorious."

The key, in Li Ching's synthesis of Sun-tzu's thought, lies in exploiting the vacuous and avoiding the substantial, as indicated in the quotation cited in the tactical discussion: "The unorthodox and orthodox are the means by which to bring about the vacuous and substantial in the enemy. If the enemy is substantial, then I must use the orthodox. If the enemy is vacuous, then I must use the unorthodox." Their actual implementation becomes almost transcendent in its implications, as T'ang T'ai-tsung's comments reveal: "If we take the unorthodox as the orthodox and the enemy realizes it is the unorthodox, then I will use the orthodox to attack them. If we take the orthodox as the unorthodox and the enemy thinks it's the orthodox, then I will use the unorthodox to attack them. I will cause the enemy's strategic power to constantly be vacuous and my strategic power to always be substantial."

42 The Orthodox 正

Tactical Discussion

Whenever engaging an enemy in battle, if the roads are impassable, preventing the movement of provisions and supplies, your plans cannot inveigle the enemy, nor can proffered advantages and threatened harm confuse them; then you must employ orthodox troops. For an orthodox army you must train the officers and troops well, make the weapons advantageous, ensure that the rewards and punishments are clear, and make certain that edicts and commands are trusted. If you then engage in combat and advance, you will be victorious. A tactical principle from the *Questions and Replies* states: "Without orthodox troops, how can one venture out far?"

Historical Illustration

During the Southern Sung dynasty in the Northern and Southern Dynasties period, T'an Tao-chi launched an attack in the north on behalf of the emperor, his advance forces eventually reaching Lo-yang. Throughout the campaign he seized cities and destroyed fortifications, taking more than four thousand prisoners. His subordinates suggested that he should slay them all and erect a victory mound with the dead. T'an Tao-chi said: "At this time we have attacked the guilty and consoled the people. The army of a true king takes the upright (orthodox) as its standard, so why is it necessary to slay people?" He released all the prisoners and sent them back to their homes.

Thereupon the barbarians dwelling in the region were elated, and a great many led each other to come forward and give their allegiance.

Commentary

This selection, which compliments the previous one on "unorthodox" warfare, addresses the concept of "orthodox" combat, the norm for most battles and engagements throughout history. The execution of orthodox tactics has always depended upon well-disciplined and ordered troops, although the requirements for segmentation, independent and coordinated action, and flexibility are far less rigorous than in the imaginative execution of unorthodox tactics in maneuver warfare. This explains the value of orthodox measures in plodding out far, as Li Ching is quoted as noting in the discussion and as was previously discussed in our commentary to "Chariots."

The paradigm explanation of the nature and interrelationship of the unorthodox and orthodox is preserved in Sun Pin's chapter "Chariots in Warfare," the critical portions of which follow:

> The patterns of Heaven and Earth, reaching an extreme and then reversing, becoming full and then being overturned, these are yin and yang. In turn flourishing, in turn declining, these are the four seasons. Having those they conquer, having those they do not conquer, these are the five phases. Living and dying, these are the myriad things. Being capable, being incapable, these are the myriad living things. Having that which is surplus, having that which is insufficient, these are form and strategic power.
>
> Thus as for the disciples of form, there are none that cannot be named. As for the disciples that are named, there are none that cannot be conquered. Thus the Sage conquers the myriad things with the myriad things; therefore his conquering is not impoverished.
>
> In warfare, those with form conquer each other. There are not any forms which cannot be conquered, but none know the form by which one conquers. The changes in the forms of conquest are coterminal with Heaven and Earth and are inexhaustible.
>
> As for the forms of conquest, even the bamboo strips of Ch'u and Yüeh would be insufficient for writing them down. Those that have form all conquer in accord with their mode of victory. Employing one form of conquest to conquer the myriad forms is not possible. That by which one controls the form is singular; that by which one conquers cannot be single.
>
> Thus when those who excel at warfare discern an enemy's strength, they know where he has a shortcoming. When they discern an enemy's insufficiency, they know where he has a surplus. They perceive victory as easily as seeing the sun and moon. Their measures for victory are like using water to conquer fire.

When form is employed to respond to form, it is orthodox. When the formless controls the formed, it is unorthodox. That the unorthodox and orthodox are inexhaustible is due to differentiation. Differentiate according to unorthodox techniques, exercise control through the five phases, engage in combat with your three forces. Once differentiations have been determined, things take form. Once forms have been determined, they have names.

Things that are the same are inadequate for conquering each other. Thus employ the different to create the unorthodox. Accordingly, take the quiet to be the unorthodox for movement, ease to be the unorthodox for weariness, satiety to be the unorthodox for hunger, order to be the unorthodox for chaos, and numerous masses to be the unorthodox for the few.

When action is initiated it becomes the orthodox; what has not yet been initiated is the unorthodox. When the unorthodox is initiated and is not responded to, then it will be victorious. One who has a surplus of the unorthodox will attain surpassing victories.

Thus if when one joint hurts the hundred joints are not used, it is because they are the same body. If, when the front is defeated the rear is not employed, it is because they are the same form.

Thus to realize strategic combat power, increase the victorious, alter the defeated, rest the weary, and feed the hungry. Accordingly the people will see the enemy's men but not yet perceive death; they will tread on naked blades and not turn their heels. Thus when one understands the patterns of flowing water, he can float rocks and break boats. When, in employing the people, one realizes their nature, then his commands will be implemented just like flowing water.

43 The Vacuous 虛

Tactical Discussion

If, when you engage an enemy in battle, your strategic power is vacuous, you should create the facade of a substantial disposition to make it impossible for the enemy to determine where you are vacuous, where substantial. When the enemy does not dare recklessly engage your forces, you can preserve your regiments and protect your army. A tactical principle from the *Art of War* states: "If the enemy does not dare engage us in battle, it is because we thwart his movements."

Historical Illustration

During the Three Kingdoms period, General Chu-ko Liang of Shu was in Yin-p'ing while Wei Yen and several other generals united their forces in the east and went down river. Chu-ko Liang only retained about ten thousand men to defend the city. Ssu-ma Yi of Wei led 200,000 troops to crush Chu-ko Liang, moving along an alternate route to Yen's forces, stopping to oppose Chu-ko Liang about sixty miles away. An observer returned and reported to Ssu-ma Yi that there were few soldiers in Liang's city and their overall strength was weak. Chu-ko Liang also knew that Ssu-ma Yi's armies would soon reach them and feared they would severely press them. He wanted to join his forces with Yen's army, but they were too far apart and his own strategic power was insufficient to achieve it. His generals and officers all lost their composure, not knowing what the plan might be. However, Chu-ko Liang's determination and spirit were unchanged, and he issued an edict that within the army everyone should furl their battle flags and set their drums aside, nor should anyone irresponsibly go forth. Moreover, he ordered that the four city gates be thrown wide open and instructed that they should sweep the grounds and sprinkle them with water. Ssu-ma Yi constantly viewed Chu-ko Liang as a serious commander, so when Liang manifested a weak appearance, he suspected him of holding troops in ambush. Accordingly, Ssu-ma Yi led his numerous troops in a retreat to the northern mountains. By mealtime Liang and his assistants were clapping their hands and laughing. Liang said: "Ssu-ma Yi thinks I am deliberately displaying fear because I have troops in ambush, so he will go around the mountains and depart." An observer returned and reported that it was as Liang had said. Later, when Ssu-ma Yi learned of it, he hated him deeply.

Commentary

Sun-tzu probably first articulated the concepts of vacuity and substance, although competent generals had certainly employed them in previous centuries to determine which positions to strike and which to avoid. The military writers all incorporated them into their thinking but, with the exception of Li Ching in the passages already cited in the previous two selections on the unorthodox and orthodox, little discussed them beyond such singular statements as the T'ai Kung's admonition, "When you see vacuity in the enemy you should advance; when you see substance you should halt." Moreover, Wu Ch'i advised: "In employing the army you must ascertain the enemy's voids and strengths and then race to take advantage of his endangered points." Even Sun-tzu's chapter entitled "Vacuity and Substance" never specifically explicates his concept but instead addresses the question of manipulating the enemy through movement and deceit so as to force the commander to disperse his men to cover all possible targets and thus inadequately defend any point at all. However, in essence the principle entailed striking voids and gaps while avoiding substantial deployments and impregnable surfaces. Accordingly, the astute commander struggled to keep his own weaknesses from being detected and thereby prevent the enemy from concentrating their forces at a soft point to wrest a victory.

The historical incident provides an interesting illustration of the tactical discussion, but it may be exaggerated or simply apocryphal, characteristic of many episodes originating in the Three Kingdoms period. In fact, to a large extent the historical material has been obscured by the famous novel loosely based upon the characters and events of the era entitled the *Romance of the Three Kingdoms,* with numerous incidents from it forming the basis for contemporary films, novels, short stories, and even cartoon versions for both children and adults in China and Japan.

44 The Substantial 實

Tactical Discussion

Whenever you engage an enemy in battle, if their strategic power is substantial you must rigorously deploy your troops in order to prepare against them, for then the enemy will certainly not recklessly move. A tactical principle from the *Art of War* states: "If they are substantial, prepare for them."

Historical Illustration

During the Three Kingdoms period, when Shu's future ruler was still king of Han-chung, he appointed Kuan Yü as commander of his advance army. Kuan Yü was granted the seals of office and the symbolic axe of command, and encamped at Chiang-ling. Later in the year Kuan Yü retained holding forces at Kung-an and Nan-chün in preparation against the kingdom of Wu, while he personally led troops to attack General Ts'ao Jen of the kingdom of Wei at Fan. Ts'ao Ts'ao of Wei dispatched Yü Chin and others to rescue Ts'ao Jen. During the heavy autumnal rains that fell at this time, the Han River overflowed and flooded the area, causing the seven armies under Yü Chin's supervision to all be lost. Yü Chin surrendered to Kuan Yü and General P'ang Te was captured. Some among the enemy forces in the Liang-chia and Lu-hun districts came from far away to submit to Kuan Yü's authority and become his supporters, so that Kuan Yü's awesomeness shook the realm.

Commentary

Although this selection focuses upon the "substantial" in warfare, the tactical discussion is rather weak in comparison with the rest of the book and essentially repeats the previous selection's lesson on the "insubstantial." Moreover, the historical illustration turns upon natural causes—or "advantages of Heaven and Earth" as the ancients phrased it—rather than conscious activities of men. Kuan Yü was indeed the victor, at least temporarily, and his fame soared, but not because of excellence in command or tactical planning. In short, this selection seems rather deficient, particularly when Sun-tzu and the other military writers devoted considerable thought to the problem of manipulating substantial enemies to create disorder and thus opportunities to attack, as discussed in the earlier selections on confronting strong and numerous forces.

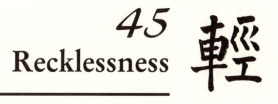

45 Recklessness 輕

Tactical Discussion

Whenever engaging in battle, you must first analyze the enemy, investigating them carefully, and only thereafter send the army forth. If you advance without estimations and engage in battle without plans, you will inevitably be defeated by the enemy. A tactical principle from the *Wu-tzu* states: "Inevitably, the courageous recklessly join battle with the enemy. They recklessly engage without knowing whether it is advantageous."

Historical Illustration

During the Spring and Autumn period, when Duke Wen of Chin was about to engage the state of Ch'u in battle he knew that Ch'u's commanding general Tzu Yü was obstinate and volatile, so he detained Tzu Yü's emissary Wan Ch'un in order to irritate him. Tzu Yü indeed became angry and immediately launched an attack against Chin's army. Ch'u's forces were then badly defeated.

Commentary

Throughout the ages, beginning with Sun-tzu's chapter "Initial Estimations," Chinese military writers have emphasized the importance of knowledge, thorough preparation, and detailed plans before embarking upon military actions. For example, the *Wei Liao-tzu* states:

> In general, whenever about to mobilize the army you must first investigate the strategic balance of power both within and without the borders in order to calculate whether to mount a campaign. You must know whether the army is well prepared or suffers from inadequacies; whether there is a surplus or shortage of foodstuffs. You must determine the routes for advancing and returning. Only thereafter can you mobilize the army to attack the chaotic and be certain of being able to enter his state.
>
> Now one must make decisions early and determine plans beforehand. If plans are not first determined, if intentions are not decided early, then neither advancing nor retreating will be ordered. When doubts arise defeat is certain. Thus an orthodox army values being first; an unorthodox army values being afterward. Sometimes being first, sometimes being afterward, this is the way to control the enemy. Generals throughout the ages who have not known this method, after receiving their commission to go forward, were first to launch an attack, relying upon courage alone. There were none who were not defeated.

The quotation excerpted from the *Wu-tzu* found in this selection actually appears in a discussion of generals and their defects rather than one focusing on planning and its process. The original passage runs:

> Now the commanding general of the Three Armies should combine both military and civilian abilities. The employment of soldiers requires uniting both

> hardness and softness. In general, when people discuss generalship they usually focus on courage. However courage is but one of a general's many characteristics, for the courageous will recklessly join battle with the enemy. To recklessly join battle with an enemy without knowing the advantages and disadvantages is not acceptable. Now the affairs that the general must pay careful attention to are five: First, regulation. Second, preparation. Third, commitment. Fourth, caution. And fifth, simplification. Regulation is governing the masses just as one controls a few. Preparation is going out the city gate as if seeing the enemy. Commitment means entering combat without any concern for life. Caution means that even after conquering one maintains the same control and attitude as if just entering a battle. Simplification means the laws and orders are kept to a minimum and are not abrasive.
>
> To accept the mandate of command without ever declining, destroy the enemy, and only afterward speak about returning is the proper form of behavior for a general. Thus when the army goes forth his only thought should be of the glory that death will bring, not the shame of living.

Remarkably, although certain defects, such as arrogance and anger, are mentioned in isolation, none of the selections in the *Unorthodox Strategies* focus upon the requisite talents and characteristics of commanders despite the topic having been much discussed by the military writers, particularly as armies became stronger and the scope of warfare escalated.

The historical incident summarizes the "Battle of Ch'eng-p'u," one of the great battles of ancient (632 B.C.) Chinese history in which Chin's ruler became the second hegemon or de facto military ruler under the pretext of sustaining the Chou emperor, whose power had already been seriously eroded. The battle itself, which was actually quite complex, receives extensive treatment in the *Tso Chuan,* the main record of the period. In essence, Ch'u and its allies had besieged the capital of Sung, causing the latter to appeal to Chin for assistance. Although Chin's forces were significantly outnumbered, Ch'u's commander Tzu Yü, (better known as Ch'eng Te-ch'en) had antagonized his king and didn't really enjoy his full support. Duke Wen actually retreated three times in the face of Ch'u's offensive to visibly repay an old moral debt, causing Tzu Yü (as well as his own frustrated soldiers) to think they wouldn't fight. However, just as at the battle of Marathon, the collapsing middle drew the enemy's forces inward, automatically allowing the flanks to extend beyond the aggressors on both sides and eventually execute a double envelopment. Thus Ch'u was defeated and Chin became both famous and powerful.

46 Weightiness 重

Tactical Discussion

Whenever engaging an enemy in battle, you must concentrate upon maintaining the army's weightiness. When you perceive advantage, move; when you do not perceive advantage, halt. You cannot recklessly initiate actions. In this fashion you will never be forced onto fatal terrain. A tactical principle from the *Art of War* states: "Be unmoving like a mountain."

Historical Illustration

During the Spring and Autumn period, General Luan Shu of Chin attacked the state of Ch'u and was about to engage in battle. At daybreak Ch'u's forces pressed forward and deployed into formation, causing Chin's officers to be troubled. Lieutenant General Fan Kai raced forward and said: "Fill in the wells and destroy the stoves, assume formation right here in camp, and then disperse outward so that the army can advance." Luan Shu said: "Ch'u's army is recklessly provoking us into battle. If we preserve our gravity and solidify our fortifications in order to outwit them, in three days they will certainly withdraw. If we then suddenly strike them while they are retreating, we will invariably gain a complete victory." In the end they defeated Ch'u's army.

Commentary

The complimentary concepts discussed in this selection and the preceding one entail a less quantifiable yet essential characteristic of armies, their "weightiness" and "lightness" or "recklessness." While somewhat indefinable, weightiness (or perhaps *gravitas*) marks armies that are not only powerful, solid, and well disciplined but also strictly commanded, making it impossible to easily provoke them to precipitous actions, ensuring they could refuse battle as discussed in "Defense" and "Refusing Battle." Thus it is not a question of numbers or force size, but rather an army's unity, control, and total impact. When committed to action, such forces methodically execute predetermined plans; when encamped or assuming a defensive posture, they remain unshakable. Thus, in an original passage whose conceptions thereafter echoed throughout the military writings, Sun-tzu asserted, "The army is established by deceit, moves for advantage, and changes through segmenting and reuniting. Thus its speed is like the wind, its slowness like the forest; its invasion and plundering like a fire; unmoving, it is like the mountains. It is as difficult to know as the darkness; in movement it is like thunder."

The historical illustration perhaps too enigmatically describes one of the five famous battles found in the *Tso Chuan,* that of Yen-ling in 575 B.C., roughly the middle of the Spring and Autumn period. In this incident, Ch'u's army well illustrated the danger of recklessly engaging in battle, of lacking the weightiness that presumably characterized Chin's forces. Moreover, the full account in the *Tso Chuan* indicates that Ch'u's forces suffered from acrimonious dissension among the senior commanders; its troops were exhausted from long campaign service; the units were mixed in type and origin, some of them being disorganized and undisciplined; and the best troops were concentrated in the middle under the king's personal command, making the flanks vulnerable to Chin tactics to focus upon them and collapse them inward. However, Chin's forces were also troubled, as Fan Kai's decisive but hasty advice indicates. In fact, the brief depiction recorded here is somewhat misleading, implying—especially in the context of a selection on weightiness—that they followed Luan Shu's advice and outwaited the enemy's impetuosity. In actuality, under the ruler's direction they filled in their wells and smashed the cookstoves—indicating a resolute commitment to press forward in the face of death—and quickly mounted an attack to exploit Ch'u's recklessness and internal dissension. The battle, although ostensibly marked by decorous encounters reminiscent of an earlier age, lasted well into nightfall, indicating the fighting was both extensive and intense. However, the turning point came later that night when the King of Ch'u, undertaking the urgent task of reorganizing in preparation for the next morning's onslaught, discovered his chief commander had gotten drunk and could not be queried on tactical plans. The king therefore fled with his core forces, leaving the encampment empty and the field to Chin.

47 Profit 利

Tactical Discussion

Whenever engaging an enemy in battle, if their commander is stupid and does not understand change, you can entice him with apparent profits. If he covets profit without perceiving potential harm, you can establish ambushes and have your forces suddenly strike him. Then his army can be defeated. A tactical principle from the *Art of War* states: "Display profits to entice them."

Historical Illustration

During the Spring and Autumn period, the state of Ch'u attacked the minor state of Chiao. Ch'u's Military Superintendent Ch'ü Hsia said: "Chiao is small and reckless. Being reckless they make few plans. I suggest that we entice them with some unprotected foraging parties sent out for grass and firewood." The commander followed his plan, and Chiao's troops easily captured some thirty men. The next day Chiao's soldiers competed with each other to race after a number of Ch'u's infantrymen similarly employed in the mountains. Ch'u's forces then blocked Chiao's north gate and unleashed ambushes from below the mountains, severely defeating them.

Commentary

By the Spring and Autumn period an army's fate often rested solely upon the commander's wisdom and decisions; even the strongest, best-prepared forces could no longer overcome their commander's stupidity. Moreover, as the battlefield became more complex and the number of troops multiplied, fixed-piece battles became less possible and maneuver warfare, requiring flexibility, began to emerge. Thus in "Nine Changes" Sun-tzu said: "The general who has a penetrating understanding of the advantages of the nine changes (associated with terrain) knows how to employ the army. If a general does not have a penetrating understanding of the advantages of the nine changes, even though he is familiar with the topography, he will not be able to realize advantages of terrain." Immediately thereafter Sun-tzu pointed out that competent generals can discern both advantages (or potential profits) and disadvantages in any situation and can therefore determine an action's advisability. Conversely, the stupid general fails to note them and blunders into disaster.

Employing the lure of apparent profit or the enticement of potential battlefield gain or advantage—the Chinese term *li* being understood as either "profit" or "advantage"—was fundamental to manipulating an enemy and compelling them to initiate desirable actions. Sun-tzu's statement "display profits to entice them" became the watchword thereafter and was particularly employed by Sun Pin in the *Military Methods.* Recklessness in a commander, such as that appearing in the historical illustration and discussed in the earlier selection on recklessness, facilitated the attempt, but the successful execution of enticements required the presence of greed. An overwhelming desire for profit was recognized as one of the fundamental flaws, although it had to be distinguished from the praiseworthy aggressiveness in exploiting opportunities displayed by outstanding commanders.

Among the many military writers who commented upon the general's traits and flaws, few failed to identify greed as one of the foremost deficiencies. For example, the *Huang Shih-kung* states: "If the general is greedy, treachery will be unchecked and the masses will not submit." The T'ai Kung listed being greedy and loving profit as one of the ten errors of generals: "One who is greedy and loves profit can be bribed." And in the first part of a lengthy passage Wu Ch'i remarked: "In general the essentials of battle are as follows: You must first attempt to divine the enemy's general and evaluate his talent. In accord with the situation exploit the strategic imbalance of power, then you will not labor but still achieve results. A commanding general who is greedy and unconcerned about reputation can be given gifts and bribed." In Chiao's case, the entire army seems to have been unaware of the lessons taught in Chapter 89, "Bait," and therefore befuddled by easy gains into recklessly pursuing them.

48 害 Harm

Tactical Discussion

In general, whenever you and an enemy are both defending a common border, if they make raids across your border to plunder and disrupt your settlers in the nearby region, you can establish ambushes at critical points and erect obstacles to block and intercept them. Then the enemy certainly will not recklessly advance. A tactical principle from the *Art of War* states: "What can cause the enemy not to come forth is the prospect of harm."

Historical Illustration

During the T'ang Dynasty the Commander-in-Chief for the Northern Region, Sha-t'o Chung-yi, was defeated by the Western Turks, so the emperor designated Chang Jen-yüan to serve as Censor-in-Chief and replace him. By the time he reached the region the brigands had already fled; therefore, he led his troops into the hills and mounted a sudden attack, overwhelming and destroying the enemy's camp that very night.

In the beginning Sha-t'o's army and the Turkish forces had taken the Yellow river as their respective borders. On the river's northern bank stood the Temple of the Dispersing Clouds, where the Turks first made offerings and prayed for success every time they were about to make a border incursion, only thereafter leading their troops down to the south. At this time the khan of the Eastern Turks had gathered all his troops to launch an attack in the west against the Western Turks. Chang Jen-yüan requested permission from the emperor to exploit the newly created void and seize the area north of the river, erecting cities for the surrendered peoples in order to cut off potential southern incursions. However, T'ang Hsiu-ching advised the emperor that ever since the Western Han all the Chinese dynasties had defended the Yellow River as their border. Therefore, to now erect cities in the heart of barbarian territory would only result in the cities falling to them. Chang Jen-yüan persistently requested that it be permitted, and eventually Emperor T'ang Chung-ts'ung assented.

Since the memorializing process had taken a full year, some two hundred men in the supplementary labor force had fled back to their native places. Chang Jen-yüan captured them and had them all executed outside the city walls, causing everyone within the army to tremble with fright. The labor forces then exhausted their energies, completing the three cities in just sixty days. Chang took the location of the Temple of Dispersing Clouds as the site for the central city in the southern special administrative region, located the western city in the southern special administrative region of Lin-wu, and the eastern city in the southern special administrative region of Yü-lin, all in the Northern Region. The three fortresses were more than four hundred miles apart from each other, while to the north there was nothing but rocks and boulders. In this extended territory of more than three hundred miles, and moreover north of Niu-ch'i-miao-na mountain, Chang Jen-yüan also established eighteen hundred signal towers. From this time onward the Turks never dared cross the mountains to pasture their horses, and the Northern Region was spared border incursions for many years. These measures saved inestimable amounts, and the T'ang was able to reduce its occupation forces by several tens of thousands.

Commentary

The selection's title suggests it should simply be the correlate to the preceding one on profit, taking Sun-tzu's concept of the deterrent value of potential harm as its central theme. In fact, the original quote—from "Vacuity and Substance"—reads: "In order to prevent the enemy from coming, show them the potential harm." Thus understood, it comprises one of Sun-tzu's fundamental methods for manipulating an enemy, compelling them to move their troops toward desired positions. The potential harm, of course, might either be real, as in heavily fortified areas, or apparent, as in highly visible flags and straw troops, both equally capable of accomplishing the envisioned aim. However, the author has extrapolated the idea to include the notion of a static defensive line—in this case erected along China's northern border—to secure strategic locations and effectively command a much larger area. In part this stems from the underlying compound for the Chinese term for such strategically held locations, *yao hai,* containing the term for harm, *hai,* as its second part. Still, the historical incident well illustrates the tactical discussion's premise and also provides a further glimpse of the difficulties that the Chinese dynasties experienced throughout their history with the highly mobile steppe peoples.

49 Security 安

Tactical Discussion

Whenever an enemy comes from afar and their spirit is sharp, it is advantageous for them to quickly engage in battle. Accordingly, you should deepen your moats and increase the height of your fortifications, securely defending your position without making any response in order to await their enervation. Even if they irritate you with taunts and insults, trying to provoke combat, you still cannot move. A tactical principle from the *Art of War* states: "The secure can be tranquil."

Historical Illustration

During the Three Kingdoms period, General Chu-ko Liang of Shu led a mass of more than one hundred thousand troops through Hsieh-ku and established a fortified encampment south of the Wei river. The kingdom of Wei dispatched Grand General Ssu-ma Yi to oppose him. His generals all wanted to go to the northern bank of the Wei River to await Chu-ko Liang, but Ssu-ma Yi said: "Our people and accumulated supplies are all south of the Wei river. It is territory we must fight for." Then he led the army in fording the river and established fortifications with their backs to the river. Thereupon he addressed his generals: "If Chu-ko Liang is courageous, he will go forth from Wu-kung and follow the mountains to the east. However, if he goes west and ascends Wu-chang-yüan, there will not be any problems." Chu-ko Liang indeed ascended Wu-chang-yüan. By coincidence a shooting star dropped down over Liang's fortifications so Ssu-ma Yi knew he would certainly be defeated.

At that time the king of Wei thought that since Chu-ko Liang had led his army out far to cross into their territory, it would be advantageous for Liang to fight quickly; therefore he repeatedly ordered Ssu-ma Yi to remain steadfast and await changes. Chu-ko Liang attempted to provoke Wei's forces into battle several times, but Ssu-ma Yi would not go forth. Thereupon Chu-ko Liang sent Ssu-ma Yi some material for a dress and some women's jewelry, but Ssu-ma Yi still refused to engage in combat. Ssu-ma Yi's younger brother Ssu-ma Fu sent him a letter to inquire about the state of military affairs and Yi replied, saying: "Chu-ko Liang's ambition is great but he does not perceive opportunities. He makes many plans but few decisions. He loves military studies but lacks the tactical means to effect them. Even though he controls a hundred thousand soldiers, he has already fallen into my plans, and his destruction is certain."

Ssu-ma Yi maintained his fortifications opposite Liang for more than a hundred days. It happened that Chu-ko Liang fell ill and died, so his subordinates burned their camp and the army snuck away. The common people raced to report it to Ssu-ma Yi, who sent his forces to pursue them. Liang's Chief-of-Staff Yang Yi unfurled Liang's command flag and beat the drums as if they were about to counterattack. Ssu-ma Yi did not press them as they were retreating. Thereupon Yang Yi collapsed his formations and departed. A day later Ssu-ma Yi walked through their deserted fortifications, observed the items left behind after their departure, and obtained their maps, documents, and considerable provisions. Ssu-ma Yi decided that Chu-ko Liang must have died, and said: "He was an extraordinary talent." General Hsin Pi thought it was still unclear. Ssu-ma Yi said: "Army commanders emphasize military writings, secret plans, weapons and horses, and supplies and provisions. Now he has abandoned them all. Do you think a man can lose his five viscera and still live? We should urgently pursue them." Within the pass Shu's army had placed numerous caltrops, so Ssu-ma Yi had three thousand of his soldiers wear soft shoes with flat wooden soles to walk ahead of the army because the caltrops would stick to their shoes. Thereafter the cavalry and infantry advanced together, pursuing Shu's forces as far as the banks of the Red River before they truly knew that Chu-ko Liang had died. At the time the local people circulated a saying that "Even in death Chu-ko Liang was able to walk away from the living Ssu-ma Yi." Ssu-ma Yi laughed about it: "It's because I am able to fathom the living, not the dead."

Commentary

This, the first in the paired selections on security and danger, largely focuses upon the use of fortifications and temporizing defenses, although the later were already raised in Chapter 40, "Response." The tactical discussion explicates the insight that confronting strong, spirited forces is foolish when prolonged delays will witness them inevitably weakening because they have ventured far from their supplies and are forced to constantly pressure the defenders. (A variant of this situation is discussed in "Refusing Battle," which reaches similar conclusions.) The historical incident vividly illustrates the tactic's effective adoption, although the final outcome was precipitated by Chu-ko Liang's unexpected death.

The tactical quotation—cited from Sun-tzu's chapter entitled "Strategic Military Power"—is somewhat transformed from the initial intent, for it was originally employed in an extended analogy for strategic power, being the italicized portion in the following passage:

> One who employs strategic power commands men in battle as if he were rolling logs and stones. The nature of wood and stone is *to be quiet when stable* but to move when on precipitous ground. If they are square they stop; if round they tend to move. Thus the strategic power of one who excels at employing men in warfare is comparable to rolling round boulders down a thousand-fathom mountain. Such is the strategic configuration of power.

The author has thus shifted the emphasis and created a tactical principle with its own attestable validity.

The historical illustration recounts some interesting battlefield measures. First, Ssu-ma Yi deliberately chose to deploy along the river rather than a comfortable distance away from the banks—contrary to Sun-tzu's admonitions previously cited in the commentary to "Amphibious Strategies" as well other views found in Chapter 65, "Rivers"—thereby precluding any landing by the enemy but also putting himself onto potentially fatal terrain. Second, the watchword when pressed—"increase the height of your fortifications and deepen your moats and ditches"—is found in many of the military writings. While none of the *Unorthodox Strategies* focus upon fortifications, even temporary encampments could quickly erect palisades and reasonably solid exterior walls behind which extensive earthworks and ditches, extremely difficult to breech or scale without siege equipment, could then be constructed. Third, deflating an enemy's animated spirit, or *ch'i*, by waiting for them to become enervated was first espoused by Sun-tzu and became basic doctrine thereafter, as will be discussed in Chapter 74, the selection focusing on *ch'i*. It was also a general principle, although opposing viewpoints existed (as will be explicated by the commentary in Chapter 60, "Retreating") that retreating forces should not be pressed too closely; otherwise, being compressed onto fatal terrain, they might suddenly find the resolve to fight fervently. Finally, the employment of caltrops—several spikes sticking out from a common center (something like jacks) arranged so that no matter how they fall, one spike is always sticking up—to delay pursuing forces should be noted, as well as Ssu-ma Yi's clever solution for rapidly clearing them. The caltrops, which functioned as the land mines of their day, were also used to deny or control an enemy's movement, such as by forcing them onto less desirable terrain. For example, Sun Pin stated: "caltrops are employed as ditches and moats," while the T'ai Kung enumerated several very large types and provided some brief instructions for their use:

> "The army's equipment should include wooden caltrops that stick out of the ground about two feet five inches, one hundred twenty. They are employed to defeat infantry and cavalry, to urgently press the attack against invaders, and to intercept their flight.
>
> "For narrow roads and small bypaths, set out iron caltrops eight inches wide, having hooks four inches high and shafts of more than six feet, twelve hundred. They are for defeating retreating cavalry.
>
> "If, in the darkness of night the enemy should suddenly press an attack and the naked blades clash, stretch out a ground net, and spread out two arrow-headed caltrops connected together with 'weaving women' type caltrops on both sides. The points of the blades should be about two feet apart. Twelve thousand sets."
>
> King Wu said: "Suppose there aren't any hills or mounds, ravines or defiles. The enemy arrives, and it is both numerous and martial. Their chariots and cavalry outflank us on both sides, and they are making sudden thrusts against our front and rear positions. Our Three Armies are terrified and fleeing in chaotic defeat. What should we do?"
>
> The T'ai Kung said: "Order our officers and troops to set up the spiked horse barriers and wooden caltrops, arraying the oxen and horses by units of five in their midst, and have them establish a four-sided martial assault formation. When you see the enemy's chariots and cavalry are about to advance, our men should evenly spread out the caltrops and dig ditches around the rear, making them five feet deep and wide. It is called the 'Fate of Dragon Grass.'
>
> "Our men should take hold of the horse barriers and advance on foot. The chariots should be arrayed as ramparts and pushed forward and back. Whenever they stop set them up as fortifications. Our skilled soldiers and strong crossbowmen should prepare against the left and right flanks. Afterward order our Three Armies to fervently fight without respite."

50 Danger 危

Tactical Discussion

Whenever engaging an enemy in battle, if you should suddenly penetrate terrain where you are in danger of perishing, you should arouse your generals and officers, encouraging them to commit themselves to fight to the death, for you cannot seek to live and hope to be victorious. A tactical principle from the *Art of War* states: "When the officers and soldiers have penetrated deeply they will not be afraid."

Historical Illustration

During the Later Han dynasty, when general Wu Han, engaged in a punitive expedition against Kung-sun Shu, had advanced across the border of Chieh-hui commandery, the various district forces in the commandery all ensconced themselves in their fortified cities. General Wu assaulted the city of Kuang-tu and seized it. He then dispatched light cavalry units to burn the bridges in Ch'eng-tu, thereby frightening all the towns east of Wu-yang into surrendering.

The emperor admonished General Han: "Ch'eng-tu has more than a hundred thousand troops so you cannot treat them lightly. However, you can solidly occupy Kuang-tu and wait for them to come and attack rather than fight them head-on. If they do not dare come forth, you should shift your encampment in order to pressure them. Wait for their strength to abate; then they can be attacked." General Wu Han did not obey but instead exploited the advantages presented by the situation to personally lead more than twenty thousand cavalrymen to advance and press Ch'eng-tu, setting up his camp some ten miles away, north of the Yangtze River, which blocked them. Then he had floating bridges constructed and dispatched General Liu Shang in command of approximately ten thousand cavalrymen to establish a camp about twenty miles away, south of the river.

When the emperor learned of these developments he was greatly startled and dispatched a missive upbraiding Wu Han: "I instructed you many times, so what do you mean by embarking on a military action in this confused and rebellious manner? Now you have already treated the enemy lightly and deeply penetrated their territory, and moreover have established Liu Shang in a separate encampment. If affairs should suddenly turn inauspicious, you will not be able to reunite. If the brigands come forth and entangle your forces while a large mass attacks Liu Shang, Liu will be destroyed and then you in turn will also be destroyed. There is no alternative but to hastily lead your troops back to Kuang-tu."

The imperial missive had not yet reached Wu Han when Kung-sun Shu indeed dispatched two generals—Hsieh Feng and Yüan Chi—with more than a hundred thousand troops to attack Han, and had other generals, with more than ten thousand men, suppress Liu Shang, preventing him from providing any rescue forces. Wu Han fought a fierce battle with the enemy for a full day, but was defeated and forced back within his fortifications, where he was encircled by Hsieh Feng.

Wu Han summoned his generals and incited them by saying: "You and I have overstepped danger and obstacles, conducting running battles for more than a thousand miles, killing the enemy and being victorious everywhere, and have thus penetrated deep into enemy territory. Now we have arrived outside their capital city but we and Liu Shang are surrounded in two different locations. The damage caused by our inability to unite is inestimable, but I want to secretly move our army south of the river toward Liu Shang to mount a defense. If we are able to be united in both mind and strength and every man is willing to fight fervently, great achievements can be attained. If not, nothing but defeat looms ahead. The crux of success and defeat lies in this single effort." His generals all assented.

Accordingly, they feasted the soldiers and fed the horses, closed the gates to the encampment, and did not venture forth for three days. Then they set up numerous pennants and flags and raised smoke and fire continuously. That night, with their horses and men gagged to prevent any sound, they went forth and joined with Liu Shang's army. General Feng and the other enemy commanders were not aware of it, so the next day Feng divided his forces, retaining some to fight a holding action north of the river while he personally led his soldiers in an attack on Liu Shang south of the river. General Wu Han employed all his forces in a counterattack, fighting from dawn to dusk, and eventually severely defeated Feng's army, killing both Hsieh Feng and Yüan Chi.

Then Wu Han led his soldiers back to Kuang-tu, leaving Liu Shang behind to resist Kung-sun Shu. Moreover he reported the situation to the emperor and severely reproached himself. The emperor responded: "It is highly appropriate that you have returned to Kuang-tu, for Kung-sun Shu will certainly not dare try to seize Liu Shang and simultaneously attack you. If he attacks Liu Shang first, you can mobilize all your cavalry and infantry forces to go the fifty miles from Kuang-tu to them. When they are caught in this fatal difficulty, their destruction will be certain."

Thereupon Wu Han and Kung-sun Shu clashed between Kuang-tu and Ch'eng-tu, with Wu Han winning eight out of the eight engagements, advancing the army into Shu's outer perimeter. Kung-sun Shu, in personal command of several tens of thousands of troops, sallied forth from the city walls for a decisive battle. Wu Han had the Military Protectors Kao Wu and T'ang Han, in command of a similar number of elite troops, suddenly attack him. Kung-sun Shu's army was defeated and fled; Kao Wu rushed into their formations and stabbed Kung-sun Shu, killing him. The next day the city surrendered and Kung-sun Shu's severed head was sent to Lo-yang. Thereafter Shu was peaceful.

Commentary

The psychology of troops facing certain death was much discussed by the ancient Chinese military writers and in fact consciously exploited by generals throughout history, including the Vietnam War. Chapter 18, "The Guest," has already described the solidity that can be achieved when soldiers find themselves surrounded and cut off deep inside enemy territory, whereas this selection indicates a need for arousing the soldiers to an awareness of their fate in order to elicit a similarly desperate effort from them. The quotation cited in the tactical discussion, however, is only a rough paraphrase of a line from "Nine Terrains," as will be seen in the commentary to the next selection, which considers the same topic from a slightly different perspective.

51 Fighting to the Death 死

Tactical Discussion

Whenever the enemy is strong and vigorous while your officers and troops are doubtful and confused, unwilling to obey orders, you must thrust them onto fatal terrain. Issue orders to the Three Armies showing that there is no intent to preserve yourselves. Slaughter the oxen and burn your wagons in order to provide a final feast for your generals, officers, and troops. Incinerate your fodder and cast aside your provisions, fill in the wells and smash your cooking utensils, severing and abandoning all thoughts of life, for then you will be victorious. A tactical principle from the *Wu-tzu* states: "When death is certain, they will live."

Historical Illustration

After the Ch'in general Chang Han had vanquished Ch'u's army under General Hsiang Liang, he felt that the forces still remaining in Ch'u were not worth worrying about and so crossed the Yellow River and launched a sudden attack on the state of Chao, extensively destroying it. At this time Chao Hsieh was king of Chao, Chen Yü was commanding general, and Chang Erh was prime minister. When their army was defeated they all raced into the city of Chü-lu. Chang Han, Wang Li, and Sheh Chien surrounded Chü-lu. South of his army Chang Han built a protected corridor to transport their grain.

Meanwhile, King Huai of Ch'u appointed Sung Yi as commanding general, Hsiang Yü as general, and Fan Tseng as lieutenant general, with the remaining generals all subordinate to them, to mount an expedition to rescue Chao. Sung Yi proceeded as far as An-yang, where he remained for more than forty days without advancing, dispatching his son Sung Hsiang as ambassador to Ch'i with a great feast, personally escorting him as far as Wu-yen. Hsiang Yü said: "Now, when our state's army has recently been defeated, the king does not sit securely on his throne, and the country has been scoured for every soldier who might be placed under the general's command, the fate of the entire state lies in this one effort. However, instead of being concerned about his officers and troops, Sung Yi has placed his personal affairs first. He is not a true minister of the state."

The next morning he entered the general's tent, killed Sung Yi, and then circulated an announcement throughout the army: "Sung Yi was plotting a revolt with the state of Ch'i, so our king of Ch'u secretly ordered me to execute him." At this time the various feudal lords submitted in terror, none daring to assert themselves. They all said: "The first to establish Ch'u was a general, and now a general has executed the rebellious." In consort, they designated Hsiang Yü as provisional commanding general and had men pursue Sung Yi's son Sung Hsiang as far as Ch'i, where he was killed. Separately they sent men to report the incident to King Huai of Ch'u, who accordingly commissioned Hsiang Yü as commanding general with the lord of Tang-yang and General P'u subordinate to him. Because he had slain Sung Yi, Hsiang Yü's awesomeness shook the state of Ch'u, and his fame was established among the feudal lords.

The king dispatched the Lord of Tang-yang and General P'u with some twenty thousand troops to cross the Yangtze river and rescue the city of Chü-lu. However, the battle went badly. General Chen Yü of Chao again requested troops from Hsiang Yü, so Hsiang Yü assembled all his troops and forded the Yangtze River, then sank their boats, smashed their cooking utensils, and burnt their huts, setting out with only three days rations to show the officers and troops that they would certainly die and should not have any thoughts of returning alive. When they reached the city they surrounded Wang Li's forces, severed his protected supply corridor, and badly defeated him, killing Su Yung and capturing Wang Li. Initially, when Ch'u's forces were about to rescue Chü-lu, every one of their soldiers opposed ten of the enemy. Their shouts and yells shook Heaven and Earth, and Ch'in's feudal lords all shook with terror. They then proceeded to utterly destroy Ch'in's army.

Commentary

This chapter advocates deliberately ordering highly visible measures to impress upon the troops the finality of their situation, to convince them they are about to engage in battle with no hope of survival. This was a psychological technique derived from the common observation that men thrown into desperate situations tend to exert maximum effort (even though history equally records numerous examples of forces, even armies, suddenly losing the will to fight in exactly the same circumstances). Moreover, the author has extended the method's applicability even further, favoring its adoption simply to coerce a unified effort rather than because a desperate situation demands it. However, the historical illustration, while recording such dramatic steps as casting aside their rations and provisions, describes Hsiang Yü's heavily outnumbered forces still emerging victorious in a truly hopeless situation over Ch'in's mighty army during the chaotic final years of the Ch'in dynasty.

Many of the military writers remarked upon this psychology of spirit, or *ch'i,* in desperate battles (as will be further discussed in Chapter 74, "Spirit"), although Sun-tzu was probably the first to consciously articulate it as a theoretical principle. In the *Art of War* he states:

> Cast them into positions from which there is nowhere to go and they will die without retreating. If there is no escape from death, the officers and soldiers will fully exhaust their strength.
>
> When the soldiers and officers have penetrated deeply into enemy territory, they will cling together. When there is no alternative, they will fight. Cast them into hopeless situations and they will be preserved; have them penetrate fatal terrain and they will live. Only after the masses have penetrated dangerous terrain will they be able to craft victory out of defeat.
>
> For this reason even though the soldiers are not instructed, they are prepared; without seeking it, their cooperation is obtained; without covenants they are close together; without issuing orders they are reliable. Prohibit omens; eliminate doubt so that they will die without other thoughts. Thus it is the nature of the army to defend when encircled, to fight fervently when unavoidable, and to follow orders when compelled by circumstances.

Accordingly, he said: "On fatal terrain I show them that we will not live."

The early *Ssu-ma Fa* also preserves a succinct analysis of spirit, or *ch'i,* in the soldiers:

> In general, in battle one endures through strength, and gains victory through spirit. One can endure with a solid defense but will achieve victory through being endangered. When the heart's foundation is solid, a new surge of ch'i will bring victory. With armor one is secure; with weapons one attains victory. When men have minds set on victory, all they see is the enemy. When men have minds filled with fear, all they see is their fear.

The *Ssu-ma Fa* also observes that highly visible measures, such as smashing the cookstoves, was an ancient practice:

> Writing letters of final farewell is referred to as "breaking off all thoughts of life." Selecting the elite and ranking the weapons is termed "increasing the strength of the men." Casting aside the implements of office and carrying only minimal rations is termed "opening the men's thoughts." From antiquity this has been the rule.

Thus, when men are committed to death and oblivious to life, they become strong and reckless, fighting with abandon, and therefore extremely powerful in comparison to reluctant soldiers hoping to avoid being wounded or killed, as both the *Wei Liao-tzu* and *Wu-tzu* record:

> If a warrior wields a sword to strike people in the marketplace, among ten thousand people there will not be anyone who doesn't avoid him. If I say it's not that only one man is courageous, but that the ten thousand are unlike him, what is the reason? Being committed to dying and being committed to seeking life are not comparable.
>
> I have heard that men have strengths and weaknesses, that their *ch'i* flourishes and ebbs. Now if there is a murderous villain hidden in the woods, even though a thousand men pursue him they all look around like owls and glance about like wolves. Why? They are afraid that violence will erupt and harm them personally. Thus one man oblivious to life and death can frighten a thousand.

Obviously Hsiang Yü's forces were oblivious to life and death and therefore overwhelmed the enemy.

52 Seeking Life 生

Tactical Discussion

Whenever engaging in battle with an enemy, if you have realized the terrain's advantages, your officers and troops are already deployed, the laws and orders have been well circulated, and your unorthodox troops already established, you should abandon yourself to fate and engage in combat, for then you will be victorious. A tactical principle from the *Wu-tzu* states: "Those who cling to life will perish."

Historical Illustration

During the Spring and Autumn period, the prince of Ch'u attacked the minor state of Cheng, but an army from Chin came to their rescue. The battle was fought between Ao and Hao. Chao Ying-ch'i of Chin dispatched some of his troops to prepare boats at the river, wanting to be able to cross first if they should be defeated. In consequence his generals and officers became lax, and his troops were unable to be victorious.

Commentary

The quotation, cited from Wu Ch'i's chapter entitled "Controlling the Army" in the *Wu-tzu,* summarizes not only this chapter's tactical discussion, but also the previous one's as well. The author has merely reoriented the fundamental insight slightly in order to provide two selections upon the pair "death/life," in consonance with similarly correlated pairs throughout the text, although he revisits the topic from another perspective in Chapter 96, "Fear."

The historical incident clearly illustrates the danger of clinging to life because Chin's general severely undermined his troops' moral and commitment by revealing his own doubts and fears. While this is not a simple issue, for only an irresponsible commander would neglect making at least minimal preparations for a possible retreat, it was distinctly contrary to the spirit of commitment prevailing in ancient China, particularly as the disgrace of defeat could well result in the commander's execution.

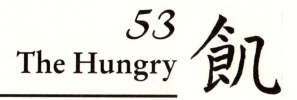

53 The Hungry 飢

Tactical Discussion

In general, whenever you mobilize the army to go forth on a punitive campaign to extirpate an enemy and have deeply penetrated their territory, fodder and provisions will be scarce and lacking, so you must segment your troops to forage and plunder. If you occupy the enemy's storehouses and granaries and seize his accumulated resources in order to continuously provision your army, you will be victorious. A tactical principle from the *Art of War* states: "If one relies upon gaining provisions from the enemy, the army's food will be sufficient."

Historical Illustration

During the Northern and Southern Dynasties period, General Ho Juo-tun of the Northern Chou led his troops across the Yangtze River to seize the minor state of Chen, so General Hou Ch'i of Hsiang-chou in Chen came forth to exterminate him. The autumnal rains overflowed the land, flooding the roads along the river, cutting off Ho's provisions and support. His men were terrified by their predicament. General Ho then segmented his troops to forage and plunder in order to supply their requirements. Meanwhile, as he feared Hou Ch'i would learn that their provisions were scarce, he raised a number of earthen mounds within the encampment and covered them over with a layer of grain. He then summoned some people from the nearby villages, pretending to ask them about local conditions, and afterward sent them away. When Hou Ch'i heard about these grain mounds, he assumed Ho's provisions were substantial. General Ho also improved and increased his fortifications and built reed huts to show that they intended to remain indefinitely. Thus, between Hsiang-chou and Luo-shan the people abandoned their agricultural pursuits and Hou Ch'i did not know what to do.

In the beginning the local people had employed light boats to ferry rice, millet, and baskets of chickens and ducks in order to feed Hou Ch'i's army. General Ho was troubled by their success, so he fabricated some boats in the local style but hid armored soldiers in them. When Hou Ch'i's soldiers saw them off in the distance, they thought their supply boats were coming and therefore competed with each other in rushing into the river to bring in their supplies, whereupon Ho's mailed troops captured them. Furthermore, several times mounted deserters from Ho's army sought refuge with Hou's forces and were taken in every time. Ho accordingly had some horses led down to board their boats and then had the men on the boats whip them. After this was repeated a few times, the horses were afraid of the boats and would not dare climb aboard. Thereafter, General Ho concealed troops in ambush along the river bank and had some soldiers ride the boat-shy horses and pretend to seek refuge with Hou Ch'i's army. Hou Ch'i dispatched some soldiers by boat to receive them, but they fought among themselves to take the horses' reins. Moreover, the horses were afraid of the boats and would not climb aboard. During the confusion the ambush was sprung and all of

Hou's troops were killed. Thereafter, when real supply boats or deserters appeared, Hou Ch'i still feared that they might be disguised troops and did not dare accept them. The two armies maintained their positions for more than a year, but Hou Ch'i was unable to wrest a victory.

Commentary

This chapter and the next ponder the question of supplying campaign armies from the guest's (invader's) and host's (defender's) perspectives. (The nature and roles of the guest and host have previously been examined in Chapters 17 and 18.) By the end of the Spring and Autumn period, and certainly in the Warring States period, logistics had become critical because mobilizing, moving, and feeding an army of a hundred thousand men plus their horses required an extensive supply train and numerous support personnel. This prompted Sun-tzu to voice concern over the adverse economic effects of prolonged campaigns and stress the need to opportunistically capitalize upon whatever supplies and provisions might be gained en route and in the enemy's own territory, whether through purchase or seizure. Naturally the latter would be preferable, as it would minimize the adverse effects on the state's coffers. In a famous passage in "Waging War" he asserted:

> One who excels in employing the military does not conscript the people twice or transport provisions a third time. If you obtain your equipment from within the state and rely on seizing provisions from the enemy, then the army's foodstuffs will be sufficient.
>
> The state is impoverished by the army when it transports provisions far off. When provisions are transported far off, the hundred surnames are impoverished. Those in proximity to the army will sell their goods expensively. When goods are expensive, the hundred surnames' wealth will be exhausted. When their wealth is exhausted, they will be extremely hard pressed to supply their village's military impositions.
>
> When their strength has been expended and their wealth depleted, then the houses in the central plains will be empty. The expenses of the hundred surnames will be some seven-tenths of whatever they have. The ruler's irrecoverable expenditures, such as ruined chariots, exhausted horses, armor, helmets, arrows and crossbows, halberd-tipped and spear-tipped large, movable protective shields, strong oxen, and large wagons, will consume six-tenths of his resources.
>
> Thus the wise general will concentrate on securing provisions from the enemy. One bushel of the enemy's foodstuffs is worth twenty of ours; one picul of fodder is worth twenty of ours.

While most of the military writers agreed, and campaign armies in China, just as in ancient Greece, frequently resorted to plundering and foraging for essential supplies (as well as personal material rewards), there were also dissenting voices that felt wanton destruction and the seizure of foodstuffs was counterproductive, serving only to stiffen an enemy's resistance and undermine any claim to be pursuing a righteous cause. While the earlier period—particularly as preserved in the *Ssu-ma Fa*—witnessed a concern with righteous warfare, with punishing tyrannical and debauched monarchs while sparing the people, the excesses of the Warring States period also provoked a humanistic reaction and the desire to minimize the destruction being wrought. Unfortunately, the scope of battle continued to escalate and there was little relief or refuge for the people from the carnage and rampages of the period.

54 The Sated 飽

Tactical Discussion

Whenever an enemy comes from afar, their supplies and provisions will not be continuous. If the enemy is hungry while you are full, you can make your walls solid and not engage in battle, maintaining your stance for a prolonged period in order to enervate them while severing their supply routes. When they withdraw, you can secretly dispatch unorthodox troops to intercept them along their route of retreat and release troops to pursue and suddenly attack them. Then their destruction will be certain. A tactical principle from the *Art of War* states: "With the well-fed await the hungry."

Historical Illustration

In the Wu-te reign period at the beginning of the T'ang dynasty, Liu Wu-chou, who had occupied T'ai-Yüan, dispatched General Sung Chin-kang to encamp east of the Yellow River. When T'ang T'ai-tsung went out to conduct a punitive campaign against him, he addressed his subordinate generals:

"Sung Chin-kang has hung up his army a thousand miles into our territory. His elite forces and brilliant generals are all here. Liu Wu-chou occupies T'ai-yüan by himself, totally dependent upon Sung Chin-kang for support. I believe that even though Sung's forces are numerous, their internal condition is actually empty and vacuous and that they are relying upon foraging and capturing provisions, so they intend to quickly engage in battle. We ought to solidify our encampment and await their hunger; it is not yet appropriate to quickly engage in battle." Thereupon he dispatched Liu Hong and others to sever their supply lines. When Sung Chin-kang's troops subsequently became hungry, he secretly withdrew them.

Commentary

This chapter addresses the issue of supplying troops in the field from the defender's perspective. While Sun-tzu had advocated plundering and foraging in order to minimize the state's expenses, and the previous chapter's historical incident provides a successful illustration of that policy, here the author points out the tenuousness of such plans and the difficulty of relying upon them for sustained periods. Moreover, although unmentioned here but noted by many of the military writers, when a defender is confronted by an invading army, normally the first response is to move all the supplies and provisions into fortified locations and, if necessary, even burn the crops in the fields to deny them to the enemy. An invader finding nothing to seize must either rely upon his own supply lines or abandon the campaign after one or two desperate thrusts at the enemy. Consequently, it is advantageous for the defender to move second, as discussed in Chapter 40, "Response," and witnessed in previous historical illustrations, to wait for the invader's supplies to be exhausted and their energy to sap. Thereafter, when they attempt to retreat and their disorder grows, they will become easy targets for ambushes, flanking attacks, and outright onslaughts from the rear.

55 Fatigue 勞

Tactical Discussion

Whenever engaging an enemy in battle, if they deploy their troops first and occupy advantageous terrain while you are forced to race onto the battlefield afterward, your troops will be tired and easily defeated by the enemy. A tactical principle from the *Art of War* states: "Whoever occupies the battleground second and must race to the engagement will be fatigued."

Historical Illustration

During the Wei-Chin period, the Commandant of Prisons in the Western Chin dynasty, Liu Kun, dispatched General of the Army Chi Tan, in command of more than one hundred thousand troops, to conduct a punitive campaign against Shih Leh. Shih Leh came forth to oppose him. Someone remonstrated with Shih Leh, saying: "General Chi has elite soldiers and vigorous horses, their vanguard cannot be withstood. But if we deepen our moats and raise the height of our fortifications, we can blunt their fierceness. Attack and defense being a matter of different strategic configurations of power, we can then gain complete victory."

Shih Leh said: "Chi Tan's forces have come far; their bodies are tired and their strength exhausted. They are like dogs and horses thrown together while their commands and orders are not unified. With one battle we can achieve victory, so what strength do they have? Moreover, reinforcements will soon arrive, so how can we abandon the effort? If we attempt to move our large army all at once and Chi Tan takes advantage of our withdrawal, we won't even have a chance to glance around, much less deepen the moats and raise fortifications. This would be the way to exterminate ourselves without ever fighting." Then he had the advisor beheaded and deputed K'ung Ch'ang as supervisor for the forward deployment, ordering that anyone who started late would be executed. He also established two ambushing forces in the mountains. Thereafter, Shih Leh led his forces to engage Chi Tan in battle, eventually pretending to collapse his troops and retreat. Chi Tan released his own soldiers to purse them, whereupon Shih Leh's forces lying in ambush mounted a sudden attack. Chi Tan was badly defeated and withdrew.

Commentary

This chapter introduces the conceptual pair "fatigued/rested," which may be reduced to the simple realization that it is decisively advantageous for a rested force to engage a much fatigued enemy. A succinct articulation, already partially quoted in the tactical discussion, appears in Sun-tzu's "Vacuity and Substance": "In general, whoever occupies the battleground first and awaits the enemy will be at ease; whoever occupies the battleground afterward and must race to the conflict will be fatigued. Thus one who excels at warfare compels men and is not compelled by other men." The last line enunciates the ultimate principle: compel others rather than be compelled by them, thereby making it possible to create advantageous conditions. Compelling the enemy into movement, forcing them to waste time and energy, was the basic method for causing fatigue throughout Chinese military history. Sun-tzu advised:

> In order to cause the enemy to come of their own volition, extend some apparent profit. In order to prevent the enemy from coming forth, show them the potential harm. Thus if the enemy is rested, you can tire him; if he is well fed, you can make him hungry; if he is at rest, you can move him. Go forth to positions to which he must race. Race forth where he does not expect it.

Rigorously applying these tactical principles should eventually produce the ideal conditions for an easy victory, as Sun Pin indicated in this concise overview from the *Military Methods:*

> Those who excel in warfare can cause the enemy to roll up his armor and race far off, to travel two days normal distance at a time, to be exhausted and sick but unable to rest, to be hungry and thirsty but unable to eat. An enemy emaciated in this way certainly will not be victorious! Sated, we await his hunger; resting in our emplacement we await his fatigue; in true tranquillity we await his movement.

The historical illustration provides an interesting example of an ill-fated tactician suffering execution for advising Shih Leh to adopt the temporizing tactics expounded in several previous chapters of the *Unorthodox Strategies* until the enemy exhausts themselves. In contrast, Shih Leh, the eventual founder of the Later Chao dynasty, moved boldly and took the initiative in exploiting the perceived opportunity presented by the enemy's internal disorder. His victory may be seen as evidence that warfare, despite its apparent principles and parameters, remains an art rather than a science.

56 Ease 逸

Tactical Discussion

Whenever you engage an enemy in battle, you cannot allow yourselves to become lax after attaining victory but should increase your strictness and sharpness in order to prepare for the enemy's next move. Even though you are at ease, you should still labor. A tactical principle states: "One who is prepared will not suffer misfortune."

Commentary

The concept of ease, of being rested and therefore prepared, forms the second half of the tactical conceptual pair "fatigued/rested" introduced in the previous chapter. In consort with the rest of the book, further discussion on the advantages of being rested when the enemy is tired, the simple correlate for "Fatigue," should be expected. Instead, the author warns about the overconfidence that victory brings, a subject raised in the succeeding chapter as well where arrogance instead threatens. Moreover, none of the several available editions record any historical illustration for this chapter even though many battles would easily suffice. For example, the idea of ease, of being rested, is well exemplified by Sun Pin's campaigns against P'ang Chüan and the state of Wei, for he compelled the enemy into motion and then awaited them with his own troops well rested and fully deployed, as previously discussed in Chapter 30, "Knowledge."

The military writers constantly warned against negligence and laxity, of being taken unaware, probably because vigilance naturally grows lax when men feel unthreatened. However, apart from Sun-tzu's admonition to fully exploit new victories, there was a distinct countercurrent that stressed the dangers of victory and even suggested that the more numerous the victories, the greater the army's or state's debilitation. Sun Pin's "Lunar Warfare" in the *Military Methods* exemplifies this fear, while Wu Ch'i said:

> Now being victorious in battle is easy, but preserving the results of victory is difficult. Thus it is said that among the states under Heaven that engage in warfare, those that garner five victories will meet with disaster, those with four victories will be exhausted, those with three victories will become hegemons, those with two victories will become kings, and those with one victory will become emperors. For this reason those who have conquered the world through many victories are extremely rare, while those who thereby perished are many.

57 Victory 勝

Tactical Discussion

Whenever you emerge victorious after engaging an enemy in battle, you cannot become arrogant or lax but should undertake rigorous preparations night and day in order to await the enemy. Then, even if they launch another assault, since you are prepared no harm will result. A tactical principle from the *Ssu-ma Fa* states: "After a victory one should act as if victory had not been achieved."

Historical Illustration

During the reign of the second Ch'in emperor, Hsiang Liang had Liu Pang and Hsiang Yü attack the city of Hsiang-yang from different directions and slaughter the defenders. Meanwhile, he personally went west and largely destroyed another Ch'in army east of P'u-yang. Ch'in gathered its remnant forces into P'u-yang. Liu Pang and Hsiang Yü attacked Ting-t'ao and then seized territory to the west as far as Yung-ch'iu, where they severely defeated the Ch'in forces there and killed their commander, Li Yu. Thereafter they returned to seize the city of Wai-huang.

Hsiang Liang increasingly despised Ch'in's forces and had an arrogant look. Sung Yi advanced to offer a remonstrance to Hsiang Liang: "One who achieves victory only to have the troops grow lax and the general arrogant will be defeated. Now you my lord have begun to grow lax while Ch'in's army increases daily. I am therefore worried about it on your behalf." Hsiang Liang would not listen but instead dispatched Sung Yi as an emissary to the state of Ch'i. While Yi was en route he encountered Ch'i's ambassador, the Lord of Kao-ling, and inquired of him: "Is my lord going to see Hsiang Liang?" The ambassador replied that he was, so Sung Yi said: "Soon Hsiang Liang will certainly be defeated. If you travel slowly you will avoid death; if you proceed quickly, you will meet with disaster." Ch'in indeed mobilized all its soldiers in support of General Chang Han, who suddenly attacked Hsiang Liang's armies, badly defeating them. Hsiang Liang perished in the conflict.

Commentary

"Victory" again warns against allowing laxity after great victories, coupling it with the observation that arrogance may prove an equally dangerous tendency. The original passage, from "Strict Positions" in the *Ssu-ma Fa,* equally cautions against allowing the troops to become arrogant:

> In general, whether the troops are numerous or few, even though they have already attained victory, they should act as if they had not been victorious. The troops should neither boast about the sharpness of their weapons, nor speak of the stoutness of their armor, nor the sturdiness of their chariots, nor the quality of their horses, nor should the masses take themselves to be many—for they have not yet gained the Tao.

As already discussed in Chapter 21, "Arrogance," arrogance in a commander was recognized as a fatal flaw, one easily exploited if it had not already led to serious errors in judgment. However, while trying to prevent the soldiers from becoming arrogant, the commander had to avoid excessively deflating or repressing their spirit and instead strive for a balance between self-confidence and pride. The subsequent passage in the *Ssu-ma Fa* provides some suggestions for attaining the proper attitude:

> In general, if in warfare you are victorious, share the achievement and praise with the troops. If you are about to reengage in battle, then make their rewards exceptionally generous and the punishments heavier. If you failed to direct them to victory, accept the blame yourself. If you must fight again, swear an oath and assume a forward position. Do not repeat your previous tactics. Whether you win or not, do not deviate from this method, for it is referred to as the "True Principle."

58 Defeat 敗

Tactical Discussion

Whenever suffering a defeat after engaging an enemy in battle, you must not become fearful but should instead ponder the potential advantages within the harm that has befallen you. If you order your forces, sharpen your weapons, and incite your officers and troops, awaiting the moment when the enemy grows negligent and lax to suddenly attack them, you will be victorious. A tactical principle from the *Art of War* states: "If one reacts to harm, calamities can be resolved."

Historical Illustration

During the internal strife at the end of the Chin dynasty in the Wei-Chin period, Ssu-ma Yung, king of Ho-chien, who was in Kuan-chung, dispatched Chang Fang to extirpate Ssu-ma Yi, the king of Ch'ang-sha. Chang Fang led his troops out of Han-ku to the south of the Yellow River, where they encamped, so Emperor Hui of the Chin dispatched his General of the Left Huang-fu Shang to counter him. Chang Fang employed concealed troops to destroy Huang-fu Shang's army and subsequently enter Lo-yang. Huang-fu Shang, still obeying the emperor's order to conduct a campaign against

Chang Fang, proceeded to engage Chang's forces in the city itself. When Chang Fang looked out and observed that the emperor's carriage was approaching, he grew fearful. Soon his forces proved unable to stop Huang-fu Shang's soldiers, and they suffered a severe defeat, the dead and wounded filling the streets and alleys.

Chang Fang retreated to establish a temporary position at a bridge thirty miles outside the city. His men were beaten and defeated, with no way to restore and firm their will, and in fact they mostly encouraged him to secretly depart during the night. However, Chang Fang replied: "It is normal for an army's spirit to fluctuate between being sharp and blunted. What is important is making something out of defeat. If we construct fortifications before nightfall where the enemy does not expect it, we will be employing our troops in an unorthodox manner." Then, before night fell, he advanced again, pressing within seven miles of the city of Lo-yang. Huang-fu Shang, having just been victorious, did not pay any attention. Suddenly he learned that Chang Fang's fortifications were finished, so he went forth to engage him in battle but was soundly defeated and forced to retreat.

Commentary

"Defeat" revisits the theme of the last two selections—the danger of complacency and arrogance following victory—but from the perspective of the defeated rather than the conqueror. Assuming the vanquished can reassemble their forces, instill the requisite discipline, scrounge the needed materials, and incite their soldiers, if they have not been completely decimated they may still exploit the victor's natural laxity to launch a highly effective surprise offensive. The historical incident, which provides a glimpse of the internecine strife at the end of the Chin dynasty in the very first years of the fourth century A.D., in fact records two illustrations of the chapter's tactical insight within the ebb and flow of this extended engagement. First, Huang-fu Shang's forces suffered severe losses from the unexpected ambush but then pressed on to engage Chang Fang on the highly constricted urban terrain that can be advantageously utilized by weaker forces to wrest a temporary victory. However Chang Fang, who understood the nature of human spirit in combat, resisted the temptation to despair and instead reformed his troops into a viable force, maneuvering his troops to surprise a Huang-fu Shang who had quickly become oblivious to his battlefield experience. (The discussion found in Chapter 95, "Nurturing Spirit"—which ponders measures for revitalizing a defeated army—might well be compared with the above reversals.)

59 Advancing 進

Tactical Discussion

Whenever engaging an enemy in battle, if you truly know that the enemy has a weakness that can be exploited to yield victory, you should quickly advance your army and pound it, for then you will always be victorious. A tactical principle states: "Advance when you see it is possible."

Historical Illustration

During the T'ang dynasty, when Li Ching was serving as Commander-in-Chief for the Ting-hsiang Circuit campaign army, he suddenly attacked and destroyed the Turks. Chieh-li, khan of the tribe, raced back to the protection of Mount T'ieh and dispatched an ambassador to the T'ang court to acknowledge his offense and request that his state be allowed to submit in allegiance to the T'ang. The emperor dispatched Li Ching to accept their surrender.

Although the khan had visibly requested the privilege of visiting the imperial court, he still harbored doubts. Li Ching guessed his intentions. At this time the emperor summoned the Director of Rites, T'ang Chien, and dispatched him and others to officially condole with and placate the khan. Li Ching said to Chang Kung-chin, the Military Commissioner attached to his command: "With the arrival of imperial ambassadors, the Turks will certainly feel quite secure. If we were to have ten thousand cavalrymen, each carrying three days rations, proceed via the Pai Road we could suddenly attack them and certainly gain our objectives."

Chang Kung-chin said: "The emperor has already assented to their surrender. And what about the men who have gone out there?" Li Ching said: "The opportunity cannot be lost. This is the way Han Hsin destroyed Ch'i during the founding reign of the Han dynasty. As for men of Tang Chien's advanced age, what is there to regret?" He supervised the soldiers in an urgent advance. When they had proceeded as far as Mount Yin they encountered more than a thousand of the khan's perimeter defense troops, all of whom surrendered and joined Li's army.

When the khan received the T'ang's ambassadors he was greatly elated and neglected the army's supervision. Li Ching's vanguard took advantage of a heavy fog to advance within seven miles of the khan's command center before the khan first became aware of them. Before the Turkish formations could be deployed, Li Ching released his troops in an assault that resulted in killing more than ten thousand enemy soldiers. They also took more than a hundred thousand men and women prisoners, captured the khan's son Ku-luo-shih, and killed Princess Yi-ch'eng. The khan fled but was subsequently captured by Chang Pao-hsiang, the Commander-in-Chief of the Ta-t'ung Circuit campaign army, and sent back to the emperor. The T'ang thus enlarged its territory from Mount Yin north to the Gobi Desert.

Commentary

Advancing when appropriate, discussed in this chapter, forms a natural pair with retreating when necessary, the subject of the next selection. The tactical discussion is essentially a variant of that found in Chapter 37, "Offense," with much of the situational wording even being the same. The thrust of both chapters is to aggressively exploit opportunities presented by weakness in the enemy, whatever they may be. Virtually all the military classics not only recognized this principle, but enumerated many concrete conditions that rendered the enemy susceptible to attack, such as hunger, thirst, exhaustion, and disorder. Central to the concept is the notion of timeliness, of the subtle moment or crux of circumstances (as describe by Wu Ch'i in the *Wu-tzu*) when events are susceptible to shaping and determining. Such a moment cannot be lost if an army is to advance and prove victorious.

The historical illustration recounts Li Ching's infamous but crucial assault on the Turkish khan after he had ostensibly surrendered. Several interesting points are raised by the incident. First, commanders should never become lax, whether in treaty negotiations or simply in a state of nonaggression. Second, Li Ching acted contrary to all the dictates of Confucianism, which stressed righteousness, trust, and good faith in undertaking the attack, and was frequently condemned thereafter by the hypocritical literati for his perfidy, particularly as it damaged the emperor's credibility. However, the official histories, as well as the emperor at the time, have allowed him the rationalization of perceiving that the khan's true intent was to deceive the emperor and continue his warlike ways. The *Questions and Replies* purportedly preserves a discussion between Li Ching and T'ang T'ai-tsung, the emperor, on this matter:

> The T'ai-tsung said: "Formerly, when T'ang Chien was an emissary to the Turks, you availed yourself of the situation to attack and defeat them. People say you used T'ang Chien as an expendable spy. Up until now I have had doubts about this. What about it?"
>
> Li Ching bowed twice and said: "T'ang Chien and I equally serve your Majesty. I anticipated that T'ang Chien's proposals would certainly not be able to persuade them to quietly submit. Therefore I took the opportunity to follow up with our army and attack them. In order to eliminate a great danger I did not concern myself with a minor righteousness. Although people refer to T'ang Chien as an expendable spy, it was not my intention.
>
> According to Sun-tzu, employing spies is an inferior measure. I once prepared a discussion of this subject and at the end stated, 'Water can float a boat, but it can also overturn the boat. Some use spies to be successful; others, relying on spies, are overturned and defeated.'
>
> If one braids his hair and serves the ruler, maintains a proper countenance in court, is loyal and pure, trustworthy and completely sincere, even if someone excels at spying, how can he be employed to sow discord? T'ang Chien is a minor matter. What doubts does your Majesty have?"
>
> The T'ai-tsung said: "Truly, without benevolence and righteousness one cannot employ spies. How can the ordinary man do it? If the Duke of Chou, with his great righteousness, exterminated his relatives, how much the more so one emissary? Clearly, there is nothing to doubt."

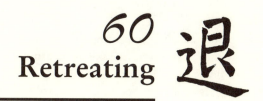

60 Retreating 退

Tactical Discussion

Whenever one engages in battle with an enemy, if the enemy is numerous while you are few, the terrain is not advantageous, and you lack the strength to engage in battle, you should quickly retreat in order to avoid them and thereby preserve your army intact. A tactical principle states: "When one perceives difficulty he should retreat."

Historical Illustration

During the Three Kingdoms period, General Ts'ao Shuang of Wei attacked the kingdom of Shu. Ssu-ma Yi of Wei also came forth on this campaign, and they went out through Lo-ku and then came to Hsing-yüan. The Shu general Wang Lin took advantage of nightfall to suddenly launch a surprise attack, but Ssu-ma Yi ordered his troops to firmly maintain their positions without making any response. When Wang Lin withdrew, Ssu-ma Yi said to his generals: "General Fei Hui will occupy the ravines and prepare a stout defense, so we will not be able to advance and gain victory in battle. In attacking them we cannot be hasty. It would be better to turn the army about in order to plan for a future engagement." Ts'ao Shuang and his forces then retreated. Fei Hui indeed pushed his soldiers to race to San-ling and contest the ravines. Shuang continued his retreat, secretly crossing the army through the ravines of that region, and then withdrew.

Commentary

The tactical discussion boldly advises simply retreating in the face of insurmountable odds or impossible strategic difficulties, much in contrast to Sun-tzu and most of the other military writers who suggested immediately employing the methods of maneuver warfare and other unorthodox measures to recreate and redefine the tactical situation. (For example, see Chapter 12, "Small Numbers." While Sun-tzu himself said, "One who cannot be victorious assumes a defensive posture," this was his minimalist position, for he also discussed extensive measures for converting disadvantageous circumstances into advantageous ones and forcing the enemy to accede to one's tactical wishes. Moreover, he said: "The army does not esteem the number of troops being more numerous for it only means one cannot aggressively advance. It is sufficient for you to muster your own strength, analyze the enemy, and take them." However, static defensive measures, such as increasing the height of fortifications and deepening the moats, designed to outwait the enemy, were also much advocated, as discussed in previous chapters and will be seen in "Refusing Battle.") Furthermore, undertaking a retreat, always a dangerous enterprise, may be an aggressive measure if commenced before actually engaging in battle rather than when on the point of succumbing to a superior enemy, providing a means to seize the initiative and control the situation.

The historical illustration has been radically simplified, omitting the fact that Ts'ao Shuang ignored Ssu-ma Yi's directive and did not really withdraw but instead attempted to penetrate the ravines and fought an unsuccessful battle with Fei Hui, only thereafter retreating. Thus, actual historical events even more dramatically prove the wisdom of retreating in the face of impossible circumstances.

61 Provocation 挑

Tactical Discussion

Whenever engaging an enemy in battle, if your two fortified encampments are some distance apart and your strategic power approximately equal, you can employ light cavalry in a provocatory attack supported by forces in ambush that await their response. Then their army can be destroyed. However, if the enemy uses this tactic, you cannot employ your entire army to strike them. A tactical principle from the *Art of War* states: "When an enemy far off provokes us into battle, they want our men to advance."

Historical Illustration

During the Five Dynasties period, Yao Hsiang—leader of the Ch'iang peoples—occupied Huang-lo, so King Fu Chien of the Eastern Chin dispatched generals Fu Huang-mei and Teng Ch'ai, in command of both infantry and cavalry forces, to extirpate Yao Hsiang. Deepening his moats and increasing the height of his fortifications, Yao Hsiang maintained a solid defense without giving battle. Teng Ch'ai said: "By nature Yao Hsiang is obstinate and rash, so it will be easy to provoke him into action. If we race forth in an extended line to directly press his fortifications, Yao Hsiang will certainly get angry and come forth to fight us. Then we will be able to capture him in a single encounter."

General Fu Huang-mei followed his tactics, dispatching Teng Ch'ai to lead three thousand cavalrymen to deploy outside the gate to Yao's fortifications. Yao Hsiang was enraged and sent all his elite forces forth into battle. Teng Ch'ai feigned being unable to achieve victory and led his cavalrymen off in retreat. Yao Hsiang then pursued them as far as San-yüan, where Teng Ch'ai suddenly wheeled about and resisted Hsiang's advance. Fu Huang-mei came up and a great battle ensued in which Yao Hsiang was slain and his troops were made prisoners.

Commentary

Employing minimal troops to harass and provoke an enemy, thereby exploiting any weakness in the commander and enraging his soldiers, was apparently common practice in ancient warfare. As Sun Pin summarized in the *Military Methods,* the tactic can destabilize armies and compel them into movement, setting the stage for an effective ambush:

> King Wei of Ch'i, inquiring about employing the military, said to Sun Pin: "If two armies confront each other, their two generals looking across at each other, with both of them being solid and secure so that neither side dares to move first, what should be done?"
>
> Sun Pin replied: "Employ some light troops to test them, commanded by some lowly but courageous officer. Focus on fleeing, do not strive for victory. Deploy your forces in concealment in order to abruptly assault their flanks. This is termed the 'Great Attainment.'"

The historical incident, as well as several earlier ones, such as the one described in "The Cavalry," indicates that the tactic frequently proved successful. Accordingly, Sun-tzu conspicuously warned against probing forces whose main strength remained distant, as noted in the tactical discussion. However, such measures could also be employed to simply probe an enemy, as advocated by Wu Ch'i in a famous passage:

> Marquis Wu asked: "When our two armies are confronting each other but I don't know their general, if I want to fathom him what methods are there?"
>
> Wu Ch'i replied: "Order some courageous men from the lower ranks to lead some light shock troops to test him. When the enemy responds they should concentrate on running off instead of trying to gain some objective. Then analyze the enemy's advance, whether their actions, such as sitting and standing, are in unison and their organization well preserved. Whether, when they pursue

> your retreat, they feign being unable to catch you, or when they perceive easy gain they pretend not to realize it. A commander like this may be termed a wise general. Do not engage him in battle.
>
> If their troops approach yelling and screaming, their flags and pennants in confusion, while some of their units move of their own accord and others stop, some weapons held vertically, others horizontally—if they pursue our retreating troops as if they are afraid they won't reach us, or seeing advantage are afraid of not gaining it, this marks a stupid general. Even if his troops are numerous they can be taken."

Clearly, any commander who reacted precipitously or permitted his troops to become disorganized simply failed to understand the technique that was being implemented against him.

The tactical quotation, from Sun-tzu's chapter "Maneuvering the Army," typifies his observations on enemy behavior commonly seen at the end of the Spring and Autumn period. A few examples from the chapter indicates the range of practices observed and their explanations:

> If an enemy in close proximity remains quiet, they are relying on their tactical occupation of ravines. If large numbers of trees move, they are approaching. If there are many visible obstacles in the heavy grass, it is to make us suspicious. If the birds take flight, there is an ambush. If the animals are afraid, enemy forces are mounting a sudden attack.
>
> If dust rises high up in a sharply defined column, chariots are coming. If it is low and broad, the infantry is advancing. If it is dispersed in thin shafts, they are gathering firewood. If it is sparse, coming and going, they are encamping.
>
> One who speaks deferentially but increases his preparations will advance. One who speaks belligerently and advances hastily will retreat.
>
> One who seeks peace without setting any prior conditions is executing a stratagem. One who has emissaries come forth with offerings wants to rest for a while.
>
> One whose troops half advance and half retreat is enticing you.
>
> Those who stand about leaning on their weapons are hungry. If those who draw water drink first, they are thirsty. When they see potential gain but do not know whether to advance, they are tired.
>
> Where birds congregate it is empty. If the enemy cries out at night, they are afraid. If the army is turbulent, the general lacks severity. If their flags and pennants move about, they are in chaos. If the officers are angry, they are exhausted.
>
> If their troops are aroused and approach our forces, only to maintain their positions without engaging in battle or breaking off the confrontation, you must carefully investigate it.

62 Compulsion 致

Tactical Discussion

Whenever you compel an enemy to come forth and engage in battle, their strategic disposition of power will usually be vacuous, so they will be incapable of going into combat, while your strategic power will always be substantial. If you employ many methods to compel the enemy to come forward while you occupy improved terrain and await them, you will always be victorious. A tactical principle from the *Art of War* states: "Compel others; do not be compelled by others."

Historical Illustration

In the fourth year of the Chien-wu reign period (29 A.D.) of the Later Han dynasty, Emperor Kuang-wu summoned Keng Yen and designated him as Military Commissioner responsible for assembling all the troops who had submitted to the Han and militarily organizing them, as well as appointing the military and civilian officials. Keng Yen led the Commandant of the Cavalry, Liu Hsin, and the Protector General for T'ai-shan, Ch'en Chün, in taking command of these troops and going east. When Chang Pu, who had rebelled against the Han, heard about it, he had his general Fei Yi deploy at Li-hsia and separately ordered troops to encamp at Chu-a. In addition, he established a line of some forty fortified camps between T'ai-shan and Chung-ch'eng in preparation for them.

Keng Yen crossed the Yellow River and advanced to attack Chu-a first. When seizing it he deliberately left one corner of the encirclement open in order to allow some of their troops to flee back to their base. When the men in Chung-ch'eng heard that Chu-a had already collapsed, they were terrified and fled, leaving behind a deserted shell. General Fei Yi split up his forces, dispatching his younger brother Fei Kan to defend Chü-li. When Keng Yen advanced, he first threatened Chü-li. At this point he strictly ordered everyone within the army to rush about repairing their assault equipment, visibly planning to employ all their strength to assault the fortifications of Chü-li in three days. However, he had secretly left an opening for some soldiers within the city to escape and race back to Fei Yi and report at what time Keng Yen would be attacking the city.

On the appointed day Fei Yi, in command of their elite troops, came forth to rescue it. Keng Yen addressed his subordinate generals: "The reason I had our assault equipment repaired was to compel them to come up. If we do not attack their field army, what use would an assault on the city be?" Then he split up his forces, some maintaining the effort at Chü-li while he personally commanded the valiant, elite units to ascend the surrounding hills and ridges. Accordingly, they were able to exploit the heights when joining battle with Fei Yi and thereby managed to severely defeat his army and kill Fei Yi himself. They then took Fei Yi's decapitated head and displayed it to the defenders in Chü-li, putting all those within the city into fear. Fei Kan, accompanied by some of his forces, fled back to Chang Pu's headquarters. Keng Yen gathered all the provisions and supplies left behind and then loosed his soldiers in assaults on all those who had not yet surrendered, pacifying more than forty encampments and settling Chi-nan commandery.

Commentary

This chapter discusses the fundamental principle of maneuver warfare: compel the enemy rather than be compelled yourself. Accordingly, Sun-tzu's famous dictum, here quoted from "Vacuity and Substance," essentially became the watchword for manipulating the enemy, for creating the advantageous circumstances that would allow achieving an easy victory. Naturally the military writers differed on the measures that might be employed to achieve this end, but no voices were heard in opposition—unlike the tactical debates witnessed in the U.S. Marines in the early 1990s when maneuver warfare doctrine was adopted.

The historical incident illustrates one of Sun-tzu's basic premises, "Warfare is the Tao of deception." In his first chapter, "Initial Estimations," Sun-tzu elaborated a few tactical guidelines for acting deceptively in order to manipulate the enemy and attain a desired objective:

> Warfare is the Tao of deception. Thus, although you are capable, display incapability to them. When committed to employing your forces, feign inactivity. When your objective is nearby, make it appear as if distant; when far away, create the illusion of being nearby.

Several of the historical illustrations in the *Unorthodox Strategies* record a variety of deceptive measures, ranging from the simplest use of straw men or dragging brushwood to increase the apparent number of forces, to more complex and carefully executed plans, such as Keng Yen's elaborate facade for assaulting the town upon a fixed day. As Sun Pin said, "Hidden plans and concealed deceptions are the means by which to inveigle the enemy into combat. Deliberate tactical errors and minor losses are the means by which to bait the enemy."

The historical illustration also provides an excellent example of manipulating the enemy's *ch'i,* for Keng Yen repeatedly structured his actions to nurture fear in the opposing forces and thereby undermine their resistance potential. First, when his troops were seizing Chu-a he deliberately allowed a few terrified men to escape with the sorrowful tale of their defeat and thus infect the other strongholds with their fright, certainly causing consternation and anxiety as well. Later he ostentatiously had Fei Yi's head displayed at Chü-li, a common practice in the period, to further discourage the defenders with the futility of their efforts. (No thought seems to have been given to the danger of provoking the opposite result, anger and a determination to fight to the death. Clearly he well understood the enemy's character and mental state.) Thus he rigorously debilitated the enemy's spirit while methodically executing his own plans and won an overwhelming victory.

63 The Distant 遠

Tactical Discussion

Whenever you and an enemy oppose each other along opposite banks of a river, if you want to ford the river far off, you should prepare numerous boats and oars to show that you intend to cross nearby. The enemy will certainly mass troops in response and you can then effect a crossing at some vacuous point. If you lack boats and oars, you can employ such things as bamboo, reeds, large wine vessels, cooking utensils, or spears and lances lashed together to serve as rafts and thereby cross the river. A tactical principle from the *Art of War* states: "When your objective is distant, make it appear as if nearby."

Historical Illustration

At the beginning of the Han dynasty, King Pao of the newly reestablished state of Wei at first submitted to the Han and was staying in the capital, but then requested permission to go back to his state because of a close relative's illness. Once he reached Wei he cut off the passes and fords and on the contrary signed a peace treaty with the state of Ch'u. The Han king dispatched an ambassador to persuade him otherwise, but King Pao would not listen. The Han king then appointed Han Hsin as Counselor-in-Chief of the Left with orders to mount a sudden strike on King Pao. King Pao deployed his forces throughout P'u-pan and blocked Lin-chin. Han Hsin then augmented the number of troops he had initially assigned to deceive the enemy and set out his boats as if he wanted to ford the river at Lin-chin. However, he actually drew his troops away to cross the river from Hsia-yang by employing earthenware jars lashed to ridgepoles to ferry them over. After effecting the crossing they suddenly struck An-yi. King Pao of Wei was startled and led his army to counter Han Hsin but ended up being defeated and captured. Thereafter the area east of the Yellow River was settled.

Commentary

This chapter provides specific instructions for successfully making an unopposed river crossing through the use of deliberate misdirection, through creating the appearance of undertaking an action at one point while actually planning to move at another. Yet the narrow scope of the principle's utilization—"when distant, make it appear as if nearby"—is somewhat surprising because it must have frequently been employed throughout history in land engagements. However, river crossings being particularly hazardous, as also discussed in Chapters 7 and 65, the author apparently felt they should be singled out for its rigorous application. (The commentary to the previous selection has already cited the full quotation from Sun-tzu's "Initial Estimations," excerpted by the tactical discussion.)

Both the tactical discussion and the historical illustration provide evidence of the inventive, if extemporaneous, nature of river crossings, for every combination of buoyant materials, stiffened by poles and lashed together, seems to have been employed because an army proceeding overland would already be heavily burdened with the ordinary supplies and provisions needed for the men and animals without carrying boats and oars. Thus, as the T'ai Kung said, "Unorthodox technical skills are the means by which to cross deep waters and ford rivers." Conversely, Sun Pin (among others) spoke about exploiting the army's vulnerability at such moments: "Unusual movements and perverse actions are the means by which to crush the enemy at fords." Essentially, the army had to have skilled carpenters and artificers capable of fabricating rafts, boats, and floating bridges when necessary, just as they would construct various types of siege engines as required.

64 The Nearby 近

Tactical Discussion

Whenever you or an enemy deploy on opposite banks of a river, if you want to attack them close by your position, you should, on the contrary, show them that you are going to attack far off. You must establish the facade of numerous troops preparing to ford the river both upstream and downstream. The enemy will certainly divide their forces in response, and you can then secretly launch a sudden attack with your nearby hidden forces, destroying their army. A tactical principle from the *Art of War* states: "When an objective is nearby, make it appear as if distant."

Historical Illustration

During the Spring and Autumn period, the state of Yüeh attacked the state of Wu. Wu's army mounted a defense at Li-che, deploying their forces on the far side of the river. Yüeh deployed its forces to the left and right on its side of the river, and when night fell beat the drums, yelled loudly, and advanced across the water. Wu divided its forces in order to defend each flank in response. Thereupon, Yüeh's commander led the three armies that he had retained in the middle to secretly ford the river right opposite the middle of Wu's encampment and only then beat the attack. Wu's army was badly defeated, and the state was subsequently annihilated.

Commentary

The tactical discussion raises the corollary to the principle enunciated in the previous selection, "When your objective is distant, make it appear as if nearby." Both are simply variants of the general concept of misdirection, of never letting the enemy know where you intend to initiate actions, although somewhat more concrete because a specific ruse is employed rather than just a general facade that forces the enemy to defend at all points. The virtue of the specific lies in pulling even the limited number of men found in a dispersed defense away from the actual objective when striving to concentrate forces for greatest effectiveness.

The battle reprised here previously appeared as the historical illustration for Chapter 26, "Night," which focused upon tactical measures for overwhelming an enemy during night engagements. Wu's failure to stand fast in the face of flank crossings exposed it to a surprise assault in the middle, and the losses were so significant that the state never recovered, being extinguished soon thereafter. (An extensive discussion with phase maps may be found in the historical introduction to our translation of Sun-tzu's *Art of War*.)

65 Rivers 水

Tactical Discussion

Whether deploying your forces along the banks or anchoring your vessels in the middle of a river to engage an enemy in battle, it is referred to as river warfare. When you approach a river, you must deploy your lines some distance from the edge because then you will entice the enemy to cross and also show there is nothing to be suspicious about. If you definitely want to engage in battle, do not approach too close to the river to confront the enemy, because they might fear being unable to ford the river successfully. If you do not want to engage in battle, then resist their forces right at the river to impede them, making it impossible for them to ford the river. If an enemy is crossing a river to come up and engage you in battle, it will be advantageous to wait at the water's edge until half have crossed before striking them. A tactical principle from the *Wu-tzu* states: "When half their force has forded the river they can be attacked."

Historical Illustration

During the Han dynasty, the Han high official Li Sheng attempted to persuade the King of Ch'i to give his allegiance to the Han, but every day the king and Li Sheng debauched themselves with wine while the king neglected his defensive preparations. K'uai T'ung advised Han Hsin of the situation, who then forded the river with the Han troops and suddenly attacked and destroyed Ch'i's forces. The king of Ch'i, thinking that Li Sheng had sold him out, had him boiled in oil before himself fleeing to Kao-mi and requesting a rescue force from Ch'u.

Ch'u dispatched Lung Ch'ieh in command of a rescue army to Ch'i. Someone said to him: "Since Han's forces are fighting far from their state, they are desperate invaders whose front cannot be withstood. In contrast, both Ch'i's and Ch'u's armies will be fighting in their homeland, so when they engage in battle their soldiers will easily be defeated and scatter. Accordingly, it would be best for us both to augment our fortified walls. If you have the king of Ch'i order his loyal subordinates to summon together all those from the ravished cities, when they hear that their king is seeking aid from Ch'u, they will certainly revolt against the Han. When Han's forces, occupying the cities in Ch'i and Ch'u some two thousand miles from their land, find that everyone has turned against them, even with their power they will not be able to obtain food, and they will surrender without fighting."

Lung Ch'ieh said: "I have always felt Han Hsin to be inconsequential. He relied on a washer woman for food, so he never had any plans to support himself; he was insulted by having to crawl between a man's legs, so he lacks the courage to confront people. He is not worth worrying about. Moreover, if Ch'i is rescued without any fighting on our part, what achievement will we realize? But if we now engage them in combat and conquer them, we will gain half of Ch'i, so why should we desist?" He then proceeded to join battle with Han Hsin.

Both sides deployed along opposite banks of the Wei River. That night Han Hsin ordered some men to make more than ten thousand sacks and solidly stuff them with sand and stones in order to block the river's flow upstream. The next day he led half his troops to ford the river and strike Lung Ch'ieh. However, once engaged he feigned being unable to wrest victory, and instead turned his forces about and fled. Lung Ch'ieh, truly elated, exclaimed: "I knew Han Hsin was a coward!" Thereupon he ordered his army to ford the river and pursue Han Hsin's forces. Han Hsin had his men break the temporary sandbag dam upstream and a torrent of water came down. More than half of Lung Ch'ieh's troops could not ford the river, and Han Hsin immediately attacked those who had, killing Lung Ch'ieh. The remaining troops all scattered and fled. King Kuang of Ch'i also fled, so Han Hsin pursued him north to Ch'eng-yang, where he captured him. Ch'u's troops all surrendered, and Han Hsin eventually pacified Ch'i.

Commentary

As previously noted, in antiquity fighting along rivers was both hazardous and difficult, especially when they were as wide as the Yellow River or as powerful as some of the rushing torrents found outside the central plains. Two armies moving in parallel up or down a river, unable to strike because of the obstacle it posed, could merely glare at each other. However, wherever the river might be crossed—and such points would have long been common knowledge—either side could potentially assault the other. Accordingly, some general principles were formulated for river environments, both for crossing over to attack and for defending against often numerically superior foes successfully fording the river. Where the water ran insufficiently shallow, the soldiers would be compelled to employ makeshift rafts or boats, as seen in Chapter 63, "The Distant." A reasonably accessible landing point would have to be chosen to facilitate ascending the opposite bank, but otherwise the possibilities would be numerous. In contrast, an army fording a river would naturally be confined to the few shallows where slower currents had allowed sand and rock deposits to build up or the river bed had widened sufficiently for the depth to drop to only two or three feet. In either case the defender, well entrenched on the shore, enjoyed an enormous superiority, one usually sufficiently great to deter any such attempt. In fact, Sun Pin listed "crossing rivers" as one of the five situations in which one cannot be victorious in "Treasures of Terrain," along with confronting hills, going contrary to the current's flow, occupying killing ground, and confronting masses of tress. Thus the tactical discussion advises deploying some distance from the riverbank, to entice the enemy into thinking he might win a foothold. (However, allowing such a foothold could prove fatal, as Fu Chien learned in the battle at Fei River, previously reprised as the historical illustration for Chapter 11, "Large Numbers.")

Even though river warfare was little discussed, both Sun-tzu and Wu Ch'i advised allowing half the enemy to cross before launching the attack. Wu Ch'i's original statement, from "Evaluating the Enemy" in the *Wu-tzu,* is just one of a series of tactical principles for exploiting enemy weakness in common situations:

> In employing the army you must ascertain the enemy's voids and strengths and then race to take advantage of his endangered points. When the enemy has just arrived from afar and their battle formations are not yet properly deployed they can be attacked. If they have eaten but not yet established their encampment they can be attacked. If they are running about wildly they can be attacked. If they have labored hard they can be attacked. If they haven't yet taken advantage of the terrain they can be attacked. When they have lost the critical moment and not followed up opportunities they can be attacked. When they have traversed a great distance and the rear guard hasn't had time to rest yet they can be attacked. When fording rivers and only half of them have crossed, they can be attacked. In narrow and confined roads they can be attacked. When their flags and banners move about chaotically they can be attacked. When their formations frequently move about they can be attacked. When a general is separated from his soldiers they can be attacked. When they are afraid they can be attacked. In general in circumstances such as these select crack troops to rush upon them, divide your remaining troops and continue the assault, pressing the attack swiftly and decisively.

The historical incident vividly illustrates two points: first, Han Hsin not only studied Sun-tzu and Wu-tzu but also applied their tactics, feigning defeat when the enemy attacked half his forces to lure them onto fatal ground. Second, commanders evaluated their counterparts and proceeded to act upon their impressions. Accordingly, depending upon the accuracy of their interpretations, they either succeeded brilliantly or failed dramatically. Han Hsin, who played a major role in the establishment and consolidation of the Han dynasty (and therefore has one of the longest biographies in the *Shih Chi,* the history of the period), was ambitious but impoverished as a youth, and so—at least in the romantic rationalization of his biography—felt compelled to endure embarrassment in order to survive. Lung Chieh's information was correct and his projection of Han Hsin's likely behavior based upon the reasonable assumption of constancy of character, but he neglected the influence that great power might have upon men in such positions and ignored sound tactical advice to adopt a temporizing strategy consonant with the beliefs found in the military writings. He therefore misled himself and virtually crafted his own defeat.

Han Hsin also developed a more comprehensive plan for the engagement, utilizing sandbags to temporarily reduce the river's flow and entice the enemy into following his retreat across the shallow depths. Apart from being interesting in itself (and puzzling as to why Lung Chieh's reconnaissance patrols, if any, did not detect their activity), it was a tactic sometimes seen from the Spring and Autumn period on. Rivers were diverted to flood camps or prevent advances, while temporary dams were constructed on smaller rivers and streams to stem the flow until enough water accumulated to constitute a "ram" that might be released to batter an encampment down river situated too close to the banks or in a marshy area. Han Hsin's genius lay in conceiving a tactical sequence that integrated the exploitable features of the terrain with tendencies in command behavior, and he thus manipulated the enemy into defeat.

66 Incendiary Strategies 火

Tactical Discussion

In warfare, whenever the enemy occupies a position near grass and brush, constructs his shelters from ramie and bamboo, or has gathered grass for fuel and piled up his provisions, if the weather has been hot and dry you can exploit the wind's direction to set fires and incinerate them. If you immediately follow up by striking with elite troops, their army can be destroyed. A tactical principle from the *Art of War* states: "Implementing an incendiary attack depends on the proper conditions."

Historical Illustration

During the initial year of the Chung-p'ing reign period of Emperor Ling in the Later Han dynasty, Huang-fu Sung conducted a campaign to suppress the Yellow Turban Revolt. The Han general Chu Chün engaged a Yellow Turban force under Po Ts'ai in battle and was defeated. Po Ts'ai then surrounded Huang-fu Sung at Ch'ang-she and set up their own encampment amidst the tall grass of the area. A strong wind happened to arise, so Huang-fu Sung had his soldiers make torches and ascend the fortification walls while also ordering some elite troops to escape through gaps in the encirclement and go out beyond the enemy. Once having succeeded these men started fires behind the enemy accompanied by much yelling and shouting, whereupon those manning the walls initiated fires in response. Huang-fu Sung then beat the war drums and had his troops race out into the enemy's deployment. Po Ts'ai's army, startled and confused, fled. An army under Ts'ao Ts'ao's command, separately dispatched by the emperor, happened to arrive and immediately joined the battle, severely defeating the rebel forces and killing more than ten thousand of them.

Commentary

Incendiary warfare was historically employed but little discussed except by Sun-tzu, the T'ai Kung (whose writings on defensive measures have already been included in the commentary for Chapter 27, "Preparation"), and Sun Pin. In the most extensive ancient discussion, Sun-tzu devoted an entire chapter entitled "Incendiary Attacks" to the so-called enlightened use of fire. Abstracted, the key passages run:

> There are five types of incendiary attack: The first is to incinerate men, the second to incinerate provisions, the third to incinerate supply trains, the fourth to incinerate armories, and the fifth to incinerate formations.
>
> Implementing an incendiary attack depends on the proper conditions. Equipment for incendiary attacks should be fully prepared before required. Launching an incendiary attack has its appropriate seasons, igniting the fire the proper days.
>
> In general, in incendiary warfare you must respond to the five changes of fire: If fires are started within their camp, then you should immediately respond with an attack from outside. If fires are ignited but their army remains quiet, then wait; do not attack. When they flare into a conflagration, if you can follow up, then do so; if you cannot, then desist. If the attack can be launched from outside without relying on inside assistance, initiate it at an appropriate time. If fires are ignited upwind, do not attack downwind.

Sun Pin further expanded the discussion in his *Military Methods* with some specific tactics:

> If the enemy is downwind in an area abundant with dry grass where the soldiers of their Three Armies would not have anywhere to escape, then you can mount an incendiary attack. When there is a frigid fierce wind, abundant vegetation and undergrowth, and firewood and grass for fuel already piled up while their earthworks have not yet been prepared, in such circumstances you can mount an incendiary attack. Use the flames to confuse them, loose arrows like rain.

> Beat the drums and set up a clamor to motivate your soldiers. Assist the attack with strategic power. These are the tactics for incendiary warfare.

Other parts of his text provide additional details for mounting a rudimentary defense against such strikes, but in general the best method was to avoid encamping in dangerous environments or exposing flammable stores to an enemy's attack.

67 Slowness 緩

Tactical Discussion

In general, assaulting fortified enemy cities is the lowest form of strategy, to be undertaken only when there is no alternative. However, if their walls are high and their moats deep, their people many and supplies few, while there is no prospect of external rescue and you can thoroughly entangle and take the city, then it will be advantageous. A tactical principle from the *Art of War* states: "Their slowness is like the forest."

Historical Illustration

During the Northern and Southern dynasties period, General Mu-jung Ch'ieh of the Former Yen suddenly attacked Tuan K'an at Kuang-ku, eventually besieging him. His generals all urged Mu-jung Ch'ieh to urgently mount an assault, but Ch'ieh said: "There are situations in which it is appropriate to proceed slowly. If we and the enemy were equal in strength while they had strong support from without, since we would have to fear facing attacks from both the interior and exterior, quickly attacking them would be unavoidable. If we were strong while they were weak and had no external support or hope of relief, then we should entangle and contain them, waiting for them to grow fatigued. The *Art of War* states: 'If you outnumber the enemy ten to one, surround them; if five to one, attack them.' It truly refers to this situation. Right now Tuan K'an's faction is still numerous and not yet divisive. Relying on their moats and the solidity of the walls, the upper and lower ranks are, without exception, exerting the maximum effort. If we fully employ our elite forces to assault them, they can be taken in several weeks, but we will also kill many of our own officers and troops. It is critical in this situation to wait for them to change by themselves so that we can then implement appropriate measures." Thereupon he had them construct countervailing walls and towers in order to contain them, and in the end managed to conquer Kuang-ku.

Commentary

This chapter and the next form a correlated pair in which the tactics to be employed are essentially defined by the ratio of people to food coupled with the prospects for outside support or rescue. (Chapter 80, "Sieges," also discusses the psychology of mounting sieges and should be consulted. Questions of defense are discussed in the commentary to the next chapter, "Quickness.") "Slowness in Warfare" presumes a large occupation force that lacks adequate food supplies to withstand a long siege and moreover has no hope of rescue. Therefore, the siege need not be prolonged, and as the fortifications are basically good—high walls and deep moats—once taken, will prove highly defensible. In contrast, the situation in the next chapter, "Quickness," assumes the opposite: ample food, few men to resist, and the danger of external forces attacking from without if the siege were to be prolonged. Thus, in the former case the attackers can afford to wait for the besieged to grow weaker, but in the latter must act quickly to achieve their tactical objectives, as Mu-jung Ch'ieh's excellent analysis in the historical illustration also summarizes. (These criteria are also raised by one of the speakers in the historical illustration for Chapter 78, "Inevitable Combat.")

In Sun-tzu's era, roughly the end of the Spring and Autumn period, cities still represented formidable targets that required considerable expenditures of time and effort to capture or reduce. As siege technology was just beginning to evolve, impetuous assaults on vigorous defenders could easily decimate the attackers rather than result in conquering the defenders. Moreover, even though cities were the military and economic centers of the surrounding area, they had not evolved into critical targets and could easily be bypassed as armies moved through reasonably open countryside. Accordingly, Sun-tzu discouraged urban assaults, classifying them as the lowest form of warfare, rather than dogmatically asserting they should never be undertaken as many later tacticians mistakenly believed:

> The highest realization of warfare is to attack the enemy plans; next is to attack their alliances; next to attack their army; and the lowest is to attack their fortified cities. This tactic of attacking fortified cities is adopted only when unavoidable. Preparing large movable protective shields, armored assault wagons, and other equipment and devices will require three months. Building earthworks will require another three months to complete. If the general cannot overcome his impatience but instead launches an assault wherein his men swarm over the walls like ants, he will kill one-third of his officers and troops, and the city will still not be taken. This is the disaster that results from attacking fortified cities.

By the middle of the Warring States period when Sun Pin was formulating his tactics, cities had become important political and economic centers, demanding capture not only for their valuables and resources but also to eliminate the local political powers and reduce the military threat. Thus the *Wei Liao-tzu,* probably a late Warring States work, contains passages stressing the need to focus upon the enemy's cities:

> In general, when assembling an army a thousand miles away ten days are required, and when a hundred miles one day, while the assembly point should be the enemy's border. When the troops have assembled and the general has arrived, the army should penetrate deeply into their territory, sever their roads, and occupy their large cities and large towns. Have the troops ascend the walls and press the enemy into endangered positions. Have the several units of men and women each press the enemy in accord with the configuration of the terrain and attack any strategic barriers. If you occupy the terrain around a city or town and sever the various roads about it, follow up by attacking the city itself. If the enemy's generals and armies are unable to believe in each other, the officers and troops unable to be in harmony, and there are those unaffected by punishments, we will defeat them. Before the rescue party has arrived a city will have already surrendered.
>
> If fords and bridges have not yet been constructed, strategic barriers not yet repaired, dangerous points in the city walls not yet fortified, and the iron caltrops not yet set out, then even though they have a fortified city they do not have any defense!
>
> If the troops from distant forts have not yet entered the city, the border guards and forces in other states not yet returned, then even though they have men, they do not have any men! If the six domesticated animals have not yet been herded in, the five grains not yet harvested, the wealth and materials for use not yet collected, then even though they have resources they do not have any resources!
>
> Now when a city is empty and void and its resources are exhausted, we should take advantage of this vacuity to attack them. The *Art of War* states, "They go out alone; they come in alone. Even before the enemy's men can cross blades with them, they have attained victory." This is what is meant.

Accordingly, Sun Pin even classified cities as to whether they might be easily attacked or should be avoided because the cost would be too great. However, throughout the Warring States period siege warfare rapidly evolved, producing specialized techniques and machines, making it possible to take a city far more expeditiously, sometimes in a matter of days. The *Six Secret Teachings* preserves an informative analysis of the tactical situation:

> King Wu asked the T'ai Kung: "Suppose, being victorious in battle, we have deeply penetrated the enemy's territory and occupy his land. However, large walled cities remain that cannot be subjugated, while their second army holds the defiles and ravines, standing off against us. We want to attack the cities and besiege the towns, but I'm afraid that their second army will suddenly appear and strike us. If their forces inside and outside unite in this fashion, they will oppose us from both within and without. Our Three Armies will be in chaos; the upper and lower ranks will be terrified. What should be done?"
>
> The T'ai Kung said: "In general, when attacking cities and besieging towns, the chariots and cavalry must be kept at a distance. The encamped and defensive units must be on constant alert in order to obstruct the enemy both within and without. When the inhabitants have their food cut off, those outside being unable to transport anything in to them, those within the city walls will be afraid, and their general will certainly surrender."

Even more than a half millennium later, in the mid-fourth century A.D. when sieges had been routinely executed for centuries, Mu-jung Ch'ieh still adhered to the same tactical principles and analyzed their feasibility by the same parameters, ever conscious of the wasteful stupidity of courageous headlong assaults.

68 Quickness 速

Tactical Discussion

Whenever attacking an encircled town, if the enemy's supplies are ample but their men few, while they have a prospect for external aid, you must quickly assault them and then you will be victorious. A tactical principle states: "The army values spiritual speed."

Historical Illustration

During the Three Kingdoms period, General Meng Ta of Shu surrendered with his forces to the kingdom of Wei and was subsequently appointed by Wei as Protector General for Hsin-ch'eng Commandery as a reward. Before long he agreed with Wu to again give his allegiance to Shu and turn against Wei. Ssu-ma Yi led an army from Wei that secretly advanced to extirpate him. However, his generals all advised that since Meng Ta had just reestablished relationships with Shu, it would be appropriate to observe him from a distance and subsequently take action. Ssu-ma Yi retorted: "Meng Ta lacks trust and righteousness. Moreover, this is the moment when he is filled with doubt. We should cut him off from Shu while he has not yet prepared adequate defenses." Thereupon they proceeded continuously at double pace until they arrived below the city. Since Wu and Shu had each dispatched forces to rescue Meng Ta, Ssu-ma Yi segmented his troops to oppose them.

At the beginning Meng Ta had sent a letter to Chu-ko Liang that stated: "The district of Wan where Ssu-ma Yi is garrisoned is eight hundred miles from Lo-yang, where his emperor is. Moreover, he is twelve hundred miles from the kingdom of Wu. Thus from the time that he learns I have revolted until his report reaches the emperor and he receives a reply will be at least a month. By then my fortifications will already be solid. As you, general, can easily discern, we are deployed at a strategic strongpoint, so Ssu-ma Yi will certainly not come himself. If any of his other generals appear, I will not have any worries." But when Ssu-ma Yi's troops actually arrived, Meng Ta again reported to Chu-ko Liang: "I revolted only eight days ago, but Wei's troops are already arrayed below our walls. How could their speed have been so spiritually quick?"

The city of Shang-yung had water obstacles on three sides, and just outside the city's perimeter Meng Ta had also erected wooden palisades to provide further security. However, Ssu-ma Yi forded the river, broke through the palisades, and directly besieged the city walls. Within ten days Li Fu and other commanders within the city had executed Meng Ta, opened the city gates, and surrendered.

Commentary

This chapter, the second part of the paired tactical discussion on the advisability of assaulting versus besieging a particular fortified city, examines the conditions under which mounting a prolonged siege would be foolhardy: vigorous defenders with ample food supplies and strong prospects for being rescued by a formidable external force. To procrastinate under such circumstances would expose the attackers to a crushing external assault combined with a simultaneous interior counterattack by highly motivated defenders. Quickness and speed are also evident in the historical incident, which, however, does not actually result in mounting a final assault, but just records the dramatic effects of Ssu-ma Yi's sudden appearance and successful attack on the outer defenses. His unexpected arrival and rapid penetration of their secondary barriers so startled the defenders that they were frightened into quickly surrendering in the absence of any prospect for immediate rescue, eliminating the need for a final attack. As the *Six Secret Teachings* states: "Being as swift as a flying arrow and attacking as suddenly as the release of a crossbow are the means by which to destroy brilliant plans."

The *Wei Liao-tzu* contains extensive passages on the nature of sieges and fortified defenses, including a brief analysis of the defender's psychology, that merit examining in this context:

> In general, when the defenders go forth, if they do not occupy the outer walls of the cities or the borderlands, and when they retreat do not establish watch towers and barricades for the purpose of defensive warfare, they do not excel at defense. The valiant heroes and brave stalwarts, sturdy armor and sharp weapons, powerful crossbows and strong arrows should all be within the outer walls, and then all the grain stored outside in the earthen cellars and granaries collected, and the buildings outside the outer walls broken down and brought into the

fortifications. This will force the attackers to expend ten or a hundred times the energy, while the defenders will not expend half theirs. The enemy aggressors will be harmed greatly, yet generals through the ages have not known this.

Now the defenders should not neglect their strategic points. The rule for defending a city wall is that for every ten feet you should employ ten men to defend it, artisans and cooks not being included. Those who go out to fight do not defend the city; those that defend the city do not go out to fight. One man on defense can oppose ten men besieging them; ten men can oppose a hundred; a hundred men can oppose a thousand; a thousand men can oppose ten thousand. Thus constructing a city's interior and exterior walls by accumulating loose soil and tamping it down does not wantonly expend the strength of the people, for it truly is for defense.

If a wall is ten thousand feet long, then ten thousand men should defend it. The moats should be deep and wide, the walls solid and thick, the soldiers and people prepared, firewood and foodstuffs provided, the crossbows stout and arrows strong, the spears and halberds well suited. This is the method for making defense solid.

If the attackers are not less than a mass of at least a hundred thousand, while the defenders have an army outside that will certainly come to the rescue, it is a city that must be defended. If there is no external army to inevitably rescue them, then it isn't a city that must be defended.

Now if the walls are solid and rescue certain, then even stupid men and ignorant women will all, without exception, protect the walls, exhausting their resources and blood for them. For a city to withstand a siege for a year, the strength of the defenders should exceed that of the attackers, and the strength of the rescue force exceed that of the defenders.

Now if the walls are solid but rescue uncertain, then the stupid men and ignorant women, all without exception, will defend the parapets but they will weep. This is normal human emotion. Even if you thereupon open the grain reserves in order to relieve and pacify them, you cannot stop it. You must incite the valiant heroes and brave stalwarts with their sturdy armor, sharp weapons, strong crossbows, and stout arrows to exert their strength together in the front, and the young, weak, crippled, and ill to exert their strength together in the rear.

If an army of a hundred thousand is encamped beneath the city walls, the rescue force must break open the siege, and the city's defenders must go out to attack. When they sally forth they must secure the critical positions along the way. But the rescue forces to the rear of the besiegers should not sever their supply lines, and the forces within and without should respond to each other.

In this sort of rescue display a half-hearted commitment. If you display a half-hearted commitment, it will overturn the enemy and we can await them. They will put their stalwarts in the rear, and place the old in the forefront. Then the enemy won't be able to advance or be able to stop the defenders from breaking out. This is what is meant by the tactical balance of power in defense.

The T'ai Kung, analyzing the problem of suddenly finding oneself under siege, suggested somewhat different tactics in the *Six Secret Teachings:*

> King Wu said: "Suppose the enemy divides his forces into three or four detachments, some fighting with us and occupying our territory, others stopping to round up our oxen and horses. Their main army has not yet completely arrived, but they have had their swift invaders press us below the city walls. Therefore our Three Armies are sorely afraid. What should we do?"
>
> The T'ai Kung said: "Carefully observe the enemy. Before they have all arrived, make preparations and await them. Go out about four miles from the walls and establish fortifications, setting out in good order our gongs and drums, flags and pennants. Our other troops will comprise an ambushing force. Order large numbers of strong crossbowmen to the top of the fortifications. Every hundred paces set up an 'explosive gate,' outside of which we should place the horse barricades. Our chariots and cavalry should be held outside, while our courageous, strong, fierce fighters should be secreted in this outer area. If the enemy should reach us, have our light armored foot soldiers engage them in battle, then feign a retreat. Have the forces on top of the city wall set out the flags and pennants and strike the war drums, completing all preparations to defend the city. The enemy will assume we are going to defend the wall and will certainly press an attack below it. Then release the forces lying in ambush, some to assault their interior, others to strike the exterior. Then the Three Armies should urgently press the attack, some striking the front lines, others the rear. Even their courageous soldiers will not be able to fight, while the swiftest will not have time to flee. This is termed 'explosive warfare.' Although the enemy is numerically superior, they will certainly run off."

The tactics for mounting effective sieges are again pondered in Chapter 80, "Sieges," where additional textual passages will be examined.

69 Order 整

Tactical Discussion

Whenever engaging an enemy in battle, if the enemy's rows and formations are well ordered and uniform, while their officers and troops are composed and tranquil, you cannot lightly initiate an attack. It would be advantageous to await some change or movement and then suddenly strike them. A tactical principle from the *Art of War* states: "Do not intercept well-ordered flags."

Historical Illustration

During the Three Kingdoms period, General Ssu-ma Yi of Wei went out on campaign against Kung-sun Yüan. Ssu-ma Yi floated his army across the Liao River by boat and encircled the enemy. However, he abandoned the siege and ordered a march toward Kung-sun Yüan's home base of Hsiang-p'ing. His generals criticized his actions, saying: "Failing to assault the city after mounting a siege is not the way to display strength of numbers."

Ssu-ma Yi retorted: "The brigand's camp is solid and his fortifications high, so he wants to wear out our army. If we attack them, we will fall into his plans. The vast majority of the brigand's troops are here, so their homeland is empty and vacuous. By going directly to Hsiang-p'ing their soldiers will inevitably become fearful about the state's interior. If they engage in battle while fearful, we will certainly destroy them." Thereupon he deployed his forces in good order and proceeded past the city. When the brigands saw the army proceeding to their rear, they indeed sallied forth to intercept them. Ssu-ma Yi then released his soldiers in a counterattack and severely defeated them.

Commentary

This chapter and the next review the advantages of attacking disordered forces and avoiding well-disciplined ones, and Sun-tzu's full statement, found in "Military Combat," emphasizes the principle in concluding "do not attack well-regulated formations." All the military writers concurred, ranging from the *Ssu-ma Fa* through the late *Questions and Replies,* and therefore devoted considerable thought to formulating methods for creating and exploiting disorder in the enemy. The concise sequence preserved in the historical incident illustrates the effectiveness of this approach. Based upon his realization that the enemy had adopted a temporizing strategy, Ssu-ma Yi initiated a highly visible, bold movement to "seize what they love" by attacking their heartland, thereby panicking them into precipitous, extremely disordered movement. Once the enemy's forces had thus been destabilized, Ssu-ma Yi launched a well-crafted attack and scored an easy victory. (This method of "seizing what they solely love" was of course the essence of Sun Pin's strategy in the two famous battle of Kuei-ling and Ma-ling, as previously discussed. Also of note is Ssu-ma Yi's ability to employ unorthodox troops in his encounter with Kung-sun Yüan, for he concealed his attack orientation within a well-ordered march toward a distant destination. His methods are also explored in the historical illustration for Chapter 78, "Inevitable Conflict," where the same campaign is again examined.)

Ssu-ma Yi's strategy exploited a fundamental psychology principle: the worried and fearful do not fight well. For example, in the *Six Secret Teachings* it states: "Taking advantage of their fright and fear is the means by which one can attack ten," while the conservative *Ssu-ma Fa* advised: "Mount a sudden strike on their doubts. Attack their haste. Force them to constrict their deployment. Launch a sudden strike against their order. Take advantage of their failure to avoid harm. Obstruct their strategy. Seize their thoughts. Capitalize on their fears."

70 Disorder 亂

Tactical Discussion

Whenever engaging an enemy in battle, if the enemy's rows and formations are disordered while their officers and men clamor and shout, it would be appropriate to send the army forth to strike them, for then you will be victorious. A tactical principle from the *Art of War* states: "Create disorder in their forces and take them."

Historical Illustration

During the Spring and Autumn period, when the state of Wu attacked the minor state of Chou-lai, the state of Ch'u led the armies of several other feudal lords to rescue it. The future king of Wu, Ho Lü, said: "The feudal lords following Ch'u may be many, but they are all small states that cannot avoid coming because they fear Ch'u. I have heard it said that when awesomeness conquers love in military affairs, although one is small he will certainly be well ordered. The rulers of Hu and Shen are young and extremely reckless; the highest ranking official in Chen is experienced but stupid; Tun, Hsü, and Ts'ai detest Ch'u's government; and Ch'u's commander is held in little esteem but has many favorites so their administrative orders are not unified. Although these seven states have undertaken a joint military effort, they are not united in mind. Since Ch'u's commander is slighted and unable to order the troops, his orders lack majesty, so Ch'u can be defeated. If we segment our regiments to initially attack Hu, Shen, and Chen, they will certainly be first to run off. When these three states have been defeated, the armies of the other feudal lords will be shaken. With the feudal lords in confusion and disarray, Ch'u will certainly be badly defeated and race off. I suggest we first send forth some insignificant, little-prepared troops while simultaneously making the formations to the rear dense and ensuring the regiments are well ordered." His father, the king, followed his advice.

On the day recorded as *hsü-ch'en,* the last day of the moon, they fought at Chi-fu, employing three thousand convicts to first rush against Hu, Shen, and Chen. The troops from these three states fought with them. Wu divided its forces into three armies in order to follow behind the initial thrust and attack. The king assumed command of the center army, Ho Lü that of the army on the right flank, while the other regiments were deployed on the left flank. Some of Wu's convict forces fled, others stood and fought. The forces of the three states were thrown into confusion and Wu's regiments pressed the attack against them, eventually defeating them and capturing their rulers. Wu then released their recently captured prisoners from Hu and Shen so that they might flee back into the armies of Hsü, Ts'ai, and Tun, foolishly proclaiming that their rulers were dead. The soldiers in these three states, clamoring and shouting, followed them in fleeing the battlefield. When these armies had run off, Ch'u's army was in turn engaged and routed.

Commentary

This chapter concludes the two-part discussion on the advisability of attacking disordered forces, a well-recognized principle throughout the military writings. For example, the *Six Secret Teachings* lists disorder among the fourteen vulnerable conditions in an enemy:

> Anyone who wants to launch a strike should carefully scrutinize and investigate fourteen changes in the enemy. When any of these changes become visible, attack, for the enemy will certainly be defeated: When the enemy has begun to assemble they can be attacked. When the men and horses have not yet been fed they can be attacked. When the seasonal or weather conditions are not advantageous to them they can be attacked. When they have not secured good terrain they can be attacked. When they are fleeing they can be attacked. When they are not vigilant they can be attacked. When they are tired and exhausted they can be attacked. When the general is absent from the officers and troops they can be attacked. When they are traversing long roads they can be attacked. When they are fording rivers they can be attacked. When the troops have not had any leisure time they can be attacked. When they encounter the difficulty of precipitous ravines or are on narrow roads they can be attacked. When their battle array is in disorder they can be attacked. When they are afraid they can be attacked.

Wu Ch'i similarly listed several manifestations of disorder that might be fortuitously assaulted:

> In employing the army, to invariably attack the enemy one must ascertain the enemy's voids and strengths and then race to take advantage of their endangered points. When the enemy has just arrived from afar and their battle formations are not yet properly deployed they can be attacked. If they have eaten but not yet established their encampment they can be attacked. If they are running about wildly they can be attacked. If they have labored hard they can be attacked. If they haven't yet taken advantage of the terrain they can be attacked. When they have lost the critical moment and not followed up opportunities they can be attacked. When they have traversed a great distance and the rear guard hasn't had time to rest yet they can be attacked. When fording rivers and only half of them have crossed, they can be attacked. In narrow and confined roads they can be attacked. When their flags and banners move about chaotically they can be attacked. When their formations frequently move about they can be attacked. When a general is separated from his soldiers they can be attacked. When they are afraid they can be attacked. In general, in circumstances

such as these select crack troops to rush upon them, divide your remaining troops and continue the assault, pressing the attack swiftly and decisively.

Among thirty-two errors of commanders that Sun Pin felt might be advantageously exploited, he listed the following indications of disarray and disorder:

Second, if he gathers together turbulent people and immediately employs them, or if he stops retreating troops and immediately engages in battle with them, then he can be defeated. . . . Fourth, if his commands are not implemented, the masses not unified, he can be defeated. Fifth, if his subordinates are not submissive and the masses not employable, he can be defeated. . . . Ninth, if the soldiers are deserting he can be defeated. Tenth, if the soldiers are disordered he can be defeated. Eleventh, if the army has been frightened several times he can be defeated. . . . Eighteenth, if commands are frequently changed and the masses are furtive, he can be defeated. Nineteenth, if the army is disintegrating while the masses do not regard their generals and officials as capable, he can be defeated. . . . Twenty-first, if he has numerous doubts so the masses are doubtful, he can be defeated. . . . Twenty-fifth, if their minds are divided at the appointed time for battle he can be defeated. . . . Twenty-ninth, if he deprecates the troops and the minds of the masses are hateful he can be defeated. Thirtieth, if he is unable to successfully deploy his forces while the route out is constricted, he can be defeated. Thirty-first, if in the army's forward ranks are soldiers from the rear ranks and they are not coordinated and unified with the forward deployment he can be defeated. Thirty-second, if in engaging in battle he is concerned about the front and the rear is therefore empty; or, concerned about the rear the front is empty; or concerned about the left, the right is empty; or concerned about the right the left is empty—his engaging in battle being filled with worry, he can be defeated.

The historical illustration summarizes the battle of Chi-fu, a famous engagement in Wu's ascension to power, pivotal to its campaign to subjugate the state of Ch'u. As King Ho Lü clearly outlines the campaign's imaginative strategy and the tactics are extensively discussed in our introduction to Sun-tzu's *Art of War,* further commentary can be omitted in favor of providing a translation of another historical illustration from a variant text:

The T'ang general Tuan Chih-hsüan followed general Liu Wen-ching in resisting Ch'ü T'u-t'ung at T'ung pass. Liu Wen-ching was defeated by one of Ch'ü T'u-t'ung's generals, Sang Hsing-ho. Although Liu's encampment had already collapsed, Tuan Chih-hsüan still led twenty cavalrymen to race there and strike into the enemy, killing several tens before withdrawing. While withdrawing he was struck in the foot by a falling arrow but feared that the troops could become troubled so endured it without saying anything. Thereafter he repeatedly reentered the enemy. Sang Hsing-ho's army was in chaos, so Tuan Chih-hsüan, from a position of no power whatsoever, managed to again restore order among his troops and thereafter badly defeat Ch'ü T'u-t'ung's army.

Tuan's determined actions again provide dramatic evidence that a few committed men can have a decisive effect against a much larger but less motivated mass, and that disorder, once induced, is difficult to stem but easily exploited.

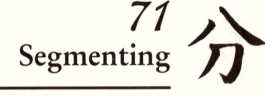

71 Segmenting 分

Tactical Discussion

Whenever engaging an enemy in battle, if you are numerous while they are few, you should select level, easy, broad, and expansive terrain for the engagement in order to be victorious. If you are five times the enemy's strength, then three-fifths of your forces should execute orthodox tactics and two-fifths should implement unorthodox ones. If you are three times the enemy's strength, two-thirds of your forces should execute orthodox tactics and one-third should implement unorthodox ones. This is what is referred to as one segment opposing their front while another attacks their rear. A tactical principle from the *Questions and Replies* states: "One who doesn't divide when he should divide entangles the army."

Historical Illustration

During the Northern and Southern Dynasties period, Generals Ch'en Pa-hsien and Wang Seng-pien of Liang conducted a punitive campaign against the army of the rebel general Hou Ching at Chang-kung Island. Their billowing pennants obscured the sky while their innumerable warships covered the river. Taking advantage of the tide, they followed the river's flow. Hou Ching stood atop a large boulder and looked out at them. Displeased, he said: "An army whose warriors have this much spirit cannot be changed." He then beat the drums and led ten thousand death-defying cavalrymen in an advance. Ch'en Pa-hsien addressed Wang Seng-pien: "One who excels at employing the army is like the snakes on Mount Ch'ang—both the head and tail respond. Now these brigands are willingly racing to their deaths, wanting to force a single decisive battle. We are numerous while they are few, so it would be best to segment their power." Wang Seng-pien followed his advice, employing stout crossbowmen to oppose their front and light, sharp cavalry forces to surge over them from the rear just as the main deployment struck their center. Eventually Hou Ching was thoroughly crushed, abandoned the city, and fled.

Commentary

The concept of segmenting and reuniting, critical to maneuver warfare and the execution of complex tactics, arose in China while Greek warfare was still confined to cumbersome phalanx clashes. Sun-tzu was apparently the first to articulate the importance of being able to segment and reunite in a succinct passage: "The army is established by deceit, moves for advantage, and changes through segmenting and reuniting." Moreover, in this context he observed:

> In antiquity those who were referred to as excelling in the employment of the army were able to keep the enemy's forward and rear forces from connecting; the many and few from relying on each other; the noble and lowly from coming to each other's rescue; the upper and lower ranks from trusting each other; the troops separated, unable to reassemble, or when assembled, not well ordered. They moved when it was advantageous, halted when it was not advantageous.

The T'ai Kung said: "Dividing your troops into four and splitting them into five are the means by which to attack their circular formations and destroy their square ones." Based upon the *Six Secret Teachings,* he frequently advised dividing one's forces, especially when in difficulty, into three operational units. This perhaps reflects Sun Pin's development of the operational reserve and his emphasis upon segmenting and reuniting to confuse the enemy and seize an advantage. Sun Pin thus concluded: "Breaking apart and intermixing like clouds are the means by which to create a tactical imbalance of power and explosive movement." He also advised applying the method to certain categories of battlefield situations. For example, when confronting a superior force in a square formation he advised dispersing to fragment the enemy: "To strike them deploy in the diffuse formation and fragment them; if they are properly assembled, separate them; engage them in battle and then feign retreat; and kill the general for their rear guard without letting them become aware of it. This is the Tao for striking a square formation." Similarly, to attack a strong foe in a horizontal formation he stressed segmenting: "To strike them you must segment our soldiers into three operational groups and select the 'death warriors.' Two groups should be deployed in an extended array with long flanks; one should consist of talented officers and selected troops. They should assemble to strike at the enemy's critical point. This is the Tao for killing their general and striking horizontal deployments."

The chapter's discussion begins with the battlefield situation previously found in Chapter 11, "Large Numbers," but the tactics are far more sophisticated and advanced. Chapter 11 is premised upon a statement found in the *Ssu-ma Fa,* a very early military text that, although definitely composed after the *Art of War,* probably incorporates older materials and never mentions the concept of the unorthodox except indirectly. In contrast, Sun-tzu and Sun Pin fully develop the concept, and the implications are exploited for two millennia thereafter, although theory and field realization always remained rather different matters. The tactical discussion in the *Unorthodox Strategies* thus represents nearly two thousand years of continuous development and perhaps its ultimate expression.

Sun-tzu is known for his assertion that "if your strength is ten times the enemy's, surround them; if five, attack them; if double, divide your forces; and if you are equal in strength to the enemy, you can engage them. If fewer, you can circumvent them. If outmatched you can avoid them." However, the tactical discussion apparently derives from passages in the *Questions and Replies* where the two concepts of the unorthodox/orthodox and segmenting/reuniting appear throughout. (The concept of the orthodox and unorthodox have already been discussed in Chapters 41 and 42 of the same names.) One section outlines some important factors in concretely realizing them on the battlefield:

> The T'ai-tsung asked: "Are the five flags in their different colors for the five directions for orthodox forces? Are the pennants and banners for penetrating the enemy for unorthodox forces? Dispersing and reforming are changes; how does one realize the appropriate number of platoons?"
>
> Li Ching replied: "I have examined and employ the methods of old. In general, when three platoons combine, their flags lean toward each other, but are not crossed. When five platoons are combined then the flags of two of them are

crossed. When ten platoons are combined then the flags of five of them are crossed. When the horn is blown then the five crossed flags are separated, and the combined unit will again disperse to form ten platoons. When two crossed flags are separated, the single unit will again disperse to form five platoons. When the two flags leaning toward each other, but uncrossed, are separated, the single unit will again disperse to form three platoons.

When the soldiers are dispersed, uniting them is unorthodox; when they are united, dispersing them is unorthodox."

General Ch'en's citing of the snake analogy to explain his tactical analysis shows the extent to which generals in the middle sixth century A.D. were thoroughly familiar with Sun-tzu's *Art of War.* Sun-tzu employed it himself in discussing the nature of a well-ordered and disciplined army commanded by a resourceful general: "Thus one who excels at employing the army may be compared to the snake called the *shuaijan.* The *shuaijan* is found on Mt. Ch'ang. If you strike its head, the tail will respond; if you strike its tail, the head will respond. If you strike the middle of the body, both the head and tail will react." General Ch'en was concerned that Hou Ching's forces, being forced to penetrate fatal terrain, would have greater resolve than his own soldiers and manage to forge a victory through sheer courage and determination. Thus, although fielding superior numbers, he elected to divide the enemy and thereby blunt their cohesiveness and power. This fully accorded with Sun Pin's method: "When your strategic power exceeds the enemy's, when deploying to approach them, employ a flanking attack on the wings."

72 Uniting 合

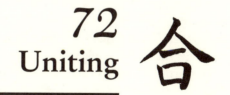

Tactical Discussion

Now it is a general principle that when an army is dispersed, its strategic power is weak, and when it is assembled, its strategic power is strong. Therefore, if your troops are encamped in several locations, should the enemy attack in force, you must reunite the army in order to counterattack. A tactical principle from the *Questions and Replies* states: "One who does not assemble when he should assemble becomes a solitary regiment."

Historical Illustration

During the K'ai-yüan reign period in the T'ang dynasty, the Turfan mounted a substantial raid across the border, and it was reported to the soldiers stationed at Hsin-ch'eng. Early in the morning the Turfan launched a cavalry attack against the government troops. As the defenders were severely outnumbered by the invaders, they were all afraid. General Wang Chung-ssu whipped his horse forward, and those on his left and right also raced forth in a sudden burst, causing the invaders to disperse. Wang and his cavalrymen went out separately and then reunited, slew several hundred of the enemy, and threw the Turfan into chaos. The army's three regiments then struck the enemy at separate points and the Turfan suffered a severe defeat.

Commentary

While this chapter ostensibly concludes the discussion of the conceptual pair segmenting/reuniting, the focus is much simpler, merely emphasizing the need to concentrate the army's power when engaging a strong enemy in battle. In contrast, the historical incident well illustrates the application "segmenting and then reuniting," much as Sun Pin recommended for coping with a sharp formation: "To strike them you must segment into three operational groups to separate them. One should be stretched out horizontally, two should go off to strike their flanks. Their upper ranks will be afraid and their lower ranks confused. When the lower and upper ranks are already in chaos, their Three Armies will then be severely defeated. This is the Tao for striking a sharp deployment."

The thrust of the tactical discussion flows from the quotation, "One who does not assemble when he should assemble becomes a solitary regiment." More imaginative methods fall by the wayside when faced with the reality of confronting overwhelming power. Sun-tzu of course spoke of concentrating one's forces against the enemy but after causing his positions to be weak and vacuous. Conversely, actual historical battles, being fought on simpler tactical lines than theoretical ones, painfully teach that a certain minimum level of power is required to withstand an enemy's onslaught whenever maneuvering to escape proves impossible. Accordingly, throughout the ages warfare theory in the West has emphasized attaining numerical and firepower superiority to achieve the quickest victory possible with the lowest casualty rates, although commanders then proceeded to act contrary to their (sometimes) avowed desire for the latter by mounting headlong assaults, often from plodding standing formations.

The *Questions and Replies,* the source for the tactical quotations in both these chapters, contains an interesting overview of the question framed in terms of two well-known campaigns that have already appeared in the *Unorthodox Strategies:*

> The T'ai-tsung said: "When the army divides and reassembles, in each case it is important that the actions be appropriate. Among the records of earlier ages, who excelled at this?"
>
> Li Ching said: "Fu Chien commanded a mass of a million and was defeated at Fei River. This is what results when an army is able to unite but cannot divide. When Wu Han conducted a campaign of rectification against Kung-sun Shu he split his forces with lieutenant general Liu Shang, encamping about twenty miles apart. Kung-sun Shu came forward and attacked Wu Han, whereupon Liu Shang advanced to unite with Wu Han in a counterattack, severely defeating Kung-sun Shu. This is the result that can be attained when an army divides and can reassemble. The T'ai Kung said: 'A force that wants to divide but cannot is an entangled army; one which wants to reassemble but cannot is a solitary regiment.'"
>
> The T'ai-tsung said: "Yes. When Fu Chien first obtained Wang Meng, he truly knew how to employ the army and subsequently took the central plain. When Wang Meng died, Fu Chien was decisively defeated, so is this what is meant by an 'entangled army'? When Wu Han was appointed by Emperor Kuang Wu, the army was not controlled from a distance, and the Han was able to pacify the Shu area. Doesn't this indicate that the army didn't fall into the difficulty of what is referred to as being a 'solitary regiment'? The historical records of gains and losses are sufficient to be a mirror for ten thousand generations."

Fu Chien's stupidity at the battle of Fei River has already been discussed in Chapter 11, "Large Numbers," while Kung-sun Shu's defeat was recounted in Chapter 50, "Danger."

73 Anger 怒

Tactical Discussion

Whenever you engage an enemy in battle, you must incite your officers and troops, making them angry before going into combat. A tactical principle from the *Art of War* states: "What enables men to kill the enemy is anger."

Historical Illustration

During the first year of the Chien-wu reign period in the Later Han dynasty, Emperor Kuang Wu directed Generals Wang Pa and Ma Wu to extirpate Chou Chien who was ensconced in Ch'ui-hui. Su Mao, in command of an army of more than four thousand, went to rescue Chou Chien. At first he dispatched elite cavalry to encircle and attack Ma Wu's supply routes. When Wu went out to rescue his supplies, Chou Chien then sent his soldiers forth from the city to strike him. Ma Wu's forces were relying upon Wang Pa to provide support, so they did not overly exert themselves in combat. When Ma's forces were defeated by Su Mao and Chou Chien, he proceeded back past Wang Pa's encampment and loudly called out to be rescued. Wang Pa replied: "The brigand's power is now flourishing, so if we go out both our armies will certainly be defeated. There's nothing for it but to exert yourselves!" Then he shut up his encampment and solidified the defense of his walls.

His staff members all argued with him. Wang Pa said: "Su Mao's forces are elite and sharp; moreover, his troops are extremely numerous. Our officers and soldiers are afraid. If we act to support Ma Wu, our armies will not be unified, so this will only result in our defeat. Just now I closed the encampment and solidified the defense of our walls to show that we would not support him. The enemy will certainly exploit the strategic situation to recklessly advance. Ma Wu's soldiers hate the fact that we didn't rescue them so their ferocity in combat will naturally be doubled. Accordingly, Su Mao's numerous troops will become fatigued, at which point we can conquer them."

As predicted Su Mao and Chou Chien assembled all their troops and went forth to attack Ma Wu, engaging him in a lengthy battle. Several tens of valiant warriors within Wang Pa's army dramatically asked to engage in the battle; only then did Wang open the gates for everyone to sally forth. His elite cavalry suddenly struck the enemy's rear, so that Su Mao and Chou Chien simultaneously suffered attacks front and rear, were eventually defeated, and fled.

Commentary

This chapter and the next focus upon the question of motivating men for combat, priming them to overcome their fears, face the enemy, and fight valiantly rather than simply occupy a space on the battlefield. Previous chapters (Chapters 14, "Awesomeness" and 16, "Punishment") have already discussed the necessity for punishments to instill the fear necessary to prevent the soldiers from fleeing and the granting of generous rewards to stimulate them to exert themselves (Chapter 15, "Rewards"). Moreover, Sun-tzu's theory of drastic motivation—deliberately casting the troops onto fatal terrain—has also been explored in Chapters 50 and 51, "Danger" and "Fighting to the Death." The military writers also identified a number of other motivational factors, primarily emotional, such as shame, honor, greed, patriotism, and love. For example, the early *Ssu-ma Fa* noted: "In general, men will die for love, out of anger, out of fear of awesomeness, for righteousness, and for profit. In general it is the Tao of warfare that when they are well instructed men will regard death lightly. When they are constrained by the Tao they will die for the upright." In the chapter entitled "Stimulating the Officers," Wu Ch'i stressed the motivational power of man's desire for fame and honor and accordingly mounted ostentatious feasts celebrating the valiant while also being visibly solicitous of deceased soldiers' families. As a result, he was able to stimulate his troops and defeat virtually every opponent he faced.

Another motivational factor was the obligations imposed on every soldier by the mutual responsibility system that strongly bound the squad of five together. Since every member of the squad would suffer for the combat failure of any one of them, every man had to fight courageously in order to avoid not only his own punishment but also causing his fellow squad members to suffer. The cohesiveness of the small unit has of course been the most important motivational factor for centuries because most men simply do not want to fail their comrades on the battlefield or be shamed in front of them. The Chinese military writers exploited this factor by heavily stressing the squad of five, which was, from at least the late Spring and Autumn period, the basis for all formations and the possibility of segmentation, articulation, and maneuver warfare. The *Wei Liao-tzu,* a focal text for discussions of the squad of five, stated: "Ensure that the members of the squads of five and ten are like relatives, the members of the companies and their officers like friends. When they stop they will be like a solid encircling wall, when they move like the wind and rain. The chariots will not wheel to the rear; the soldiers will not turn about. This is the Way to establish the foundation for combat." Of course fear of fellow squad members taking violent action on the battlefield or inflicting reprisals thereafter also prevented men from fleeing in the face of the enemy.

The *Wei Liao-tzu* also offered some observations on the campaign soldier's progressively narrowing focus and determination:

> Soldiers have five defining commitments: for their general they forget their families; when they cross the border they forget their relatives; when they confront the enemy they forget themselves; when they are committed to die they will live; while urgently seeking victory is the lowest. A hundred men willing to suffer the pain of a blade can penetrate a line and cause chaos in a formation. A thousand men willing to suffer the pain of a blade can seize the enemy and kill its general. Ten thousand men willing to suffer the pain of a blade can transverse under Heaven at will.

This progression is fundamental to the psychology of *ch'i* (or spirit) discussed in the next chapter.

The tactical discussion mentions the importance of motivating the soldiers with an inspirational speech prior to engaging in combat. In China, swearing an oath was part of the ritual from ancient days, somewhat displaced later on by more dramatic exhortations accompanied by strong denunciations of the enemy's vileness. The *Ssu-ma Fa,* which mentions the importance of oaths several times in various contexts, contains a passage purportedly showing how the time and place for making a formal commitment to warfare changed over the ages, concurrent with a general decline from Virtue:

> Shun made the official announcement of their mission within the state capital because he wanted the people to first embrace his orders. The rulers of the Hsia Dynasty administered their oaths amidst the army for they wanted the people to first complete their thoughts. The Shang rulers swore their oaths outside the gate to the encampment for they wanted the people to first fix their intentions and await the conflict. King Wu of the Chou waited until the weapons were about to clash and then swore his oath in order to stimulate the people's will to fight.

74 Spirit 氣

Tactical Discussion

The means by which the commanding general wages warfare is his soldiers; the means by which the soldiers engage in combat is their *ch'i* (spirit). The means by which *ch'i* proves victorious is the beating of the war drums. Since the drums are capable of inciting the *ch'i* of the officers and troops, they should not be incessantly employed. If employed too many times, the soldiers' *ch'i* will easily decline. Similarly, they cannot be employed when too far away from the enemy. If too far, the soldier's strength will easily be exhausted. You must estimate when the enemy will be within sixty or seventy paces and then beat the drums to signal the officers and troops to advance into combat. If the enemy's *ch'i* abates while yours surges, their defeat will be certain. A tactical principle from the *Wei Liao-tzu* states: "When their *ch'i* is substantial they will fight; when their *ch'i* has been snatched away they will run off."

Historical Illustration

During the Spring and Autumn period, the state of Ch'i attacked the state of Lü. Duke Chuang, commanding Lü's forces, was about to commit the army to battle when Ts'ao Kuei requested permission to join him. The Duke had him ride in his chariot and went into battle at Ch'ang-shao. The duke was about to have the drums sound the advance when Ts'ao Kuei said to him: "Not yet." Ch'i sounded their drums three times then Ts'ao said: "Now." They beat the drums and engaged in combat, and Ch'i's army was severely defeated. The duke inquired why Ts'ao Kuei had delayed the drums. Ts'ao replied: "Combat is a matter of courageous *ch'i.* A single drumming arouses the soldiers' *ch'i,* with a second it abates, and with a third it is exhausted. They were exhausted while we were vigorous, so we conquered them."

Commentary

"Spirit" provides a glimpse of a psychology of warfare that conceived courage and daring in terms of *ch'i*, the vital *pneuma* of life that powers the body and spirit. While determination, intention, and "will" were not overlooked, it is a surge of *ch'i* (or spirit) that makes combat possible and must be stimulated, nurtured, and controlled if armies are to be successful. Thus the *Ssu-ma Fa* states: "In general, in battle one endures through strength and gains victory through spirit. One can endure with a solid defense but will achieve victory through being endangered. When the heart's foundation is solid, a new surge of *ch'i* will bring victory." Accordingly, the tactical discussion opens and closes by essentially splitting an observation found in the *Wei Liao-tzu:* "Now the means by which the general fights is the people; the means by which the people fight is their *ch'i.* When their *ch'i* is substantial they will fight; when their *ch'i* has been snatched away they will run off."

The core of the tactical discussion, as well as the famous historical incident from the *Tso Chuan* recounting a battle from the seventh century B.C., is the need to avoid overstressing the soldiers by stimulating their *ch'i* too early, causing it to fruitlessly peak and then diminish. As Wu Ch'i said, *ch'i* ebbs and flourishes, and success in combat depends upon it reaching a zenith just at the moment of battle. Sun-tzu analyzed the importance of being cognizant of, and exploiting, these *ch'i* states in a famous passage widely known from the Warring States on:

> The *ch'i* of the Three Armies can be snatched away; the commanding general's mind can be seized. For this reason in the morning their *ch'i* is ardent; during the day their *ch'i* becomes indolent; at dusk their *ch'i* is exhausted. Thus one who excels at employing the army avoids their ardent *ch'i* and strikes when it is indolent or exhausted. This is the way to manipulate *ch'i.*

Many of Sun-tzu's measures were of course designed to manipulate the enemy until he became physically and emotionally exhausted, until his spirit or, in modern terms, "will to fight" had been so severely diminished that victory became certain.

Sun-tzu's passage was, however, sometimes misinterpreted as simply meaning attacks should be made only late in the day, prompting a discussion between T'ang T'ai-tsung and Li Ching on the extended meaning and implications of his analysis:

> The T'ai-tsung said: "Sun-tzu spoke about strategies by which the *ch'i* of the Three Armies may be snatched away: 'In the morning their *ch'i* is ardent; during the day their *ch'i* becomes indolent; and at dusk their *ch'i* is exhausted. One who excels at employing the army avoids their ardent *ch'i* and strikes when it is indolent or exhausted.' How is this?"
>
> Li Ching said: "Whoever has life and a natural endowment of blood, if they die without a second thought when the drums are sounded to do battle, it is the *ch'i* that causes it to be so. Thus methods for employing the army require first investigating our own officers and troops, stimulating our *ch'i* for victory, and only then attacking the enemy. Among Wu Ch'i's four vital points, the vital point of *ch'i* is foremost. There is no other Tao. If one can cause his men themselves to want to fight, then no one will be able to oppose their ardor. What Sun-tzu meant by the *ch'i* being ardent in the morning is not limited to those hours alone. He used the beginning and end of the day as an analogy. In general, if the drum has been sounded three times but the enemy's *ch'i* has neither declined nor become depleted, then how can you cause it to invariably become indolent or exhausted? Probably those who study the text merely recite the empty words and are misled by the enemy. If one could enlighten them with the principles for snatching away the *ch'i*, the army could be entrusted to them."

As previously seen in the commentary to Chapter 18, "The Guest," the soldiers have different mindsets and emotional states as they proceed from their own states deep into enemy territory. Following Sun-tzu's extensive analysis, Sun Pin formulated the psychological stages that need to be attained:

> When you form the army and assemble the masses, concentrate upon stimulating their ch'i. When you again decamp and reassemble the army, concentrate upon ordering the soldiers and sharpening their ch'i. When you approach the border and draw near the enemy concentrate upon honing their ch'i. When the day for battle has been set concentrate upon making their ch'i decisive. When the day for battle is at hand, concentrate upon expanding their ch'i.

Given the gravity of psychological preparation for battle, a lack of similar commitment in an enemy would immediately become obvious, indicated by external signs, and could be exploited, as, for example, noted by the *Wei Liao-tzu:* "One who occupies ravines lacks the mind to do battle. One who lightly provokes a battle lacks fullness of *ch'i.* One who is belligerent in battle lacks soldiers capable of victory."

75 Retreats 歸

Tactical Discussion

Whenever you engage in pitched assaults with an enemy, if for no apparent reason they should withdraw, you must carefully investigate it. If their strength is really exhausted and their spirit spent, you can select elite, fierce cavalrymen to pursue them closely. If they are truly a retreating army, you should not obstruct them. A tactical principle from the *Art of War* states: "Do not obstruct an army retreating homeward."

Historical Illustration

In the third year of the Chien-an reign period of Emperor Hsien of the Later Han dynasty, Ts'ao Ts'ao encircled Chang Hsiu at Wan. Liu Piao dispatched troops to rescue Chang Hsiu. Chang secured his troops and defended the ravines in order to sever any approach to the army's rear. Ts'ao Ts'ao's army was unable to advance, and therefore itself suffered attacks from both Chang Hsiu in the front and the rescue force from the rear. That night he improved the ravines and secreted ambushing forces to await the enemy and then feigned a retreat. Chang Hsiu employed all his troops in pursuit, whereupon Ts'ao Ts'ao released his unorthodox forces to attack them from both sides, severely destroying them. Ts'ao Ts'ao said: "The enemy obstructed our retreating army and joined battle with us on fatal terrain. This is how we emerged victorious."

Commentary

This chapter and the next are both essentially variants on the tactical considerations and advisability of pursuing a retreating army, and therefore the commentary for both will be appended here. The critical question is simply whether the enemy has really been routed or is merely executing a prearranged stratagem to draw your forces out from their positions, rendering them vulnerable to an unexpected counterblow just when the troops are flush with the joy of victory and thus growing somewhat lax despite being involved in a fervent pursuit.

Until the age of modern weapons, most battlefield casualties were inflicted when one force lost its will to fight and fled, exposing itself to withering fire and the blows of shock weapons inflicted from behind. Accordingly, any opportunity to eliminate the enemy's capability to regroup and again wage battle had to be fully exploited. However, cleverly executed tactical traps had to be avoided. This tactical contradiction led to conflicting statements throughout the military writings, depending upon whether the writer emphasized the importance of exploiting a victory or was primarily concerned with avoiding a trap. The *Ssu-ma Fa,* generally a conservative text that stressed measure and constraint, also declared (as quoted in the next chapter): "When pursuing an enemy do not be dilatory." This statement apart, the *Ssu-ma Fa*'s chief concern seems to have been avoiding disastrous surprises: "In antiquity they did not pursue a fleeing enemy too far or follow a retreating army too closely. By not pursuing them too far it was difficult to draw them into a trap; by not pursuing so closely as to catch up it was hard to ambush them."

Conversely, Sun Pin and other writers advocated swift, decisive pursuit: "The cavalry is advantageous to pursue the scattered and strike the chaotic. The whirlwind formation and swift chariots are the means by which to pursue a fleeing enemy." However, they equally advised employing feigned retreats to destabilize an enemy and lure them into the open from entrenched positions.

A passage in the *Six Secret Teachings* discusses almost exactly the same tactics that Ts'ao Ts'ao employed in the historical illustration and offers a suggestion for coping with them:

> King Wu asked: "The enemy, knowing we are following him, conceals elite troops in ambush while pretending to continue to retreat. When we reach the ambush their troops turn back, some attacking our front, others our rear, while some press our fortifications. Our Three Armies are terrified, and in confusion fall out of formation and leave their assigned positions. What should we do?"
>
> The T'ai Kung said: "Divide into three forces, then follow and pursue them, but do not cross beyond their ambush. When all three forces have arrived, some should attack the front and rear, others should penetrate the two flanks. Make your commands clear, choose your orders carefully. Fervently attack, advancing forward, and the enemy will certainly be defeated."

As recorded above, Ts'ao Ts'ao also pointed out an important reason for not obstructing (versus attacking) an army in retreat: it would force them into a hopelessly confined situation tantamount to fatal terrain, just the conditions that the Chinese military theorists felt would elicit an army's ultimate effort, as already discussed in Chapter 51, "Fighting to the Death." This would clearly be contrary to the pursuer's best interests and to all advice concerning a besieged enemy. As the T'ai Kung said, "Leave them a passage to entice them to flee." Had his words been heeded at the battle of Manila at the end of World War II, the remaining Japanese forces would probably have fled rather than mount the desperate defense with makeshift weapons that resulted in horrendous civilian casualties and the city's destruction.

76 Pursuits 逐

Tactical Discussion

Whenever racing after a fleeing enemy or pursuing a retreating one, you must distinguish real and feigned withdrawals. If their flags are well ordered and their drums responsive, while their commands and orders are unified, even though they appear to be retreating in chaos and confusion, it is not a true defeat but certainly an unorthodox tactic. You should ponder it for some time before taking any action. However, if their flags are confused and disordered and the response of their large and small drums discordant, while their commands and orders are shouted and clamorous and not at all unified, this truly is a defeated, terrified army that should be vigorously pursued. A tactical principle from the *Ssu-ma Fa* states: "Whenever pursuing an enemy do not be dilatory. However, if the enemy should stop along the road then contemplate it well."

Historical Illustration

In the first year of the Wu-te reign period of the T'ang dynasty, T'ang T'ai-tsung went forth on campaign against Hsüeh Jen-kao. General Tsung Lo-hou resisted him, but T'ang T'ai-tsung badly defeated Tsung at Ch'ien-shui-yüan and then led his cavalry to pursue them, racing to Kao-chih where they encircled Hsüeh Jen-kao. Many of Hsüeh's generals came out to the T'ang lines and surrendered. They then wanted to go back and retrieve their horses, which the T'ai-tsung permitted. Shortly thereafter they indeed returned riding their own horses. From this the T'ai-tsung truly understood Hsüeh Jen-kao's strategic situation and therefore advanced his troops to close the encirclement. Thereafter he allowed several persuasive officials to go and point out the relative benefits and disadvantages of surrendering and fighting, after which Hsüeh Jen-kao eventually submitted.

The T'ai-tsung's generals all congratulated him and then inquired: "Great king, after initially defeating the enemy you abandoned the infantry and without any siege equipment raced along the shortest route to directly press the city's fortifications. We all doubted we could conquer the enemy, so how did it come about that they surrendered?" The T'ai-tsung said: "It was a matter of the tactical imbalance of power. Moreover, the soldiers that Tsung Lo-hou commanded were all men from this area, so that even though we defeated them, we did not kill or capture many of them. However, if we proceeded slowly then they would all have entered the city where Hsüeh Jen-kao would have gathered and inspired them, so they wouldn't have been easy to conquer. By pressing them their soldiers scattered throughout the area and the city of Kao-chih was itself empty. Once Hsüeh Jen-kao lost heart and lacked any time to make tactical plans, he grew frightened and surrendered."

Commentary

This is the second chapter on the dangers of pursuing a retreating force; the main commentary is appended to the preceding chapter. However, the method for determining whether a retreat is real or feigned, described in the tactical discussion, reflects the general principle that good order always underlies a facade, whereas true disorder indicates real confusion and an opportunity to be exploited. (Apparently the theoreticians felt that armies were incapable of successfully feigning disorder to this degree, so any appearance would only be superficial.) For example, the T'ai Kung advised:

> Indications of victory or defeat will be first manifest in their spirit. The enlightened general will investigate them, for they will be evidenced in the men. When their formations are not solid; their flags and pennants confused and entangled

> with each other; they go contrary to the advantages of high wind and heavy rain; their officers and troops are terrified; and their *ch'i* broken while they are not unified. Their war horses have been frightened and run off; their military chariots have broken axles. The sound of their gongs and bells sinks down and is murky; the sound of their drums is wet and damp. These are indications foretelling a great defeat.

Wu Ch'i also described a number of manifestations that would indicate whether an army was well commanded or disordered, whether they were executing preplanned tactics, such as feigned movements, or actually suffering from internal chaos:

> If the enemy approaches in reckless disarray, unthinking, if their flags and banners are confused and in disorder, and if the men and horses frequently look about, then one unit can attack ten of theirs, invariably causing them to be helpless.
>
> If you want to understand an enemy general, order some courageous men from the lower ranks to lead some light shock troops to test him. When the enemy responds, they should concentrate on running off instead of trying to gain any objective. Then analyze the enemy's advance, whether their actions, such as sitting and standing, are in unison and their organization well preserved. Whether, when they pursue your retreat, they feign being unable to catch you, or when they perceive easy gain they pretend not to realize it. A commander like this may be termed a wise general. Do not engage him in battle.
>
> If their troops approach yelling and screaming, their flags and pennants in confusion, while some of their units move of their own accord and others stop, some weapons held vertically, others horizontally—if they pursue our retreating troops as if they are afraid they won't reach us or seeing advantage are afraid of not gaining it, this marks a stupid general. Even if his troops are numerous they can be taken.

Since the flags and drums conveyed the commander's orders throughout the army, any confusion in them was invariably viewed as a mark of true disorder.

77 Refusing Battle 不

Tactical Discussion

Whenever engaging in battle, if the enemy is numerous while you are few, if the enemy is strong while you are weak, it is not strategically advantageous for the army. If the enemy has come from afar but their supply lines are unbroken, it is also not advantageous. In both cases you cannot engage them in battle but should instead solidify your walls and maintain a prolonged defense in order to fatigue them, for then the enemy can be destroyed. A tactical principle from the *Art of War* states: "Not engaging in combat lies with us."

Historical Illustration

In the Wu-te reign period of the T'ang Dynasty, the T'ai-tsung led the army east across the Yellow River to extirpate Liu Wu-chou. At that time seventeen-year-old Li Tao-tsung, king of Chiang-hsia, who had accompanied the campaign, ascended the walls of Yü-pi fortress to observe the rebel formations. T'ang T'ai-tsung, looking about, saw him and asked: "The brigands, relying upon their large numbers, have come to intercept and engage us in battle. What do you think we should do?" He replied: "These brigand regiments cannot be directly opposed. Employing tactics to subjugate them should be easy, but using force to fight them would be difficult. We should immediately deepen our moats and raise the height of our fortifications in order to blunt their front. They are like a flock of birds temporarily assembled, unable to long endure. Soon the supplies they brought in will be exhausted and they will scatter by themselves. You should be able to capture them without any fighting." The T'ai-tsung said: "What you have perceived accords with my thoughts." Subsequently the enemy's food indeed became exhausted and they escaped during the night. The T'ai-tsung pursued them into Chieh-chou where they were defeated in a single engagement and fled.

Commentary

The interrelated issues of attack and defense are again pondered in this and the succeeding two chapters. The tactical discussion begins by positing two conditions already raised in earlier chapters—being outnumbered (Chapter 12) and confronting a stronger foe (Chapter 20)—whose extensive commentary need not be repeated. Furthermore, "The Guest" (Chapter 18), in characterizing the invader's psychology, pointed out that deep penetration increases the soldier's resolve, making them more formidable fighters. The continuation of adequate supplies further augments their strategic power, the latter always being a combination of brute force, human spirit, material resources, and position. Accordingly, the tactical discussion advises adopting a defensive posture, a method that requires, as the T'ai Kung said, "deep moats, high ramparts, and large reserves of supplies in order to sustain your position for a long time."

The historical incident similarly describes T'ang T'ai-tsung's successful adoption of a temporizing strategy, contrary to his usual dynamic, straightforward attacks. As the principles underlying this approach have been thoroughly discussed in the earlier chapters entitled "Response" and "Security," little need be added.

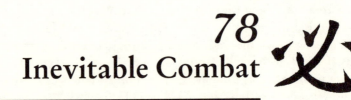

78 Inevitable Combat 必

Tactical Discussion

Whenever mobilizing an army and penetrating deep within an enemy's borders, if their walls are solid and they refuse to engage you in battle, wanting to fatigue you, you should segment and employ your regiments to attack their army. Pound their home base, cut off their routes of return, and sever their supply lines. When they reach the point that combat becomes unavoidable, you should strike them with your fiercest troops, for then they will be defeated. A tactical principle from the *Art of War* states: "If I want to engage in combat, even though the enemy has deep moats and high ramparts, he cannot avoid doing battle because I attack objectives he must rescue."

Historical Illustration

During the Three Kingdoms period, in the third year of the Ching-ch'u reign period, Emperor Ming of Wei summoned Ssu-ma Yi to Ch'ang-an and had him take command of an army to venture out to Liao-tung and extirpate Kung-sun Yüan. The emperor first inquired: "To mount a campaign of rectification that requires traversing some four thousand miles, even though you may speak about employing cavalry, it will still require great energy, developing tactics, and expenditures for supplies and provisions. What tactics do you believe Kung-sun Yüan might employ?"

Ssu-ma Yi replied: "Abandoning the city of Hsiang-p'ing and departing in advance of our arrival would be the best strategy, while deploying in Liao-tung to resist our great army would be next best. Remaining ensconced to defend Hsiang-p'ing will result in his capture."

The emperor asked: "Among these three, which one will he adopt?"

Ssu-ma Yi replied: "Only the wise are able to analyze both the enemy and themselves and abandon a course of action before it unfolds. Kung-sun Yüan is incapable of this."

"How long will the campaign require?"

Ssu-ma Yi said: "Going out there will require a hundred days, returning a hundred days, the assault a hundred days, and resting sixty days, so a year will be sufficient."

Thereafter he advanced the army. Kung-sun Yüan dispatched his generals in command of several tens of thousand of infantry and cavalry to encamp in Liao-tung, constructing a perimeter moat some twenty miles in circumference. Ssu-ma Yi's generals wanted to mount a sudden attack, but Yi resisted: "His measures are designed to wear out our army. If we attack them, we will fall into his plans. This is the strategy through which Wang Yi was shamed at K'un-yang. Since their great mass of troops are here, their home base is empty and vacuous. If we proceed directly to Hsiang-p'ing, we will be going forth where they do not expect it and their destruction will be certain." Then he had the army increase the number of flags and pennants and proceed as if he was about to go south. The brigands sent their elite troops forth to counter him. Ssu-ma Yi secretly abandoned his confrontation with the rebels and raced directly to Hsiang-p'ing, defeating the external forces and besieging Hsiang-p'ing itself.

His staff officers asked leave to attack it, but Ssu-ma Yi would not give his assent. Chien Kuei said: "Formerly, when you assaulted Shang-yung, within ten days you destroyed the solid city walls and executed Meng Ta. Today we have come so far, but you are even more tranquil and leisurely. I really am confused about this." Ssu-ma Yi replied: "Meng Ta's troops were few while he had a year's supply of food. Yüan's army is four times as large as Meng Ta's, but their supplies will not last a month. When, by just expending a month, we could successfully attack someone holding provisions for a year, why wouldn't we have acted quickly? If we could attack them with an advantageous ratio of four to one, even if we lost half our troops but were victorious, we should still do it. This approach of course focuses upon the question of supplies without calculating the number of dead and wounded. How much the more so when the rebels are numerous while we are few, the rebels are hungry while we are well fed. Moreover, right now rain still floods the land, while our assault equipment is not prepared, so why should we press forward? Since we set forth on campaign from the capital I have not been worried about the rebels attacking, only about them running off. Now their provisions have been wastefully exhausted but our encirclement has not been completely put in place. If we plunder their cattle and horses and confiscate their fodder and vegetables, this will certainly push them to depart. Now warfare is the Tao of deceit, and one who excels changes with the unfolding of events. The rebels are foolishly relying upon their large numbers, so even though they suffer from extreme hunger, they are unwilling to submit. We should manifest an appearance of incapability in order to put them at ease. If we, for the sake of some small advantage, frighten them, it would not be a good plan."

Later the rains finally stopped, so they built siege equipment to assault Hsiang-p'ing, the arrows and stones then falling like rain. The city's provisions having been exhausted, the defenders' distress was so extreme they were on the point of resorting to cannibalism. Thereupon Kung-sun Yüan had two of his generals—Wang Chien and Liu Fu—go out to request terms and that the siege be lifted. When Ssu-ma Yi and the two generals, ruler and subjects, confronted each other, Ssu-ma Yi beheaded them. Kung-sun Yüan suddenly sallied forth through the encirclement, and Ssu-ma Yi again pursued him up to Ti-shui where he killed him and subsequently pacified the Liao region.

Commentary

This chapter mirrors the previous one: Instead of defusing a strong, well-supplied invasion force with a temporizing strategy, the invader needs to provoke the defender into battle. Therefore, the aggressor must harass, threaten, and anger the local troops to force them out of their strongholds and defeat their stalling tactics. Manipulating an enemy in this fashion requires imaginative techniques and the thoroughgoing application of many of the principles previously discussed, including "seize what they love." However, as the underlying theory has been extensively reviewed in the chapter entitled "Offense" and other selections, additional explication is unnecessary.

The lengthy historical illustration contains a reference to Ssu-ma Yi's quick triumph over Meng Ta, a campaign fully described in Chapter 68, "Quickness," and again the focus of the historical illustration for Chapter 69, "Order." The logic of mounting rapid versus slow assaults against besieged forces has also been fully explored in the tactical discussions for Chapters 67 and 68, "Slowness" and "Quickness," and further detailed by Mu-jung Ch'ieh's analysis in the former's historical illustration and may be reviewed for basic doctrine.

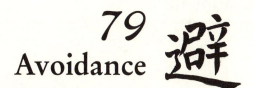

79 Avoidance 避

Tactical Discussion

In general, whenever engaging a strong enemy in battle while your own power is weak, if their spirit is sharp when they initially come forth and it will be difficult to withstand them, you should avoid them. If you watch for them to become fatigued and then suddenly strike, you will be victorious. A tactical principle from the *Art of War* states: "Avoid their ardent spirit, strike when it becomes indolent or declines."

Historical Illustration

During the sixth year of the Chung-p'ing reign period in the Later Han Dynasty, Wang Kuo, in command of rebellious forces from Liang-chou, besieged Chen-ts'ang. Emperor Ling dispatched Huang-fu Sung to extirpate them. Tung Cho suggested that they rapidly advance, but Huang-fu said: "Winning a hundred victories in a hundred battles is not as good as forcing them to submit without fighting. One who excels at employing the army first establishes himself in a position where he cannot be conquered in order to await the moment when the enemy can be conquered. Although Chen-ts'ang is a small city, it is solidly prepared and cannot yet be taken. When Wang Kuo strongly assaults Chen-ts'ang and it does not surrender, his troops will certainly be fatigued. Attacking the fatigued is the way to attain complete victory."

Wang Kuo besieged and assaulted the city, but in the end it did not fall. His troops were tired and fatigued, so he released the siege and withdrew. Huang-fu Sung then advanced his army, pursued, and struck him. Tung Cho said: "Do not pursue exhausted invaders, do not intercept an army retreating homeward." Huang-fu retorted, "It is not so." Then without Tung Cho he pursued Wang Kuo, striking and destroying him. Because of this Tung Cho had an embarrassed look.

Commentary

The tactical discussion reconsiders a fundamental principle already well discussed in the chapters entitled "Security" and "Spirit"—avoiding a strong, highly motivated enemies until their spirit abates and they become fatigued—that may be consulted for detailed explication. Of greater interest, however, are the statements from Sun-tzu's *Art of War* embedded in the dialogue found in the historical illustration, further evidence that by the third century A.D. Sun-tzu's book was thoroughly studied and frequently committed to memory. Huang-fu Sung's explanation begins with a famous, slightly abridged, quote from "Planning Offensives": "Winning a hundred victories in a hundred battles is not as good as forcing them to submit without fighting." He then continues with a sentence from "Military Disposition": "One who excels at employing the army first establishes himself in a position where he cannot be conquered in order to await the moment when the enemy can be conquered." Clearly, Huang-fu Sung not only read the text but also embraced the philosophy of winning without fighting, of destroying the enemy through tactical manipulation and the enlightened exploitation of strategic power.

The ultimate result of Huang-fu Sung's efforts also raises intriguing questions about the tactical principles previously discussed in Chapters 75 and 76, "Retreats" and "Pursuits" respectively. Tung Cho quotes the *Ssu-ma Fa*'s well-known assertion about intercepting and obstructing retreating forces, but Huang-fu Sung disparages his advice and mounts a rapid pursuit that ultimately destroys the enemy. Huang-fu thus opted to exploit a perceived opportunity rather than concern himself with the potential danger of traps and ambushes, no doubt based upon his evaluation of the invader's debilitated condition and the minor possibility of the withdrawal being a ruse.

80 Sieges 圍

Tactical Discussion

In general the Tao for conducting siege warfare is to encircle the enemy on all four sides but leave a corner open in order to display a route to life. If you are able to cause the enemy's fighting not to be stalwart, the city can be taken and their army defeated. A tactical principle from the *Art of War* states: "If you besiege an army, you must leave an outlet."

Historical Illustration

At the end of the Later Han dynasty, Ts'ao Ts'ao of Wei surrounded Huguan. Although he assaulted it, he could not take it. Ts'ao Ts'ao then announced that after he took the city, he would bury everyone in a great mound. For days on end the city would not surrender.

Ts'ao Jen said to Ts'ao Ts'ao: "When you besiege a city you must show them a gate to life in order to give them a route out and hope to live. Your announcement that they will all be buried has now caused every man to staunchly defend his position. Moreover, the city walls are solid and their provisions ample. If you assault it, our officers and troops will be wounded; if you merely continue the siege, it will go on interminably. Throwing away your soldiers against the solid city walls, assaulting a foe who will certainly fight to the death, is not a good strategy." Ts'ao Ts'ao followed his advice and was soon able to reduce the city.

Commentary

The main parameters for determining whether to mount an assault or simply besiege a city or encampment have already been raised in the tactical discussions and historical illustrations for Chapters 67 and 68, "Slowness" and "Quickness," and the extensive quotations from the classical texts noted in their commentaries may be consulted. This chapter focuses upon the inadvisability of applying viselike pressure to besieged forces because it was generally believed that "fatal terrain" would elicit an ultimate effort. Therefore, employing excessively constrictive tactics could only be considered a colossal blunder. (However, note that in the *Wei Liao-tzu* passage on the psychology of defenders quoted at length in Chapter 68, raising the morale and stimulating such effort in men condemned to certain death was neither easy nor invariably attainable. The normal tendency to despair described by the *Wei Liao-tzu*—a reaction that the Mongols and other conquerors so effectively exploited with campaigns of terror—seriously belies the traditional viewpoint even though the chapter's historical illustration gives it credence.)

Generally speaking, military thinkers from the T'ai Kung (such as in "Certain Escape" and "Urgent Battles" in the *Six Secret Teachings*) through the T'ang all encouraged enervating the enemy by undermining their resolve with highly visible prospects for life and continuing hope for escape. The psychology was identical to that underlying the principle of never obstructing a retreating army nor fully cornering an opponent, whether in the field or encamped. Sieges were among the typical situations analyzed by the T'ai Kung, such as this one in which he advises leaving an outlet to entice the enemy to flee:

> King Wu inquired: "Suppose that when the supplies inside the city are cut off, external forces being unable to transport anything in, they clandestinely make a covenant and take an oath, concoct secret plans, and then sally forth at night, throwing all their forces into a death struggle. Some of their chariots, cavalry, and elite troops assault us from within, others attack from without. The officers and troops are confused, the Three Armies defeated and in chaos. What should be done?"
>
> The T'ai Kung said: "In this case you should divide your forces into three armies. Be careful to evaluate the terrain's configuration and then strategically emplace them. You must know in detail the location of the enemy's second army, as well as his large cities and secondary fortifications. Leave them a passage in order to entice them to flee. Pay attention to all the preparations, not neglecting anything. The enemy will be afraid, and if they do not enter the moun-

tains or the forests, they will return to the large towns, or run off to join the second army. When their chariots and cavalry are far off, attack the front; do not allow them to escape. Since those remaining in the city will think that the first to go out have a direct escape route, their well-trained troops and skilled officers will certainly issue forth, with the old and weak alone remaining. When our chariots and cavalry have deeply penetrated their territory, racing far off, none of the enemy's army will dare approach. Be careful not to engage them in battle; just sever their supply routes, surround and guard them, and you will certainly outlast them."

Another passage in the *Wei Liao-tzu* identifying several factors that make a city vulnerable to siege and assault operations preserves a similar assertion:

> When the general is light, the fortifications low, and the people's minds unstable, they can be attacked. If the general is weighty and the fortifications are high, but the masses are afraid, they can be encircled. In general, whenever you encircle someone you must provide them with a prospect for some minor advantage, causing them to become weaker day by day. Then the defenders will be forced to reduce their rations until they have nothing to eat. When their masses fight with each other at night they are terrified. If the masses avoid their work, they have become disaffected. If they just wait for others to come and rescue them, and when the time for battle arrives they are tense, they have all lost their will and are dispirited. Dispirit defeats an army; distorted plans defeat a state.

Thus inducing a state of dispirit among the defenders will hasten victory and minimize the losses that might be incurred.

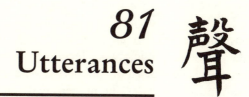

81 Utterances 聲

Tactical Discussion

In general, in warfare what is termed "utterances" refers to making some specious statement. For example, if you speak about attacking the east but instead strike the west, if you target those but attack these, you cause the enemy's forces not to know where to prepare their defenses. Therefore, the location you attack will inevitably be undefended. A tactical principle from the *Art of War* states: "When someone excels at attacking, the enemy does not know where to mount his defense."

Historical Illustration

In the fifth year of Chien-wu reign period of the Later Han dynasty, Keng Yen and Chang She opposed each other. Chang She dispatched his younger brother Chang Lan in command of twenty thousand picked troops to defend Hsi-an while the protector generals for several commanderies, with their combined forces of more than ten thousand men under Chang She himself, defended Lin-tzu. The two cities were some forty miles apart. Keng Yen advanced his army to Hua-chung, which lay between the two objectives. He observed that although Hsi-an was a small city it was well fortified and Lan's soldiers were all elite troops as well. Conversely, although Lin-tzu was large, it could easily be attacked. Thereupon he convened his subordinates to inform them that they would attack Hsi-an in five days. When Chang Lan learned of this, Hsi-an embarked on preparations day and night.

At the designated time, Keng Yen ordered his generals to have all their troops fed in the middle of the night and assemble at first light to go to Lin-tzu. Hsün Liang of the Defensive Brigade and others contested this decision, believing it would be more appropriate to quickly attack Hsi-an. Keng Yen said: "Hsi-an heard that we want to attack, so they have been making defensive preparations day and night. However, in striking Lin-tzu we will be going forth where they do not expect it, so our arrival will certainly startle and confuse them. If we assault the city, we can seize it within a day. Once we take Lin-tzu, Hsi-an will stand alone. When Chang Lan is cut off from Chang She, he will certainly flee by himself. This is what is referred to as 'striking one and gaining two.' In contrast, if we unsuccessfully attack Hsi-an, we will have thrown our soldiers against their solid walls and the dead and wounded will surely be numerous. Even if we succeed in seizing it, Chang Lan will just rush his soldiers back to Lin-tzu, where the power of their two armies will be united and they can then make strategic plans against us. We have penetrated deep into enemy territory and lack supply lines to the rear. If we do not fight within a week, we will be in difficulty. What you gentlemen have suggested is inappropriate." Thereupon he attacked Lin-tzu, took it within a half day, and occupied the city itself. When Chang Lan heard about it, he indeed led his army in withdrawing.

Commentary

Misdirection has marked the conduct of warfare since conflict began. However, in Sun-tzu's conception it is merely a more specific expression of the fundamental principle of being formless, misdirection and deceit being concrete embodiments and therefore less sophisticated than formlessness itself. Of course, the average commander could barely plan and execute the normal range of ruses and simple deceptions, including facades, feints, dragging brush, feigned retreats, and false plans, such as depicted in the historical incident. Few might successfully hide the formless within the army's physical disposition despite Li Ching's appraisal of it as the highest realization.

The chapter's title, literally "Sound," can refer to any "sound" that might be employed to misdirect the enemy. Although the tactical discussion focuses upon deliberately leaking proposed plans to lead the enemy astray, any verbal announcement—such as an initial mission statement, modern news conference, or Keng Yen's openly expressed intention to assault Hsi-an in the historical incident—would equally suffice. Moreover, on a concrete tactical level the army itself might deliberately initiate a noisy advance at one location to frighten the defenders and stimulate an inappropriate response, the real attack standing ready at another site. The phrase "to speak about the east but strike the west" has long been a Chinese idiom used to refer to deliberate verbal deceptions. History's most famous example would doubtlessly be Allied strategy prior to Normandy whereby they fabricated mountains of data and leaked numerous indirect references to invading Calais, compelling the Germans to inappropriately commit their defensive strength. They thus implemented Sun-tzu's basic principle to mislead defenders:

> When someone excels in attacking, the enemy does not know where to mount his defense; when someone excels at defense, the enemy does not know where to attack. Subtle! Subtle! It approaches the formless. Spiritual! Spiritual! It attains the soundless. Thus he can be the enemy's Master of Fate.
>
> Thus if I determine the enemy's disposition of forces while I have no perceptible form, I can concentrate my forces while the enemy is fragmented. If we are concentrated into a single force while he is fragmented into ten, then we attack him with ten times his strength. Thus we are many and the enemy is few. If we can attack his few with our many, those who we engage in battle will be severely constrained.
>
> The location where we will engage the enemy must not become known to them. If it is not known, then the positions they must prepare to defend will be numerous. If the positions the enemy prepares to defend are numerous, then the

> forces we will engage will be few. Thus if they prepare to defend the front, to the rear there will be few men. If they defend the rear, in the front there will be few. If they prepare to defend the left flank, then on the right there will be few men. If they prepare to defend the right flank, then on the left there will be few men. If there is no position left undefended, then there will not be any place with more than a few. The few are the ones who prepare against others; the many are the ones who make others prepare against them.

82 Peace Negotiations 和

Tactical Discussion

Whenever about to engage an enemy in battle, first dispatch some emissaries to discuss a peace treaty. Even though the enemy assents to the talks, the way you each understand the language of the proposals is invariably not the same. Then, relying upon their indolence and laxity, select elite troops and suddenly strike them, for their army can be destroyed. A tactical principle from the *Art of War* states: "One who seeks peace without setting any prior conditions is executing a stratagem."

Historical Illustration

At the end of the Ch'in dynasty when armies were raised throughout the realm, Liu Pang entered Wu-kuan pass, wanting to strike Ch'in's forces at Yao-kuan Pass. Chang Liang said: "Ch'in's army is still strong and cannot be taken lightly. I have learned that their generals are mostly the sons of butchers and merchants, so if we tempt them with profits it will be easy. I suggest we remain among the cliffs for now." He then deputed a party to go forward and visibly make preparations to feed fifty thousand men, and moreover increased the number of flags and pennants that the army was displaying in order to feign greater troop strength. Separately he dispatched Li Sheng and Lu Chia to entice them with bribes. As expected, Ch'in's generals wanted to agree to a peace treaty, and Liu Pang similarly wanted to listen to them.

However, Chang Liang said: "It is only their generals who want to revolt against the Ch'in; perhaps the officers and troops will not be so inclined. We should take advantage of the general's laxity to suddenly attack them." Liu Pang then led his soldiers forth to mount an attack on Ch'in's army, significantly destroying them.

Commentary

The initiation of truce or peace talks during a war or crisis invariably raises hope among those who cleave to righteousness, seek to avoid warfare, or simply hope to subjugate an enemy without fighting, well serving the interests of those seeking to buy time or disguise their true intentions. Expectations of peace immediately undermine tension and therefore alertness, providing a window of opportunity for anyone unencumbered by concepts of truth, credibility, and virtue—or, in other words, "realists" fully committed to victory in the battle for survival. The practice must have been widespread because Sun-tzu—but remarkably only Sun-tzu—already felt a need to warn against succumbing to such ruses, another trick in the deceptive array available to astute commanders. (Therefore, Chapter 84, "Surrenders," admonishes the readers of the *Unorthodox Strategies* to never become negligent in such circumstances.) However, those who practice such deceptions immediately sacrifice their future credibility, although they may well claim to have sincerely raised such proposals only to encounter disagreement over their content. Should they want to surrender or seek a truce at some later date, few would be foolish enough to extend them a second opportunity to buy time and implement new tactics.

The ostensible Japanese peace mission just prior to Pearl Harbor is frequently cited as an infamous example of this ploy as well as of a failure to heed either Sun-tzu's (no doubt unknown) warning or simple common sense. Clearly a Judeo-Christian ethic (and equally a Confucian one) that prescribes trusting the words of others simply leads men astray when vital interests are at stake, probably because of a futile desire to avoid conflict. However, perhaps more astounding was Allied willingness at the end of World War II to almost blindly trust that Japan had truly accepted the terms of surrender. When the Pacific Fleet ventured into Japanese littoral waters in strength, they could have easily suffered fatal damage from a well-prepared attack mounted under just such a ploy. On the other hand, the "failure"—if any—to take earlier Japanese peace feelers seriously, frequently cited in the atomic bomb controversy by modern critics who decry their use as inhumane, unnecessary, and unjustified, would fall into this category.

83 Enduring Attacks 受

Tactical Discussion

In warfare, if the enemy is numerous while you are few and they explosively come forth to surround you, you must investigate your respective numerical strengths and dispositions as substantial or vacuous. You cannot recklessly sneak away along an easy route for fear that the tail of their army may strike you. You should deploy into an outwardly oriented circular formation and endure the enemy's encirclement. Even if there is some gap, you should plug it in order to solidify the hearts of your officers and troops. If you fervently attack outward in all four directions, you will certainly gain an advantage. A tactical principle from the *Ssu-ma Fa* states: "If the enemy is numerous, then deploy outward toward their masses and withstand them."

Historical Illustration

During the Northern and Southern Dynasties period, in the initial year of Wei's Chin-t'ai reign period, Kao Huan conducted a punitive campaign against the Ch'in colonel encamped in Hsin-tu district, Erl-chu-chao. A year later, in the spring of the initial year of Emperor Hsiao-wu's Yung-hsi reign period, Kao Huan seized the city of Yeh. Erl-chu-kuang came forth from Ch'ang-an, Erl-chu-chao from Chin-yang, Erl-chu-tu-lü from Lo-yang, and Erl-chu-chung-yüan from Tung-chün, all assembling outside Yeh. Their combined forces of some twenty thousand encamped along both sides of the Chang River. Kao Huan went forth from Yeh and paused at Tzu-mo. His cavalry did not amount to three thousand nor his infantry to thirty thousand, so he deployed into a circular formation at the foot of Han-ling mountain. He chained the oxen and donkeys together to obstruct the route back and ensure his warriors would all be committed to fight to the death. Kao Huan then selected the elite forces among his cavalry and infantry to break out from their encirclement, attacked the enemy in all directions, and went on to severely defeat the united forces around them.

Commentary

The situation hypothesized in the tactical discussion mirrors that found in Chapter 80, "Sieges," from the perspective of the besieged. In such circumstances the commander's first task is ensuring that his men are neither tempted nor hope to escape because the enemy has deliberately left a "route to life" as Chapter 80 advised; therefore, the tactical discussion advises sealing off any gaps to guarantee that the men realize the finality of their situation. Such actions fully accord with the advice found in Chapter 50, "Danger." Furthermore, the warning about the ambushing forces that would certainly await any troops moving along a proffered escape route perhaps reflects the doctrine found in Chapter 71, "Segmenting," in which a large force surrounding a smaller one should divide its troops into orthodox and unorthodox units. Of course, it was a fundamental principle that even a small force should be destabilized into motion, particularly as it is difficult for large numbers to fully engage a compact enemy. However, in "Planning Offensives" Sun-tzu advised: "If your strength is ten times theirs, surround them; if five, then attack them."

Among the approximately twenty formations historically employed (such as discussed in Sun Pin's chapter "Ten Deployments"), the circular and square were the most basic and every competent army from the Spring and Autumn period down would have been able to swiftly change from one to the other. Sun Pin believed that "the circular formation was for unifying," critical to the situation posed in this chapter, while Sun-tzu observed: "In turmoil and confusion, their deployment is circular, and they cannot be defeated." Chapter 5, "The Infantry" in the *Unorthodox Strategies,* also recommends adopting a circular formation when infantry forces come under attack from all sides and launching multiple outward attacks at the appropriate moment: "If the enemy attacks all four sides, you should redeploy into a circular formation, dividing your troops into four in order to attack them on all fronts." Chapter 4 of Sun Pin's *Military Methods* similarly describes how to employ chariots and weapons to establish emergency field fortifications that will not only provide an outward defense—as does the T'ai Kung in several situations—but also constrain the men. Conversely, Sun Pin's method for attacking circular formations (preserved in "Ten Questions") exposes the dynamics of such engagements and thus suggests the tasks confronting a defender:

> To strike an enemy that has deployed in a circular formation in order to await us and relies upon it for his solidity, the masses of our Three Armies should be divided to comprise four or five operational groups. Some of them should assault

> them and then feign retreat, displaying fear to them. When they see we are afraid they will divide up their forces and pursue us with abandon, thereby confusing and destroying their solidity. The four drums should rise up in unison; our five operational forces should all attack together. When all five arrive simultaneously, the Three Armies will be united in their sharpness. This is the Tao for striking a circular formation.

The T'ai Kung outlined additional tactical measures for escaping from similar circumstances in a chapter entitled "Certain Battles":

> King Wu asked the T'ai Kung: "If the enemy surrounds us, severing both our advance and retreat, breaking off our supply lines, what should we do?"
>
> The T'ai Kung said: "These are the most distressed troops in the world! If you employ them explosively you will be victorious; if you are slow to employ them, you will be defeated. In this situation if you deploy your troops into martial assault formations on the four sides, use your military chariots and valiant cavalry to startle and confuse their army, and urgently attack them, you can thrust across them."
>
> King Wu asked: "After we have broken out of the encirclement, if we want to take advantage of it to gain victory, what should we do?"
>
> The T'ai Kung said: "The Army of the Left should urgently strike out to the left, and the Army of the Right should urgently strike out to the right. But do not get entangled in protracted fighting with the enemy over any one road. The Central Army should alternately move to the front and then the rear. Even though the enemy is more numerous, their general can be driven off."

84 Surrenders 降

Tactical Discussion

Whenever engaging in battle, if the enemy comes forth to surrender, you must investigate whether it is a real or feigned. To be clear about distant developments you must establish scouts and lookout posts; day and night you should also continue defensive preparations, never growing negligent or lax. You must strictly instruct your subordinate generals to rigorously order the troops in order to await the enemy, for if they should then attack you will be victorious. A tactical principle states: "Treat an enemy's surrender as you would an attack."

Historical Illustration

In the second year of the Chien-an reign period in the Later Han dynasty, Ts'ao Ts'ao conducted a punitive campaign against Chang Hsiu in Wan and forced his surrender. Afterward Chang regretted his action and again rebelled, suddenly mounting a vicious sneak attack on Ts'ao Ts'ao's army. He killed Ts'ao Ts'ao's chief of staff as well as his own son Ts'ao Ang, while Ts'ao Ts'ao himself was wounded by an arrow. When Ts'ao Ts'ao moved his forces to Wu-yin, Chang Hsiu led his cavalry forward. Ts'ao Ts'ao suddenly attacked and defeated him, so Chang Hsiu raced off to join Liu Piao. Ts'ao Ts'ao said to his generals: "Our forces were much stronger than Chang Hsiu's but I erred in not taking hostages and thereby came to this. Gentlemen, note it well and hereafter never again be defeated."

Commentary

The tactical discussion essentially repeats the admonition found in Chapter 57, "Victory": "Whenever you emerge victorious after engaging an enemy in battle, you cannot become lax, but should undertake vigorous preparations night and day in order to await the enemy. Then, even if they launch another assault, since you are prepared no harm will result." Furthermore, it imputes the possibility of feigned tactics, such as advocated in Chapter 82, "Peace Negotiations," to the enemy. Accordingly, the texts and commentaries for both chapters may be consulted for collateral material.

85 The Heavens 天

Tactical Discussion

Whenever you want to send the army out on campaign and mobilize the masses to attack the guilty and console the enemy's populace, you must rely upon the seasons of Heaven. If a ruler is obtuse and their government disordered, their soldiers arrogant and the people in hardship, they dismiss and expel worthy men, they execute the innocent, while drought, locusts, floods, or hail arise in the enemy's state and your army attacks them, it will always be victorious. A tactical principle states: "Accord with the seasons of Heaven and govern campaigns of rectification."

Historical Illustration

During the Northern and Southern Dynasties period, in the initial year of the Lung-hua reign period in Northern Ch'i, Hou Chu-wei—the ruler—selected and employed perverse sycophants, such as Lu Ling-hsüan, Ho Shih-k'ai, and Han Ch'ang-luan, to govern the realm, and Chen Te-yen and Ho Hung-chieh to exercise control over planning. Each of them maintained their own personal factions, promoting their cronies outside the normal order. The laws were relaxed, official matters advanced by wealth, lawsuits were concluded through bribes, and chaotic government harmed the people. Subsequently these actions brought about the specter of drought and flooding rains, while raiders and thieves both arose. Moreover the ruler was suspicious and jealous of the other kings, so that they suffered harm even though innocent. The Counselor-in-Chief Hu Lü-kuang and his younger brother, Duke Hsien of Chin-shan, were both executed even though not guilty of any crime. Gradually the initial signs of being overturned and drowning became manifest, and suddenly the ground could be observed collapsing. Emperor Wu of the Northern Chou took advantage of the situation to mobilize his army and extinguish them.

Commentary

The tactical discussion harks back to the early Chou dynasty when warfare was theoretically undertaken only to rectify the evil and displace the perverse, thereby rescuing the common people from tyrannical and oppressive rulers. In its idealized form, the people would be but little disturbed; only the ruler and his cohorts would be charged with, and punished for, various offenses against Heaven and man, including the most heinous, "executing the innocent." An overview of the procedure, showing its apparent formality and some typical accusations, appears in the *Ssu-ma Fa:*

> The Worthy Kings ordered the rites, music, laws, and measures, and then created the five punishments, raising armored troops to chastise the unrighteous. They made inspection tours of the feudal lands, investigated the customs of the four quarters, assembled the feudal lords, and investigated differences. If any of the feudal lords had disobeyed orders, disordered the constant, turned his back on Virtue, or contravened the seasons of Heaven, endangering meritorious rulers, they would publicize it among all the feudal lords, making it evident that he had committed an offense. They then announced it to August Heaven, and to the sun, moon, planets, and constellations. They prayed to the Gods of Earth, the spirits of the Four Seasons, mountains, rivers, and at the Great Altar of state. Then they offered sacrifice to the Former Kings. Only thereafter would the prime minister charge the army before the feudal lords saying "a certain state has acted contrary to the Tao. You will participate in the rectification campaign on such a year, month, and day. On that date the army will reach the offending state and assemble with the Son of Heaven to apply the punishment of rectification."
>
> The Prime Minister and other high officials would issue the following orders to the army: "When you enter the offender's territory do not do violence to his gods; do not hunt his wild animals; do not destroy earthworks; do not set fire to buildings; do not cut down forests; do not take the six domesticated animals, grains, or implements. When you see their elderly or very young return them without harming them. Even if you encounter adults, unless they engage you in combat, do not treat them as enemies. If an enemy has been wounded provide medical attention and return him."
>
> When they had executed the guilty, the King, together with the feudal lords, corrected and rectified the government and customs of the state. They raised up the Worthy, established an enlightened ruler, and corrected and restored their feudal position and obligations.

The *Ssu-ma Fa* also enumerates some of the offenses that would precipitate punitive action:

> Those who take advantage of weak states or encroach upon sparsely populated ones will have their borders reduced on all sides. Those who murder the Worthy or harm the people will be attacked and deposed. Those who are brutal within their state and encroach upon others outside it will be purged. Those whose fields turn wild and whose people scatter will be reduced. Those who rely on the fastness of natural advantages to disobey orders will be invaded. Those who harm or kill their relatives will be rectified. Those who depose or slay their ruler will be exterminated. Those who oppose orders and resist the government will be isolated. Those who are chaotic and rebellious both within and without their borders, who act like animals, will be extinguished.

Although several of the early military writings characterized the behavior of rulers and symptoms of government about to perish or at least susceptible to attack, the *Three Strategies* preserves the most extensive condemnations:

> When a ruler's actions are cruelly violent his subordinates will be hasty to implement harsh measures. When the taxes are onerous, impositions numerous, and fines and punishments endless, while the people mutually injure and steal from each other, this is referred to as a "lost state."
>
> If administrative officials form parties and cliques, each advancing those with whom they are familiar; the state summons and appoints the evil and corrupt, while insulting and repressing the benevolent and worthy; officials turn their backs on the state and establish their personal interests; and men of equal rank disparage each other, this is termed "the source of chaos."
>
> When strong clans assemble the evil, people without position are honored, and there are none who are not shaken by their majesty; when these practices proliferate and are intertwined, they cultivate an image of virtue, establishing it through public beneficence, and they snatch the authority belonging to those in official positions; when they insult the people below them, and within the state there is clamoring and backbiting, while the ministers conceal themselves and remain silent, this is "causing chaos at the root."
>
> When the ruler regards the good as good but doesn't advance them, while he hates the evil but doesn't dismiss them; when the Worthy are hidden and covered, while the unworthy hold positions, then the state will suffer harm.
>
> When deceitful ministers hold superior positions the entire army will be clamoring and contentious. They rely on their awesomeness to grant personal favors and act in a manner that offends the masses. Advancement and dismissal lack any basis, the evil are not dismissed, and men seek gain with any appearance possible. They monopolize appointments for themselves and in advancements and dismissals boast of their own merits. They slander and vilify those of great Virtue and make false accusations against the meritorious. Whether good or evil, all are treated the same by them. They gather and detain affairs of government so that commands and orders are not put into effect. They create a

harsh government, changing the ways of antiquity and altering what was common practice. When the ruler employs such wanton characters he will certainly suffer disaster and calamity.

When Heaven turned against a ruler, numerous evil portents and disasters might be expected, and their manifestation confirmed the tyrant had lost the sanctions of Heaven. (Heaven in this sense is essentially numinous, although not personalized. However, in the military writings its primary meaning is synonymous with "seasons of Heaven," referring to seasonal and climatic phenomena such as heat or cold, wind or rain.) When the state of Chou violently overthrew the Shang dynasty, they justified their actions by citing the Shang king's perverse, debauched behavior and the need to save his populace from further suffering, but also claimed he had lost the mandate of Heaven. The *Six Secret Teachings* purportedly preserves the T'ai Kung's overview of the Shang's errors and destiny:

> Now there is the case of Shang where the people muddle and confuse each other. Mixed up and extravagant, their love of pleasure and sex is endless. This is a sign of a doomed state. I have observed their fields—weeds and grass overwhelm the crops. I have observed their people—the perverse and crooked overcome the straight and upright. I have observed their officials—they are violent, perverse, inhumane, and evil. They overthrow the laws and make a chaos of the punishments. Neither the upper nor lower ranks have awakened to this state of affairs. It is time for their state to perish.

86 The Human 人

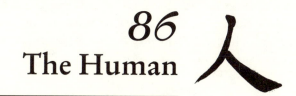

Tactical Discussion

In warfare, what is generally referred to as the "human" means that one relies solely upon men and dismisses prodigies and omens. When the army is moving forth on campaign, if owls congregate about the command flag, or if a cup of wine turns red, or a pennant staff breaks, only the commander can quash the effects of these ominous portents. If one extirpates the evil through according with Virtue, employs the straight to attack the crooked, and the worthy to strike the stupid, there should never be any doubts. A tactical principle from the *Art of War* states: "Prohibit perversity, eliminate doubt, so that they will die without other thoughts."

Historical Illustration

In the sixth year of the Wu-te reign period of the T'ang Dynasty, Fu Kung-yü rebelled, so the emperor directed Li Hsiao-kung, king of Chao Commandery, and others to mount a campaign to extirpate them. Before they were about to set out the commanders and officers gathered for a feast. The general ordered some water brought in, but the water turned into blood and everyone assembled there blanched. However, Li Hsiao-kung retained his composure and said: "No doubt this shows that Fu Kung-yü is about to give up his head!" He drank all the water and everyone was put at ease.

When they first made contact with the enemy, Fu's forces mounted skirmishing attacks on Li's army from their impregnable positions among the ravines, but Li merely solidified his fortifications and refused to go forth. However, he dispatched unorthodox forces to sever their supply routes. Soon the rebels were hungry and mounted a night attack. Li, slumbering soundly, did not move. The next day he employed some weak forces to knock against the enemy's encampment in order to provoke them into battle and separately selected elite cavalry units to await their response. Suddenly the weak troops withdrew, pursued by the rebels, who then encountered units under Lu Tsu-shang. Lu engaged and defeated them in combat, and Li Hsiao-kung immediately took advantage of the victory to destroy their remaining forces. Fu Kung-yü's position being untenable, he fled but was captured alive by cavalrymen.

Commentary

In contrast with the previous chapter that advised that signs from Heaven, such as prodigies, disasters, and eclipses, indicate that a ruler's position has become precarious, this one reflects the opposition found in most of the orthodox military writings against any credence in omens, portents, and weird phenomena because of their negative psychological effects.

In antiquity, divination always preceded the undertaking of any important state affair, especially warfare. Much of present knowledge about the Shang dynasty, including the size of their armies, organizational structure, and length of campaigns, derives from the numerous oracle writings preserved on turtle plastrons and ox bones. Even the *Six Secret Teachings,* in enumerating the commanding general's staff positions and their responsibilities, still listed three astrologers:

> Astrologers, three: responsible for the stars and calendar; observing the wind and *ch'i;* predicting auspicious days and times; investigating signs and phenomena; verifying disasters and abnormalities; and knowing Heaven's mind with regard to the moment for completion or abandonment.

Thus, from warfare's inception it and prognostication were inseparable, and they remained entangled down throughout history, both in China and the West, even though consulting omens and seeking answers through divinatory practices were frequently decried.

The greatest danger posed by omens, portents, and divinatory practices was their potential adverse psychological impact on the soldiers, for they could easily cause uneasiness, doubt, and contagious fear. Since doubt in any form was universally identified as the "greatest disaster that can befall an army," many voices were raised against allowing augury and other forms of fortune-telling (or any other distractions, such as letters from home, as discussed in Chapter 97, "Letters"). However, even when clearly mandated prohibitions were totally effective, naturally occurring chance phenomena such as eclipses, birds flying backward, and falling stars (as in the historical illustration to Chapter 49) could not be so easily stemmed. According to the *Ssu-ma Fa,* to minimize their influence commanders had to instill a level of confidence in the soldiers that would admit no doubt, that would cause them to disregard such indications:

> Whenever affairs are well executed they will endure; when they accord with ancient ways they can be effected. When the oath is clear the men will be strong, and you will extinguish the effects of baleful omens and auspicious signs. The Tao for eliminating baleful omens is as follows. One is called righteousness. Charge the people with good faith, approach them with strength, establish the foundation of kingly government, and unify the strategic power of All under Heaven.

Historically, certain famous incidents became well known wherein commanders had dramatically ignored signs foretelling doom, such as fighting on the last day of a lunar month (as already recounted in the famous battle of

Li-Che River). Li Ching, who advised retaining certain mystical practices for their potential exploitation by high-level commanders, raised one example (and also a counterexample) in these intriguing passages:

> The T'ai-tsung said: "Can the divinatory practices of yin and yang be abandoned?"
>
> Li Ching said: "They cannot. The military is the Tao of deceit, so if we apparently put faith in yin and yang divinatory practices we can manipulate the greedy and stupid. They cannot be abandoned."
>
> The T'ai-tsung said: "You once said that selecting astrologically auspicious seasons and days are not methods of enlightened generals. Ignorant generals adhere to them, so it seems appropriate to abandon them."
>
> Li Ching said: "King Chou perished on a day designated as *chia-tzu*, King Wu flourished on the same day. According to the astrologically auspicious seasons and days, *chia-tzu* is the first day. The Shang were in chaos, the Chou were well governed. Flourishing and perishing are different in this case. Moreover, Emperor Wu of the Sung mobilized his troops on a "going to perish day." The army's officers all felt it to be impermissible, but the Emperor said, "I will go forth and he will perish." Indeed, he conquered them. Speaking with reference to these cases, it's clear that the practices can be abandoned. However, when T'ien Tan was surrounded by Yen, Tan ordered a man to impersonate a spirit. He bowed and prayed to him, and the spirit said Yen could be destroyed. Tan thereupon used fire-oxen to go forth and attack Yen, greatly destroying them. This is the deceitful Tao of military thinkers. The selection of astrologically auspicious seasons and days is similar to this."
>
> The T'ai-tsung said: "T'ien Tan entrusted their fate to the supernatural and destroyed Yen, while the T'ai Kung burned the milfoil and tortoise shells yet went on to exterminate King Chou. How is it that these two affairs are contradictory?"
>
> Li Ching said: "Their subtle motives were the same. One went contrary to such practices and seized the enemy, one accorded with them and implemented his plans. In antiquity, when the T'ai Kung was assisting King Wu, they reached Mu-yeh where they encountered thunder and rain. The flags and drums were broken or destroyed. San I-sheng wanted to divine for an auspicious response before moving. This then is a case where, because of doubts and fear within the army, he felt they must rely upon divination to inquire of the spirits. But the T'ai Kung believed that rotted grass and dried up bones were not worth asking. Moreover, in the case of a subject attacking his ruler, how could there be a second chance? Now I observe that San I-sheng expressed his motives at the beginning, but the T'ai Kung attained his subsequently. Even though one was contrary to, and the other in accord with divinatory practices, their reasons were identical. When I previously stated these techniques should not be abandoned, it was largely to preserve the vital point of *ch'i* before affairs have begun to man-

> ifest themselves. As for their being successful, it was a matter of human effort, that's all."

Li Ching clearly did not believe in the power of such practices to foretell the future, but being a crafty general in Sun-tzu's mold, consistently employed every available technique to mystify his own men and thereby wrest unpredictable victories.

The *Wei Liao-tzu,* a work from the late Warring States period, begins with a famous condemnation of relying upon anything but human effort (that was later incorporated into the *Questions and Replies* as well):

> King Hui of Liang inquired of Wei Liao-tzu: "Is it true that the Yellow Emperor, through punishments and Virtue, achieved a hundred victories without a defeat?"
>
> Wei Liao-tzu replied: "Punishment was employed to attack the rebellious; Virtue was employed to preserve the people. This is not what is referred to as 'Heavenly Offices, auspicious hours and days, yin and yang, facing toward and turning your back to.' The Yellow Emperor's victories were a matter of human effort, that's all. Why was that?
>
> Now if there is a fortified city and one attacks it from the east and west but cannot take it and attacks from the south and north but cannot take it, can it be that all four directions failed to accord with an auspicious moment that could be exploited? If you still cannot take it, it's because the walls are high, the moats deep, the weapons and implements fully prepared, the materials and grains accumulated in great quantities, and their valiant soldiers unified in their plans. If the walls are low, the moats shallow, and the defenses weak, then it can be taken. From this perspective, moments, seasons, and Heavenly Offices are not as important as human effort.
>
> According to the Heavenly Offices, deploying troops with water to the rear is referred to as 'isolated terrain.' Deploying troops facing a long ridge is termed 'abandoning the army.' When King Wu attacked King Chou of the Shang, he deployed his troops with the Chi River behind him, facing a mountain slope. With 22,500 men he attacked King Chou's hundreds of thousands and destroyed the Shang dynasty. Yet, hadn't King Chou deployed in accord with the Heavenly Offices?
>
> The Ch'u general Kung-tzu Hsin was about to engage Ch'i in battle. At that time a comet appeared, with its tail over Ch'i. According to such beliefs, wherever the tail pointed would be victorious, and they could not be attacked. Kung-tzu Hsin said: 'What does a comet know? Those who fight according to the comet will certainly be overturned and conquered.' On the morrow he engaged Ch'i and greatly defeated them. The Yellow Emperor said, 'Putting spirits and

> ghosts first is not as good as first investigating my own knowledge.' This means that the Heavenly Offices are nothing but human effort."

In the *Questions and Replies* Li Ching also debunked some old superstitions that could adversely impact the army's maneuvering potential:

> The T'ai-tsung said: "The T'ai Kung has stated, 'When infantrymen engage chariots and cavalry in battle, they must take advantage of hillocks, funeral mounds, ravines and defiles.' Moreover, Sun-tzu said, 'Terrain that looks like fissures in the Heavens, hillocks, funeral mounds, and old fortifications should not be occupied by the army.' What about this contradiction?"
>
> Li Ching said: "The successful employment of the masses lies in their being of one mind. Unification of mind lies in prohibiting omens and dispelling doubts. Should the commanding general have anything about which he is doubtful or fearful, their emotions will waver. When their emotions waver, the enemy will take advantage of the chink to attack. Thus when securing an encampment or occupying terrain, it should be convenient to human affairs, that's all. Terrain such as precipitous gorges, deep canyons, ravines, and passes with high sides, natural prisons, and heavily overgrown areas are not suitable for human activity. Thus military strategists avoid leading troops into them, to prevent the enemy from gaining an advantage over us. Hillocks, funeral mounds, and old fortifications are not isolated terrain or places of danger. If we gain them it will be advantageous, so how would it be appropriate to turn around and abandon them? What the T'ai Kung discussed is the very essence of military affairs."
>
> The T'ai-tsung said: "I think that among implements of violence none is more terrible than the army. If mobilizing the army is advantageous to human affairs, how can one, for the sake of avoiding evil omens, be doubtful? If in the future any of the generals fails to take appropriate action because of yin and yang or other baleful indications, my lord should repeatedly upbraid and instruct them."

Although in this case the T'ai Kung's views surprisingly emerge as operationally superior to Sun-tzu's, the *Six Secret Teachings* still contains vestiges of prognosticatory practices, such as chapters 28 and 29, "The Five Notes" and "The Army's Indications" respectively. The former discuses a method for foretelling victory and defeat from the particular pitch pipe that resonates after the enemy has been startled in the dead of night, while the latter concludes a series of commonplace indications of strength and weakness with a paragraph for interpreting a city's character and susceptibility by its *ch'i*. In fact, *ch'i* prognostication was considered a highly developed art, one that retained currency and respectability over the centuries.

87 The Difficult 難

Tactical Discussion

In general, the essence in the Tao of generalship lies in experiencing both the bitter and the sweet with the troops. Should he encounter dangerous and difficult terrain, the general cannot abandon his troops just to save himself. When approaching difficulty a general cannot look for devious ways to avoid it, but must preserve and protect his entire regiment, living and dying with them. If he does so, how can the soldiers of the Three Armies ever forget it? A tactical principle from the *Ssu-ma Fa* states: "When you see danger and difficulty, do not forget the troops."

Historical Illustration

During the Three Kingdoms period, Ts'ao Ts'ao conducted a campaign of rectification against Sun Ch'üan and then returned. His generals Chang Liao, Leh Chin, and Li Tien, in command of more than seventy thousand troops, encamped at Ho-fei. When Ts'ao Ts'ao then went out on campaign against Chang Lu, he left a letter of instruction with the defensive commander Hsüeh Ti, marking its contents to be read only if the enemy approached. Shortly thereafter Sun Ch'üan led his troops and encircled Ho-fei so they opened the instructions which said: "If Sun Ch'üan should come, generals Chang Liao and Li Tien should go forth with their armies and engage in combat, but Leh Chin's army should act as the city's defensive force and not go out to do battle."

The three generals were puzzled by his instructions. Finally Chang Liao said: "Ts'ao Ts'ao is far off on campaign, so if an enemy arrives here it is certain we will be destroyed. That is why he gave us these instructions. However, before we engage in battle with them, we should mount a preemptive counterattack to defuse their overwhelming strategic power and thereby calm the minds of our men. Thereafter we can sustain a defensive effort. The subtle moment that determines victory or defeat lies in this one effort, so what are you gentlemen doubtful about?"

Li Tien was of the same opinion, so that night Chang Liao recruited eight hundred courageous warriors and feasted them well with freshly killed beef in preparation for a great battle the next day. At dawn Chang Liao put on his armor, and they went out to do battle. First they rushed and penetrated the enemy formations, killing several tens of the rebels and beheading two high-ranking generals. Then, loudly yelling out his own name, Chang led them to penetrate even into Sun Ch'üan's personal bodyguards. Sun Ch'üan was extremely frightened. The other troops did not know what was happening, so they ascended the heights and saw that Sun Ch'üan was defending himself with a long halberd. Chang Liao taunted Sun Ch'üan to come down but Sun did not dare move.

A number of Sun's soldiers encircled Chang Liao and his men several layers deep, but Liao broke through to the left and right, and struck fervently straight ahead until the encirclement was broken. Several tens of the men under Liao's command managed to get out of the encirclement with him, but then those remaining shouted out: "Is the general going to abandon us?" Chang Liao reentered the encirclement and aided the others in escaping, no one in Sun Ch'üan's army daring to oppose him. Their efforts consumed the whole morning and Sun's army had their spirit snatched away. Chang Liao then returned to their fortifications and had their defensive equipment put in order, thereby calming the hearts of their troops. Sun Ch'üan assaulted Ho-fei for ten days but as the city would not fall he withdrew. Chang Liao led the other generals in pursuing and striking Sun Ch'üan's army, almost capturing Sun himself.

Commentary

Chapter 13, "Love," has already discussed the need for the general to share all experiences, both pleasant and bitter, with his troops and thereby gain their emotional allegiance. "The Difficult" extrapolates the principle further, asserting that the commander must equally face danger and hardship, even lead from the front when necessary rather than command from the rear. Of course this raises the issue of effectiveness because it is difficult for a general to direct the army's complex formations and react to battlefield changes if he is deeply immersed in the fighting, a problem that plagued Greek commanders for centuries and prevented varying predetermined battlefield tactics once a battle had commenced. However, the tactical discussion emphasizes that generals should not avoid danger, because it will undermine the army's confidence and vitiate their resolve, as in the historical illustration to Chapter 52, "Seeking Life."

In general, the classic military writings stress personal leadership. For example, the *Ssu-ma Fa* states: "If you are respectful, the troops will be satisfied. If you lead in person, they will follow." The *Wei Liao-tzu* concurs, advancing the general a step further into the field: "Those who engage in combat must take leading in person as their foundation in order to incite the masses and officers, just as the mind controls the four limbs. If their minds are not incited, then the officers will not die for honor. When the officers will not die for honor, then the masses will not do battle." In the historical illustration Chang Liao not only inspired his men by leading in person, but was also the most valiant warrior in the encounter—contrary to Wu Ch'i's idea that the general should command, not wield a sword like an ordinary soldier. However, his men were committed, and as previous chapters have observed and history has frequently shown, a few committed men are able to withstand, even shatter, far larger startled and disordered enemy numbers. (It should be noted that the actual number of men at Ho-fei is unclear. Several texts state 700,000—clearly an error and certainly impossible—others only 7,000, probably far too low. The texts probably suffer from an additional multiplier for ten in the former case, and an incorrect character ["thousand" instead of "ten thousand"] in the latter, with 70,000 perhaps being the likely number. In any event Ts'ao Ts'ao's holding forces were seriously outnumbered by Sun Ch'üan, who came forth with more than 100,000 men.)

88 The Easy 易

Tactical Discussion

In general, the method for attacking an enemy is to initially target the small and easy. For example, if they have encamped and prepared to defend a number of locations, there will certainly be differences among them in power and numerical strength. You should keep their strength distant and attack their weaknesses, avoid their large numbers and strike their few, for then you will always be victorious. A tactical principle from the *Art of War* states: "Those that excel at warfare conquer those who are easy to conquer."

Historical Illustration

During the Northern and Southern Dynasties period, Emperor Wu of the Chou attacked Ch'i's district of Ho-yang. Yü Wen-jo said to him: "Ho-yang is a strategic crossroads where elite forces are concentrated. Even if we exert our full strength to encircle and attack it, I am afraid that it will be difficult to realize your desires. Conversely, in the region along the bend of the Fen River the cities are small and the mountains low, so that if we attack them they will easily be taken." The emperor did not heed his advice and in the end failed to accomplish his objectives.

Commentary

Sun-tzu's quotation, from "Military Disposition," summarizes his doctrine of maneuver and manipulation, of directing and positioning the army so that when it mounts an attack it will be virtually unopposed, the enemy's forces having been misdirected, scattered, and surprised. (These principles have already been discussed in the chapters entitled "Offense," "Defense," and "The Unorthodox," whose commentaries may be consulted for textual quotations and further explication.) In the tactical discussion's somewhat simplistic adoption of Sun-tzu's conception, one should always—and only—strike the "vacuous" while avoiding the "substantial," thereby winning victory after victory and eventually destroying the enemy. From a modern perspective that emphasizes focusing the main effort on the enemy's center of gravity, concentrating all available forces to destroy it, this approach would certainly be plodding and, even though likely to assure ultimate victory, unnecessarily tentative and wasteful. However, whenever forces strike the vacuous the resulting victory appears easily won, but only because outside observers fail to realize the tactical effort necessary to deliberately create the required situation. Thus Sun-tzu said:

> Those who excel at defense bury themselves away below the lowest depths of Earth. Those who excel at offense move from above the greatest heights of Heaven. Thus they are able to preserve themselves and attain complete victory. Perceiving a victory that does not surpass what the masses could know is not

the pinnacle of excellence. Wrestling victories for which All under Heaven proclaim your excellence is not the pinnacle of excellence. Thus lifting an autumn hare cannot be considered great strength; seeing the sun and moon cannot be considered acute vision; hearing the sound of thunder cannot be considered having sensitive ears.

Those that the ancients referred to as excelling at warfare conquered those who were easy to conquer. Thus the victories of those that excelled in warfare were not marked by fame for wisdom or courageous achievement. Thus their victories were free from errors. One who is free from errors directs his measures toward certain victory, conquering those who are already defeated.

89 Bait 餌

Tactical Discussion

In warfare what is referred to as bait does not mean that the army poisons the food and water, but is any situation in which profit entices an enemy into action. When the two fronts clash, perhaps the enemy will loose teams of cattle and horses, abandon material goods, or leave provisions and supplies behind. In every case you should not seize them, for if you do, you will certainly be defeated. A tactical principle from the *Art of War* states: "Do not take an army acting as bait."

Historical Illustration

During the fifth year of Emperor Hsien's Chien-an reign period in the Later Han dynasty, Yüan Shao dispatched an army to attack the city of Pai-ma. Ts'ao Ts'ao attacked and defeated them, killing Yüan's general Yen Liang and breaking the siege of Pai-ma. Ts'ao Ts'ao then moved the city's population to the west, but Yüan Shao pursued them. When the army and people reached the south bank at Yen ford, Ts'ao Ts'ao established a holding force within wooden palisades on the southern slopes and then ordered his cavalrymen to remove their saddles and release their horses.

At this time their baggage train from Pai-ma was just arriving and Ts'ao Ts'ao's generals accordingly thought that, as the enemy's cavalry were numerous, it would be best to return to the protection of the encampment. Hsün Yu said: "This is what is referred to as an army acting as bait, so how can we abandon our exposure?" Yüan Shao's two cavalry generals—Wen Ch'ou and Liu Pei—in command of five or six thousand cavalrymen arrived in succession. Ts'ao Ts'ao's generals advised that they should mount their horses, but Ts'ao Ts'ao resisted. After a while the number of enemy cavalry had increased even further. Someone among the enemy yelled out: "Divide and go after the baggage train," so Ts'ao Ts'ao said: "Now!" Then they all mounted their horses and loosed their attack, severely defeating them.

Commentary

The military writers frequently speak of offering "bait"—synonymous with profits and even rewards—in the two contexts of combat engagements and employing men. On the battlefield, where astute commanders consistently seek to exploit every enemy error, potential profits or advantages (as the two meanings are encompassed by the single character *li*) may be available for only a critical moment, hardly enough time to carefully analyze even the simplest situation. Generals are thus forced to act quickly, to seize the crux in rapidly evolving circumstances, and may therefore initiate actions that divert them from their main task even though apparently contributing to that effort. The possibility of capturing an enemy's supplies would, as in the historical illustration, prove particularly alluring as most campaign armies constantly suffered from deprivation and hunger. Once destabilized and compelled into fervent motion, forces become easy prey for concerted enemy attacks launched against exposed columns or disorganized cavalry. Thus Hsün Yu, although outnumbered at least ten to one in this engagement, emerged victorious by luring the enemy into moving against his supply train, an overwhelmingly tempting bait, and creating the reinforcing facade of being unprepared to undertake any protective action.

Extending apparent profit was one of the important methods for manipulating enemies and therefore structuring the battle to one's advantage, as already considered in Chapter 47, "Profit." Sun-tzu included it as a primary measure for compelling others to react as desired, saying: "Display profits to entice them" and "One who excels at moving the enemy deploys in a configuration to which the enemy must respond. He offers something that the enemy must seize. With profit he moves them, with the foundation he awaits them." The T'ai Kung, who rigorously exploited the allure of profits, said: "To be first to gain victory, initially display some weakness to the enemy and only afterward do battle. Then your effort will be half, but the achievement will be doubled." Among others, Sun Pin emphasized deluding the enemy into perceiving potential profits in visible weakness: "Deliberate tactical errors and minor losses are the means by which to bait the enemy." One of the most dangerous and unpredictable baits was a retreating army for, as already noted in "Retreats" and "Pursuits," pursing a feigned retreat could prove disastrous but neglecting to exploit a hard-won victory equally unfortunate.

90 Estrangement 離

Tactical Discussion

Whenever engaging an enemy in warfare, you should secretly await the appearance of discord among their rulers and ministers, for then you can dispatch spies in order to estrange them further. If a ruler and his subordinates become mutually suspicious and doubtful of each other, you can employ elite troops to exploit the opportunity and inevitably gain your desires. A tactical principle from the *Art of War* states: "If they are united, cause them to be separated."

Historical Illustration

During the thirty-first year of King Nan of Chou in the Warring States period (284 B.C.), the king of Yen ordered Yüeh Yi, in alliance with armies under generals from Ch'in, Wei, Han, and Chao, to attack Ch'i. They defeated Ch'i and King Min fled to Chü. When Yen learned that the king of Ch'i was in Chü, they united their forces and attacked it. Ch'u's general Nao Ch'ih, who was in Chü, wanted to split up Ch'i's territory with Yen, so he seized King Min, proclaimed his crimes, and then executed him. However, he was himself killed by the inhabitants who then stoutly defended the two cities of Chü and Chi-mo, resisting Yen's army for several months without flinching. Yüeh Yi besieged both cities, and eventually the leader of Chi-mo was slain in battle. The people within the city then acclaimed T'ien Tan as commanding general. Shortly thereafter King Chao of Yen died and was succeeded by King Hui.

When King Hui had earlier been the Heir-apparent, he frequently clashed with Yüeh Yi. When T'ien Tan learned of this, he released double agents throughout Yen who said: "Yüeh Yi and the new king of Yen have had their differences. Thus Yüeh Yi is afraid of being executed and wants to unite with Ch'i's forces to become king of Ch'i. Since the people of Ch'i will not submit to him, he is mounting a slow-paced attack on Chi-mo in the expectation that internal support will develop. The only thing that the people of Ch'i fear is that some other general will be sent, for then Chi-mo will be destroyed." The new king of Yen thought it was true, so he dispatched Ch'i Chieh to replace Yüeh Yi who then fled to Chao. From this point on there was nothing but discord among Yen's generals and officers. T'ien Tan then pretended one of his soldiers was possessed by the spirit of an other-worldly strategist and visibly offered sacrifice to him in order to gain the support and raise the spirit of the troops. Then one night he employed rows of oxen enraged by having firebrands tied to their tails to break out of the encirclement and destroy Yen's army. Thereafter he went on to restore more than seventy of Ch'i's cities and welcome King Hsiang back from Chü into the capital of Lin-tzu.

Commentary

Warfare being an enterprise undertaken by states rather than just armies, the astute employ every means at their command to gather and act upon information about their enemies. Accordingly, they not only dispatch spies to observe and collect vital data but also employ them to sow discord and undermine the enemy's ability to plan and wage war, just as Wei Shu-yü did in the historical illustration to Chapter 3, "Spies." Sun-tzu himself pointed out that spreading disinformation is one of the primary responsibilities of spies located in foreign territories, an activity expertly exploited by general T'ien Tan in this chapter's lengthy confrontation. (The battle of Chi-mo immediately became famous and remained common knowledge throughout China's long history, T'ien Tan's tactical inventiveness and Ch'i's refusal to yield providing vivid material for legends and romance. It is extensively discussed in our *History of Warfare in China, The Ancient Period.*)

The *Six Secret Teachings* contains a well-known chapter entitled "Civil Warfare," which, coupled with a few other scattered passages, resulted in the

T'ai Kung being viciously condemned and the book disparaged as a forgery because the methods and psychological techniques that he described would—the critics naively claimed—never have been employed or required by the Virtuous Chou kings to defeat the dissolute Shang dynasty. (The T'ai Kung's personal history and these charges are extensively discussed in our translation of the *Seven Military Classics,* which may be consulted for further information.) A few selected paragraphs from the *Six Secret Teachings* indicate his premises and methods for undermining enemy governments and sowing discord, although largely oriented to the historic act of overthrowing the powerful Shang dynasty:

> Become familiar with those he loves in order to fragment his awesomeness. When men have two different inclinations, their loyalty invariably declines. When his court no longer has any loyal ministers, the state altars will inevitably be endangered.
>
> Covertly bribe his assistants, fostering a deep relationship with them. While they will bodily stand in his court, their emotions will be directed outside it. The state will certainly suffer harm.
>
> Assist him in his licentiousness and indulgence in music in order to dissipate his will. Make him generous gifts of pearls and jade and ply him with beautiful women. Speak deferentially, listen respectfully, follow his commands, and accord with him in everything. He will never imagine you might be in conflict with him. Our treacherous measures will then be settled.
>
> Treat his loyal officials very generously, but reduce the gifts you provide to the ruler. Delay his emissaries; do not listen to their missions. When he eventually dispatches other men treat them with sincerity, embrace and trust them. The ruler will then again feel you are in harmony with him. If you manage to treat his formerly loyal officials very generously, his state can then be plotted against. . . .
>
> Sixth, make secret alliances with his favored ministers but visibly keep his less favored outside officials at a distance. His talented people will then be under external influence, while enemy states encroach upon his territory. Few states in such a situation have survived.
>
> Seventh, if you want to bind his heart to you, you must offer generous presents. To gather in his assistants, loyal associates, and loved ones, you must secretly show them the gains they can realize by colluding with you. Have them slight their work, and then their preparations will be futile. . . .
>
> Eleventh, block up his access by means of the Tao. Among subordinates there is no one who does not value rank and wealth or hate danger and misfortune. Secretly express great respect toward them and gradually bestow valuable gifts in order to gather in the more outstanding talents. Accumulate your own resources until they become very substantial, but manifest an external appearance

> of shortage. Covertly bring in wise knights and entrust them with planning great strategy. Attract courageous knights and augment their spirit. Even when they are sufficiently rich and honored continue to increase them. When your faction has been fully established you will have attained the objective referred to as "blocking his access." If someone has a state, but his access is blocked, how can he be considered as having the state?
>
> Support his dissolute officials in order to confuse him. Introduce beautiful women and licentious sounds in order to befuddle him. Send him outstanding dogs and horses in order to tire him.
>
> Now in order to attack the strong you must nurture them to make them even stronger and increase them to make them even more extensive. What is too strong will certainly break; what is too extended must have deficiencies. Attack the strong through his strength. Cause the estrangement of his favored officials by using his favorites and disperse his people by means of the people.
>
> If you want to cause his close supporters to become estranged from him, you must do it by using what they love, making gifts to those he favors, giving them what they want. Tempt them with what they find profitable, thereby making them ambitious. Those who covet profits will be extremely happy at the prospects, and their remaining doubts will be ended.
>
> Now without doubt the Tao for attacking is to first obfuscate the king's clarity and then attack his strength, destroying his greatness and eliminating the misfortune of the people. Debauch him with beautiful women, entice him with profit. Nurture him with flavors and provide him with the company of female musicians. Then after you have caused his subordinates to become estranged from him, you must cause the people to grow distant from him, while never letting him know your plans. Appear to support him and draw him into your trap. Don't let him become aware of what is happening, for only then can your plan be successful.

As the T'ai Kung said, "when these measures are fully employed they will become a military weapon."

91 Doubt 疑

Tactical Discussion

Whenever occupying fortifications opposite an enemy, if you want to launch a sudden attack against them, you should gather large amounts of grass and different branches and make your flags and pennants numerous in order to create the appearance of a populated encampment. If you force the enemy to prepare in the east and then strike in the west, you will inevitably be victorious. If you should want to retreat, create some false, empty deployments that can be left behind when you withdraw, for then the enemy will never pursue you. A tactical principle from the *Art of War* states: "Many obstacles in heavy grass is suspicious."

Historical Illustration

During the Northern and Southern Dynasties period, when Emperor Wu of the Chou went east on a punitive campaign, he used Yü Wen-hsien as his vanguard to defend Chüeh-shu Pass. At that time Ch'en Wang-ch'ün was encamped at Shih-li-ching, Grand General Yü Wen-ch'un was encamped at Chi-hsi-yüan, and Grand General Yü Wen-sheng was defending Wen-shui Pass. Yü Wen-hsien, who was also the Regional Commander, secretly said to Yü Wen-sheng: "Warfare is the Tao of deception. In erecting your present encampment, instead of setting up tents, you should cut down some cyprus trees to construct huts as this will show it will be more than just a temporary camp. Then when your army departs and the brigands arrive, they will still be doubtful." At that time the king of Ch'i segmented an army off toward Shih-li-ching, and dispatched the bulk of his forces through Wen-shui Pass. He himself led a large contingent to confront Yü Wen-ch'un. The latter reported that Ch'i's army was making a fervent attack, so Yü Wen-hsien personally led a force to rescue them, but even after their armies joined together, they were defeated and pursued by Ch'i. That night Yü Wen-ch'un evacuated his position and retreated. However, Ch'i thought the cyprus huts indicated a fully manned defensive position and therefore dared not advance until the next morning when they realized they had been deceived.

Commentary

The chapter's discussion essentially integrates principles already raised by earlier chapters into a coherent tactical measure. The fundamental intent remains implementing measures to confuse and manipulate the enemy, with the first technique being to employ flags and fabricate other outward evidence indicating that the army is ensconced in a certain location and numerically larger than it appears to be. The same principle appeared in Chapter 25, "Daylight":

> Whenever engaging an enemy in battle during daylight, you must set out numerous flags and pennants to cause uncertainty about your forces. When you prevent the enemy from determining your troop strength, you will be victorious.

Certainly Yü Wen-hsien learned this lesson well, although he obviously anticipated a need for such a ruse because of their relative strategic weakness.

The second statement—about feinting to the east but striking in the west—repeats the lessons of Chapter 81, "Utterances," as well as the chapters entitled "The Distant" and "The Nearby," making further comments unnecessary.

The tactical quotation, cited from Sun-tzu's chapter "Maneuvering the Army," is somewhat distorted by the chapter's application. The original runs: "If there are many visible obstacles in the heavy grass, it is to make us suspicious." The tactical discussion makes the simple observation that numerous obstacles are suspicious—that is, they might conceal an ambush or have some other purpose. In contrast, Sun-tzu's statement is reflexive, pointing out that the intent of such obstacles is precisely to make an army suspicious. In the former case the obstacles are essentially "discovered," in the latter they are fathomed as a ruse. Moreover, Sun Pin also suggested exploiting such techniques to cause doubt: "Spreading out the pennants and making the flags conspicuous are the means by which to cause doubt in the enemy. Analytically positioning fences and screens is the means by which to bedazzle and make the enemy doubtful."

92 The Impoverished 窮

Tactical Discussion

In warfare, whenever you are numerous and the enemy few, they will certainly fear your army's power and retreat without engaging in battle. However, you must not strongly pursue them because things that become extreme tend to revert to their opposites. It would be appropriate to constrain your forces and slowly advance, for then you will be victorious. A tactical principle from the *Art of War* states: "Do not pursue an impoverished invader."

Historical Illustration

During the Former Han dynasty, Chao Ch'ung-kuo conducted a campaign to extirpate the Hsien-ling tribe of the Ch'iang people. When the army approached the barbarians' encampment, the Hsien-ling had long been lodged together and thus grown negligent and lax. When they saw the great Han army off in the distance, they abandoned their baggage train, forded the Huang River, and withdrew. Their route of retreat was narrow and constricted, so Chao Ch'ung-kuo proceed forward at a slow pace. Someone said: "For pursuing profit the pace is too slow." Chao Ch'ung-kuo said: "These impoverished invaders cannot be hastily pursued. If we proceed slowly then they will depart without paying much attention to us; if too quickly, they will turn about and fight to the death." His colonels agreed. The Hsien-ling subsequently entered the river to escape and several hundred drowned. The remainder fled and scattered.

Commentary

This is another chapter that largely combines previous observations under the key term "impoverished." The tactics to be employed when significantly outnumbering an enemy have already been discussed in "Large Numbers" as well as incidentally in several other selections, while the problems posed by retreats have been reviewed in the chapters entitled "Retreats" and "Pursuits." However, a fundamental Taoist view has crept in, evidenced by the statement "things that become extreme tend to revert to their opposites." Nevertheless, the historical incident (which reconsiders a campaign previously recounted in Chapter 31, "Observers") strongly illustrates the successful imposition of constraint even though the final results were perhaps highly fortuitous.

93 Wind 風

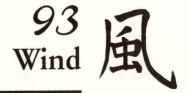

Tactical Discussion

Whenever engaging an enemy in battle, if you encounter a favorable wind, you can exploit the strategic advantage and mount a sudden attack. However, if the prevailing wind is contrary, you can unexpectedly ram an attack into the enemy and always be victorious. A tactical principle from the *Wu-tzu* states: "If the wind is favorable, exploit the strategic advantage and follow it; if the wind is contrary, solidify your formation and await the enemy."

Historical Illustration

During the Five Dynasties period, the Later Chin High Commissioner for the Suppression of Rebels, Fu Yen-ch'ing, and others engaged a Khitan force at Yang-ch'eng but were surrounded by the enemy. Their army lacked water, the well they had dug having suddenly collapsed. Moreover a strong northeast wind had arisen, allowing the enemy to exploit the wind's favorable direction to launch incendiary attacks and stir up clouds of dust to augment their strategic power. The army's officers were enraged and angrily cried out: "What kind of tactics are these? The Commissioner is wasting the lives of his officers and troops!" The generals all begged leave to fight. General Tu Wei said: "We should wait for the wind to abate somewhat, then carefully observe whether we can attack or not." Li Shou-chen said: "Amidst this wind-blown sand, although the enemy is numerous while we are few, no one knows to what extent. However, one who fights forcefully will be victorious. This really is a case where the wind's strength will assist us." Then he yelled out: "Let all the regiments attack together!"

Fu Yen-Ch'ing summoned his staff together and queried them about potential strategies. Someone said: "The enemy has gained a strategic advantage from the wind, so it would be best to wait for the wind to turn about." Fu agreed with him. However the Assistant Commissioner of the Left, Yüeh Yüan-fu, said: "The army's hunger and thirst are now already extreme. If we wait for the wind to turn, all my troops will already be in the hands of the enemy. Moreover, the enemy assumes that our armies will not go against the wind to engage in battle. Therefore we should unexpectedly go forth and fervently strike them. This is the Tao of deception." Fu Yen-ch'ing, in command of picked cavalry, then energetically attacked the Khitan force, pursuing them northward some twenty miles. When the chief of the Khitan Hsi clan had raced his chariot some ten miles away, he was suddenly attacked by pursuing cavalry but managed to get a camel and escape. Then the Chin army halted.

Commentary

Even for modern armies enjoying the luxury of such protective equipment as goggles and armored vehicles, wind and blowing sand present hidden dangers and significant obstacles to overcome, if not advantageously exploit. Ancient armies suffered even more extensively from climatic variables, such as strong prevailing winds, and sometimes perished because of their inability to counter their effects. (In "Incendiary Strategies" and the commentary to "Night" the problems of being downwind of an enemy who will exploit dry conditions to launch incendiary attacks has already been noted.) Generally speaking, armies adhered to Wu-tzu's dictum in "Controlling the Army" and refrained from attacking into the wind: "When about to engage in combat determine the wind's direction. If favorable, yell and follow it; if contrary, assume a solid formation and await the enemy." However, the tactical discussion and general Li Shou-chen in the historical illustration have both completely reversed this principle, exploiting the usual expectation that an army downwind will remain passively entrenched to boldly advocate mounting an attack. In following this advice, an imaginative commander will realize the fundamental principle of maneuver warfare, "attack when unexpected," and employ unorthodox tactics that play upon the enemy's expectations to achieve victory.

94 Snow 雪

Tactical Discussion

Whenever you and an enemy are engaged in mutual assaults, if rain or snow falls interminably and you observe that the enemy has grown unprepared, you should conceal troops in order to strike them, for then their strategic power can be broken. A tactical principle from the *Art of War* states: "Attack where they are not alert."

Historical Illustration

The T'ang emperor deputed the Military Commissioner for T'ang-teng, Li Su, to extirpate Wu Yüan-chi. Li's first action was to dispatch a general in command of more than two thousand cavalrymen to conduct a reconnaissance patrol. They happened to encounter the rebel general Ting Shih-liang, whom they engaged in battle and captured. Ting Shih-liang, one of Wu Yüan-chi's valiant commanders, had long caused problems on the eastern border so the troops all wanted to cut out his heart. Li Su assented but Ting Shih-liang never appeared fearful, and Li subsequently ordered that Ting be released from his bonds. Ting Shih-liang requested that he be given an opportunity to die in Li's service in order to repay his mercy. Li Su appointed him as a general in command of captured troops.

Ting Shih-liang spoke with Li Su: "Wu Hsiu-lin occupies Wen-ch'eng-cha and acts as the rebel's left flank. The reason government forces do not dare come near him is that he has Ch'en Kuang-hsia as his chief of planning. However, Ch'en is courageous and hasty and loves to go forth himself to wage war. I believe that if you capture him Wu Hsiu-lin will surrender by himself." Li Su heeded his advice, and after T'ieh Wen and Ch'en Kuang-hsia were captured, as predicted Wu himself surrendered. Li Su received Ch'en Kuang-hsia and queried him about strategy. Ch'en replied: "If you really want to defeat the rebels, without Li Yu it will not be possible."

Li Yu was the rebel's stalwart general, a man of courage and strategic abilities. He was defending Hsing-ch'iao-cha, and every time they went out to battle he was contemptuous of the government forces. At the time he happened to be leading his troops to cut wheat in the fields. Li Su dispatched Shih Yung-ch'eng and three hundred stout warriors to lay an ambush in the woods, and Wu Hsiu-lin managed to capture him and bring him back to Li Su. Li's generals and officers fought with each other for permission to kill him, and only Li Su treated him with the courtesies due an honored guest. From time to time Li Su spoke with him, but his subordinates were all displeased. As Li's power alone was inadequate to preserve him, he had Li Yu manacled and sent back to the capital. But first he secretly memorialized that "If you execute Li Yu, our efforts will not be successful." The emperor had Li Yu returned to Li Su, and when the latter saw him he was elated and designated him as a Commander, ordering him to wear a sword while coming in and out of headquarters.

When they first settled the strategy for defeating the forces in Ts'ai-chou, Li Su designated Li Yu, in command of three thousand quick response troops, to serve as the advance front, with Li Chung-yi subordinated to him. Li Su, as Inspector General, took command of the central army of three thousand men, while Li Chin-ch'eng directed the three thousand men serving as the rear guard. They were ordered to march east at dawn. The next day they covered sixty miles, arriving at night at Chang-ch'ai-ts'un, where they killed all the defenders. Li Su then ordered the soldiers to rest briefly, eat some dry rations, and put their cavalry equipment, bows, and edged weapons into good order. By that time it was snowing hard; the supports for the flags and pennants cracked, while the horses and men could see each other freezing to death. Everyone said they would surely die and several colonels requested that they encamp, but Li Su said: "We will enter Ts'ai-chou and seize Wu Yüan-chi." Everyone blanched. Weeping, they muttered to each other that they had certainly fallen into Li Yu's perfidious trap, but as they all feared Li Su none dared disobey him.

Around midnight the snow grew heavier so Li Su segmented his light troops to sever the rebel's support from Mount Lang and moreover cut off the bend of the Hui River and all the bridge routes, marching seventy miles until they reached Hsüan-hu-ch'eng. All around the city were duck and geese ponds, so Li Su suddenly struck the geese to startle them into raising a tumult. From the time when the people of Ts'ai-chou first rebelled against T'ang authority until then, some thirty years, no T'ang commander had succeeded in reaching the city, so the people had not made any preparations. Li Yu and a few others were the first to clamber up over the city walls and the troops followed. They slew the gate defenders and opened the gates for the troops to enter the city, leaving behind a few men to sound the watch. By the time the cock crowed the snow had stopped. Eventually they seized Wu Yüan-chi and had him sent back to the capital under restraint. Thereafter the region west of the Huai River was pacified.

Commentary

This is the second chapter to advocate exploiting adverse weather conditions to surprise an enemy who has naturally grown lax and whose soldiers are probably huddling in shelters to avoid the elements. Wind, rain, cold, and snow all present opportunities to the truly motivated, although their troops must be tough enough to endure prolonged misery and overcome deprivation. Accordingly, the T'ai Kung said : "High winds and heavy rain are the means by which to strike the front and seize the rear," while Wu Ch'i believed that any battered and distressed enemy force that had been exposed to rainy weather for a few days could be advantageously attacked. Such dedicated efforts could yield disproportionate rewards because the army attacks when—and frequently where—unexpected, as in the historical illustration, totally overwhelming the enemy to achieve startling conquests. However, Li Su's achievement in assaulting the rebel's heartland and wresting a total victory under extremely adverse circumstances must still be considered remarkable.

In the *Six Secret Teachings* the T'ai Kung analyzed the debilitating effects of extreme weather on campaign armies and provided King Wu with suggested measures for not only ameliorating them but also maintaining the army's readiness:

> King Wu asked the T'ai Kung: "Suppose we have led the army deep into the territory of the feudal lords where we are confronting the enemy. The weather has been either extremely hot or very cold, and it has been raining incessantly, day and night, for ten days. The ditches and ramparts are all collapsing, defiles and barricades are unguarded, our patrols have become negligent, and the officers and men are not alert. Suppose the enemy comes at night. Our Three Armies are unprepared, while the upper and lower ranks are confused and disordered. What should we do?"
>
> The T'ai Kung said: "In general, for the Three Armies alertness makes for solidity, while laziness results in defeat. Order our guards on the ramparts to unceasingly challenge everyone. Have all those bearing the signal flags, both inside and outside the encampment, watch each other, responding to each other's or-

ders with countersigns, but do not allow them to make any noise. All efforts should be externally oriented.

Three thousand men should comprise a detachment. Instruct and constrain them with an oath, requiring each of them to exercise vigilance at his post. If the enemy approaches, when they see our state of readiness and alertness, they will certainly turn around. As a result their strength will become exhausted and their spirits dejected. At that moment send forth our elite troops to follow and attack them."

Clearly weather conditions were much on the minds of commanders, both for the opportunities they presented and the dangers they entailed.

95 Nurturing Spirit 養

Tactical Discussion

Whenever engaging an enemy in battle, if your army has been thwarted and defeated, you must investigate the morale of your officers and troops. If their spirit is strong, then incite them and reengage in combat. However, if their spirit has waned you must nurture it for a while, waiting for the moment when they can again be employed before using them. A tactical principle from the *Art of War* states: "If you carefully nurture them and do not fatigue them, their spirit will be united and their strength will be at a maximum."

Historical Illustration

The First Emperor of the Ch'in dynasty asked Li Hsin: "If we want to seize Ch'u, how many men do you estimate it will require?" Li Hsin replied: "No more than 200,000." He then similarly questioned Wang Chien who replied: "Without at least 600,000 it will not be possible." The emperor retorted: "General, you are old! What are you afraid of?" Thereupon he commissioned Li Hsin and Meng T'ien to take command of 200,000 men and attack

Ch'u. Since Wang Chien's advice had not been employed, he returned to Pin-yang on the pretext of illness.

Li Hsin and Meng T'ien attacked Ch'u and severely defeated it. Thereafter they withdrew their armies westward, arranging to rejoin at Ch'eng-fu. Ch'u's forces followed them, proceeding for three days without pausing or resting, and then severely defeated Li Hsin's army, entered his two fortifications, and killed seven colonels. Li Hsin himself fled back to Ch'in.

The king (emperor), enraged, personally went to Pin-yang to see Wang Chien and strongly press him to assume command. Wang replied: "Your old servant is muddled and confused. However, if my great lord absolutely must employ me, without 600,000 men it will not be possible." The emperor agreed. Wang Chien took command of the army and the emperor sent him off as far as Pa-shang. When the people of Ch'u learned about of it, they mobilized all their forces in order to resist Wang Chien. Wang solidified the defense of his ramparts but did not give battle, instead allowing his officers and troops to rest, attend to their personal needs, and enjoy excellent food and drink, all in order to nurture and assure them. Moreover, he shared both the sweet and bitter with his soldiers. After a long time, he inquired: "What sort of amusements are taking place in the army?" The reply was: "Just now they competed in throwing stones and jumping obstacles." Wang Chien then said: "They can be employed in battle." Since Ch'u's forces had not succeeded in engaging them in battle, they had already withdrawn to the east. Wang Chien pursued, suddenly attacked, and shattered them. When they reached Ch'i-nan, he killed Ch'u's commanding general Hsiang Yen and subsequently defeated his troops so badly that they fled. Wang Chien then took advantage of the victory to seize and settle the cities and towns in the area.

Commentary

Chapters 95, 96, and 97 reconsider the psychology of *ch'i*, or spirit, with "Nurturing Spirit" again pondering the measures necessary to revitalize an army that has experienced frustration or defeat. Being a coherent work by a single author, the text advises essentially the same principles as advanced in Chapter 58, "Defeat," although with the emphasis now falling upon the morale and esprit de corps of one's own troops. Even the historical illustrations found throughout the *Unorthodox Strategies* offer numerous examples of armies recovering from defeat to immediately wrest victory, often (as warned against in Chapter 57, "Victory") against an enemy that had grown fatally overconfident. As the tactical discussion here observes, the critical question is whether the soldiers are dejected by defeat or remain confident enough to be incited for another effort. The enthusiasm and commitment described in Chapter 74, "Spirit," and the stages discussed in the commentary to that chapter from Sun Pin's analysis, must again be realized. Failing to attain them, failing to anger and motivate the troops as discussed in "Anger," will allow the enemy to gain repeated victories. Conversely, men expecting widespread punishments for their failure may also be shamed if they should unexpectedly not be applied and presumably roused to action, according to the *Ssu-ma Fa:*

> In cases of great defeat do not punish anyone, for both the upper and lower ranks will assume the disgrace falls upon them. If the upper ranks reproach themselves they will certainly regret their errors, while if the lower ranks feel the same they will certainly try to avoid repeating the offense.

The historical incident describes one of the great engagements fought by the state of Ch'in in 226–224 B.C. during the very last stage of their accession to ultimate power just before formally founding the Ch'in dynasty three years later. (Although the abstracted official record begins by referring to the First Emperor of the Ch'in Dynasty, he is termed the "king" at the beginning of the third paragraph because he had not yet finished consolidating imperial power or assumed the title.) By then, the very end of the Warring States period, the scope of battle had burgeoned enormously as indicated by the mobilization of first 200,000 and then 600,000 men, certainly a logistical nightmare prior to the twentieth century. Moreover, the importance of a general's ability to accurately analyze a strategic situation is also vividly evident, for Wang Chien was able to astutely estimate the force strength required, whereas Li Hsin and Meng T'ien were both overly optimistic, although they no doubt feared the emperor and didn't wish to enrage him with high numbers that might suggest they lacked confidence or ability. (At this time 200,000 men would have composed a standard operational force.) Neither paid heed to Sun-tzu's well-known discussion about calculating the number of men required to achieve an objective:

> As for military methods: The first is termed measurement; the second, estimation of forces; the third, calculation of numbers of men; the fourth, weighing relative strength; and the fifth, victory. Terrain gives birth to measurement; measurement produces the estimation of forces. Estimation of forces gives rise to calculating the numbers of men. Calculating the numbers of men gives rise to weighing strength. Weighing strength gives birth to victory. Thus the victorious

> army is like a ton compared with an ounce, while the defeated army is like an ounce weighed against a ton! The combat of the victorious is like the sudden release of a pent-up torrent down a thousand-fathom gorge. This is the strategic disposition of force.

The historical incident also illustrates a number of principles well discussed in earlier chapters. First, a commanding general must gain the soldiers' emotional allegiance by sharing pleasure and misery ("Love") and danger and security ("The Difficult") with them. Second, Wang Chien applied the principles of avoiding battle until his army was prepared, until he had rebuilt their confidence and witnessed their desire for action, as seen in such chapters as "Refusing Battle," "Avoidance," and "Defense." He thus epitomized Sun-tzu's concept of a skilled general, one who neither advances simply because he feels courageous action is expected in spite of the circumstances nor simply bends before the ruler's will.

96 Fear 畏

Tactical Discussion

Whenever engaging an enemy in battle, if there are any within the army who are fearful and afraid, who do not advance when the drums are sounded but retreat before hearing the sound of the gongs, you must pick them out and execute them in order to provide a warning to the mass of troops. However, if everyone within the army is afraid, you cannot punish them with execution. You must bestow a congenial countenance upon them, showing that there is nothing to fear, and persuade them with talk about profit and loss. Once they realize they will not die, then the minds of the masses will be eased by themselves. A tactical principle from the *Ssu-ma Fa* states: "Seize and execute deserters in order to stop fear. If they are too terrified, do not threaten them with execution but display a magnanimous countenance and speak to them about what they have to live for."

Historical Illustration

During the Northern and Southern Dynasties period, Emperor Wu of the Ch'en dynasty wanted to conduct a campaign to extirpate Wang Seng-pien, so he first summoned Ch'en Ch'ien to plan the campaign with him. At the time Wang Seng-pien's son-in-law Tu K'an was occupying Wu-hsing with a vast number of troops. Emperor Wu secretly ordered Ch'en Ch'ien to quickly return to Ch'ang-an, establish palisades, and prepare for him. Tu K'an dispatched general Tu T'ai to take advantage of the void and surprise them. When they saw Tu T'ai's forces coming, Ch'en Ch'ien's officers and generals looked at each other and blanched. However, Ch'en Ch'ien talked and laughed as before, then clearly put the deployment of the various units in order, whereupon the minds of the troops were settled.

Commentary

This chapter continues to analyze the problems of spirit or morale that arise in warfare by focusing upon the issue of fear. As all the military writers agreed, "men do not take pleasure in death" and most fear dying; therefore, the commander's critical task is rousing their anger (as discussed in "Anger") and inciting their *ch'i* (fully analyzed in Chapter 74, "Spirit") so that their fears will be overcome or displaced. As the *Ssu-ma Fa* also said: "When men have minds set on victory, all they see is the enemy. When men have minds filled with fear, all they see is their fear."

One solution, advocated in the tactical discussion and in the earlier selections entitled "Awesomeness" and "Punishments," was severely punishing cowards to deter others from deserting. However, awesomeness could become excessive; the solution could also create problems, as the *Ssu-ma Fa* noted:

> When the army excessively concentrates upon its awesomeness the people will cower, but if it diminishes its awesomeness the people will not be victorious. When superiors cause the people to be unable to be righteous, the hundred surnames to be unable to achieve proper organization, the artisans to be unable to profit from their work, oxen and horses to be unable to fulfill their functions, while the officers insult the people—this is termed "excessive awesomeness," and the people will cower. When superiors do not respect Virtue but employ the deceptive and evil, when they do not honor the Tao but employ the courageous and strong, when they do not value those who obey commands but instead esteem those who contravene them, when they do not value good actions but esteem violent behavior, so that the people insult the minor officials—this is

termed "diminished awesomeness." If the conditions of diminished awesomeness prevail, the people will not be victorious.

Furthermore, situations may arise where all the men, despite the threat of punishments (which can of course only coerce performance, not affect emotional attitude) and the prospect of rewards (which can further simulate action), are still debilitated by fear. In such cases even thrusting them onto fatal terrain will prove ineffective, so their commanders must first encourage them to think about living rather than simply despair at dying, a natural extension of the positive measures designed to stimulate the men suggested by the *Wei Liao-tzu:*

> In order to stimulate the soldiers, the people's material welfare cannot but be ample. The ranks of nobility, the degree of relationship in death and mourning, and the activities by which the people live cannot but be made evident. One must govern the people in accord with their means to life and make distinctions clear in accord with the people's activities. The fruits of the field and their salaries, the feasting of relatives through the rites of eating and drinking, the mutual encouragement in the village ceremonies, the mutual assistance in death and the rites of mourning, the sending off and greeting of the troops—these are what stimulate the people.

Naturally this entails a degree of danger and uncertainty because it was generally thought that seeking life constitutes the quickest route to defeat and death, but it may offer the only recourse. Thus the *Ssu-ma Fa* advised, "speak to them about what they have to live for." In fact, the passage preceding the tactical quotation outlines several concrete steps for managing the army's morale and coping with fear:

> In general, those soldiers who stand in their formations should advance and then crouch down; those who fire from a squatting position should advance and then kneel. If they are frightened, make the formations dense; if they are in danger, have them assume a sitting position. If the enemy is seen at a distance, they will not fear them; if, when they are close, they do not look at them they will not scatter.
>
> When the commanding general dismounts from his chariot, the generals of the left and right also dismount, those wearing armor all sit, and the oath is sworn, after which the army is slowly advanced. All officers, from the generals down to the infantry squad leaders, wear armor. Calculate the deployment of the light and heavy forces. Rouse the horses to action; have the infantrymen and armored soldiers set up a clamor. If they are afraid, also collapse them into a tighter unit. Those who are kneeling should squat down, those who are squat-

> ting should lie down. Have them crawl forward on their knees, then put them at ease. Have them get up, shout, and advance to the drums. Then signal a halt with the bells. With gagged mouths and minimal dry rations swear the oath. Have the troops withdraw, crawling back on their knees. Seize and summarily execute any deserters to stop the others from looking about to desert. Shout in order to lead them. If they are too terrified of the enemy, do not threaten them with execution and severe punishments but display a magnanimous countenance. Speak to them about what they have to live for, supervise them in their duties.

The historical illustration provides another example of how the commander's mental and emotional attitudes directly affect his men. As was well known, a commander beset by doubt undermined the entire army, while one who was afraid spawned fear in the troops. Someone who could remain composed in the face of great danger became a focal point for the soldiers, calming and inspiring them, just as Chu-ko Liang did in the historical illustration in Chapter 43, "The Vacuous."

97 Letters 書

Tactical Discussion

Whenever engaging an enemy in battle from opposing fortifications, you cannot allow your soldiers to receive letters from their families or visits from their relatives for fear that what is said will not be unified and the minds of your troops will become doubtful and confused. A tactical principle states: "When letters convey questions, the mind will have things that trouble it. When relatives visit, the mind will have things to which it is attached."

Historical Illustration

During the Later Han dynasty, General Kuan Yü of the kingdom of Shu was encamped in Chiang-ling. Just then the kingdom of Wu had Lü Meng replace Lu Hsiao as commander of the Wu forces encamped at Lu-k'ou. When Lü Meng first arrived he doubled the previous efforts at externally cultivating beneficence and virtue, and also adopted a conciliatory stance toward Kuan Yü. However, he clandestinely launched sudden strikes against Kung-an and Nan-chün, annexing them, and many of Shu's generals surrendered to Lü Meng.

When Lü Meng's forces occupied the cities, he captured the families and relatives of Kuan Yü's officers and soldiers. In every case he placated and consoled them and ordered that none of his soldiers could take anything from the households. Among Lü Meng's subordinates was an officer from his native commandery of Ju-nan who took a bamboo hat to cover an officer's helmet. Although this was for an official purpose, Lü Meng still felt it violated military ordinances and he could not, because of their common native origin, fail to apply the law. Weeping, he had the man beheaded, whereupon the entire army quaked with fear. Thereafter, no one dared even to pick up anything left on the road.

From morning to night Lü Meng had his confidants preserve and console the aged and old, inquiring about their needs. He provided medicine to the seriously ill and clothing and food to the hungry and cold. While Kuan Yü was still en route back, he dispatched men to appraise the situation. In every instance Lü Meng at once treated them well and had them brought around the towns to make inquiries among the families. When Kuan Yü's men returned to their units, the soldiers would all eagerly inquire about their families and then gave thanks that they were not suffering under the occupation and were apparently passing their days even better than normally. Accordingly, Kuan Yü's officers and men lacked the will to fight Lü Meng and Wu's forces. Just then Sun Ch'üan, ruler of Wu, also arrived with an army. Kuan Yü fled to the west, but many of his troops and the surrounding villages all surrendered.

Commentary

"Letters" proposes to resolve a common military problem—the negative effects of personal letters and visits that cause the men to think of family and home, to wonder about the tactical situation, to feel discouraged and troubled, perhaps even exploited when they realize others need not confront the hardships they daily endure—by simply banning all letters and other forms of personal contact. (Apparently the potentially positive effects such letters might have on men serving far from home were never considered.) As the psychology is essentially the same as advanced in "The Human" (with respect to omens) and mainly a variation on the theme of doubt (which debilitates armies and undermines morale), except to note that modern media, such as CNN, can equally raise doubts, further commentary may be omitted.

The historical illustration offers a somewhat different slant on the chapter's lesson, for while the soldiers were ostensibly distracted by thoughts of home, in fact it was rather a question of Lü Meng's expert implementation of psychological warfare measures undermining their will to fight. Many of Kuan Yü's soldiers originally came from the twin cities being occupied by Lü Meng's forces, and they accordingly expected their families would be enduring every sort of brutality and atrocity. However, when they learned to their relief that their families were being well treated, their fears diminished and anger deflated, so they immediately lost any incentive to rush forth and destroy Lü Meng and his forces. Lü's measures were so successful that when their armies actually clashed, Lü easily wrested a largely unopposed victory. Kuan Yü not only fled but was subsequently slain, ending his career and ambitions.

Several of the military writings advocated benevolent policies when invading and occupying enemy territory, although late in the Warring States period they were basically ignored. The fundamental intent was to defuse armed opposition if not win the allegiance of the populace. Accordingly, the T'ai Kung said:

> Do not set fire to what the people have accumulated; do not destroy their palaces or houses or cut down the trees at grave sites or altars. Do not kill those who surrender or slay your captives. Instead show them benevolence and righteousness; extend your generous Virtue to them. Cause their people to say "the guilt lies with one man." In this way the entire realm will then submit.

The *Wei Liao-tzu* subsequently expanded his thoughts:

> In general, when employing the military do not attack cities that have not committed transgressions or slay men who have not committed offenses. Whoever kills people's fathers and elder brothers, whoever profits himself with the riches and goods of other men, whoever makes slaves of the sons and daughters of other men is in all cases a brigand. For this reason the military provides the means to execute the brutal and chaotic and to stop the unrighteous. Wherever the army is applied, the farmers do not leave their occupations in the fields, the merchants do not depart from their shops, and the officials do not leave their offices, due to the martial plans all proceeding from one man. Thus even without the forces bloodying their blades, All under Heaven give their allegiance.

98 Change 變

Tactical Discussion

In general, the essence of military strategy lies in responding to change, being familiar with the past, and knowing your army. Before initiating any action you must first analyze the enemy. If a formidable enemy does not suffer any internal changes, then you must wait for them. Exploit changes, follow up and respond, for it will be advantageous. A tactical principle from the *Art of War* states: "One who is able to change and transform in accord with the enemy and wrest victory is termed spiritual."

Historical Illustration

During the Five Dynasties period, at the end of the Later Liang dynasty, General Wei Po-chen rebelled against the Liang. When General Ho Te-lun of the Liang then surrendered to the Chin, T'ang Chuang-tsung—the future Chin emperor—entered Wei-chou with his forces. General Liu Hsün of the Liang then moved his army into Hsin-hsien district, erected high ramparts and deep moats, and constructed a protected supply route to the river. The Liang emperor commanded Liu Hsün to go out and engage the enemy in battle, but Liu responded: "It will not yet be easy to attack Chin's army. I am waiting to advance and seize them. If we had encountered an opportunity when they experienced some change, would we have dared sit here worrying about harm?" The emperor dispatched another emissary to inquire what tactics he had formulated for a decisive victory. He replied: "Your servant does not have any unorthodox plans, but if you provide ten piculs of grain for every man, by the time they are fully exhausted we will have defeated the enemy." The emperor angrily said: "General, are you planning to accumulate enough grain to relieve a famine?"

The emperor again sent an emissary to supervise the battle. Liu Hsün addressed his colonels: "When a commanding general assumes sole responsibility for a campaign of rectification, there are orders from the ruler that are not accepted. Warfare is a matter of controlling change when one encounters the enemy, so how can we plan our tactics in advance? At present I believe that the enemy's spirit is flourishing, so it would be difficult to wrest an easy victory. What do you think?" His generals all wanted to go into battle. Liu Hsün was silent for a while, then ordered them all to line up outside the army's gate, gave each one a cup of river water, and ordered them to drink it. They did not yet understand his intentions; some drank, some declined. Liu Hsün then said: "If a single cup of water proves this difficult, how can you possibly exhaust the river's racing torrent?" They all blanched.

At this time the Chin army under T'ang Chuang-tsung's pressed Liu Hsün's encampment in an attack, but he still did not venture forth. The emperor dispatched several emissaries in succession to press him to fight, so Liu finally launched a powerful thrust with ten thousand men that penetrated the enemy's encampment and resulted in capturing a great many prisoners. Somewhat thereafter, Chin's main army appeared, so Liu Hsün retreated and reengaged them at Ku-yüan-ch'eng. T'ang Chuang-tsung and Fu Yen-ch'ing attacked from both sides, and Liang's army under Liu Hsün was badly defeated.

Commentary

This chapter raises the critical concept of change and the need to constantly alter tactics and revise plans in response to changes in the enemy, whether initiated or forced onto them. Sun-tzu was the first to stress the importance of change, considering it the essence of warfare, as the tactical quotation shows. Furthermore, the concept underlies his doctrine of the unorthodox, for the orthodox and unorthodox are constantly evolving, forming new combinations and taking on radically different appearances. (His doctrine was previously discussed in the commentary for Chapter 41, "The Unorthodox." Sun-tzu's integrated concepts of change and the unorthodox are mainly preserved in his chapter entitled "Strategic Military Power.")

However, Sun-tzu did not limit the concept of change solely to this context but also employed it to refer to the commander's manipulation of various configurations of terrain, as in the chapter entitled "Nine Changes." Perhaps not coincidentally, the key paragraph concludes with "there are commands from the ruler that are not accepted," exactly Liu Hsin's assertion in the historical illustration. In full, with its extended conclusions regarding the general's requisite capability in understanding and employing the changes, the section runs as follows:

> In general, the strategy for employing the military is this. After the general has received his commands from the ruler, united the armies, and assembled the masses:
>
> Do not encamp on entrapping terrain. Unite with your allies on focal terrain. Do not remain on isolated terrain. Make strategic plans for encircled terrain. On fatal terrain you must do battle. There are roads that are not followed. There are armies that are not attacked. There are fortified cities that are not assaulted. There is terrain for which one does not contend. There are commands from the ruler that are not accepted.
>
> Thus the general who has a penetrating understanding of the advantages of the nine changes knows how to employ the army. If a general does not have a penetrating understanding of the advantages of the nine changes, even though he is familiar with the topography, he will not be able to realize the advantages of terrain.
>
> One who commands an army but does not know the techniques for the nine changes, even though he is familiar with the five advantages, will not be able to control men.

The recently discovered *Art of War* tomb text contains additional, although badly damaged, material that suggests that the orders "that are not obeyed" refer specifically to the last four items: roads, armies, cities, and terrain. Accordingly, in the early tenth century A.D. Liu Hsin would have been following Sun-tzu's advice when he specifically refused to attack the enemy because "there are armies that are not attacked."

Being relatively isolated and outnumbered, Liu Hsin had chosen to adopt the familiar temporizing strategy previously discussed in "Response" and several other chapters. His failure to maintain it meant abandoning a strong position only to expose himself to enemy assaults, ultimately embracing a fatal vulnerability even though he wrested a temporary victory. The emperor's interference thus doomed a vital field army to total destruction—roughly seventy thousand men perished in the battle—while Liu Hsin barely managed to escape with a few cavalrymen. To avoid such debacles Sun-tzu had strongly warned:

> Thus there are three ways by which an army is put into difficulty by a ruler: He does not know that the Three Armies should not advance but instructs them to advance, or does not know that the Three Armies should not withdraw and orders a retreat. This is termed "entangling the army." He does not understand the Three Armies' military affairs but directs them in the same way as his civil administration. Then the officers will become confused. He does not understand the Three Armies' tactical balance of power but undertakes responsibility for command. Then the officers will be doubtful. When the Three Armies are al-

> ready confused and doubtful, the danger of the feudal lords taking advantage of the situation arises. This is referred to as "a disordered army drawing another on to victory."
>
> If the Tao of Warfare indicates certain victory, even though the ruler has instructed that combat should be avoided, if you must engage in battle it is permissible. If the Tao of Warfare indicates you will not be victorious, even though the ruler instructs you to engage in battle, not fighting is permissible.
>
> Thus a general who does not advance to seek fame or fail to retreat to avoid being charged with the capital offense of retreating but seeks only to preserve the people and gain advantage for the ruler is the state's treasure.

The *Six Secret Teachings* strongly reiterated his admonition:

> Military matters are not determined by the ruler's commands; they all proceed from the commanding general. When the commanding general approaches an enemy and decides to engage in battle, he is not of two minds. In this way there is no Heaven above, no Earth below, no enemy in front, and no ruler to the rear. For this reason the wise make plans for him and the courageous fight for him. Their spirit soars to the blue clouds; they are swift like galloping steeds. Even before the blades clash, the enemy surrenders submissively.

Finally, the *Wei Liao-tzu* made the general's independence definitively transcendent, subject neither to God, Devil, or Man:

> Now the commanding general is not governed by Heaven above or controlled by Earth below or governed by men in the middle. Thus weapons are evil implements. Conflict is a contrary virtue. The post of general is an office of death. Thus only when it cannot be avoided does one employ them. There is no Heaven above, no Earth below, no ruler to the rear, and no enemy in the front. The unified army of one man is like the wolf and tiger, like the wind and rain, like thunder and lightning. Shaking and mysterious, All under Heaven are terrified by it.

99 Enthralled with Warfare 好

Tactical Discussion

The army is an inauspicious instrument, warfare a contrary Virtue. Only when it is absolutely unavoidable should they be employed. You cannot, because the state is large and the populace numerous, exhaust all your sharpness in expeditions and attacks, fighting and exterminating without end until finally being defeated and perishing when regret will be useless. Yet, the army is like fire: if you don't eventually extinguish it, you will suffer the misfortune of burning yourself. If you constantly pursue the martial and exhaust the army, disaster will come in an instant. A principle from the *Ssu-ma Fa* states: "Even though a state may be vast, those who love warfare will inevitably perish."

Historical Illustration

Emperor Yang of the Sui dynasty, when the state was vast and the population numerous, loved the martial and was enthralled with warfare. Every day he flourished shields and halberds, conducting expeditions and attacks without interruption. But when circumstances changed and his armies were badly defeated in Korea, a disaster brought about by the imperial court, didn't he become the laughingstock of later generations! Truly, one who would be a ruler of men must be cautious.

Commentary

The *Unorthodox Strategies* closes with two chapters expanding a famous pair of sentences found in the *Ssu-ma Fa:* "Even though a state may be vast, those who love warfare will inevitably perish. Even though calm may prevail under Heaven, those who forget warfare will certainly be endangered." (The author split the lesson into two, perhaps to better stress the correlated aspects. Both are commonly found throughout the military classics and in many of the philosophical writings, but the government's view, as expressed and held by the literati staffing the bureaucracy in their constant tension with the emperor, fluctuated over the ages, generally inclining to the fatal error of "forgetting warfare.") Moreover, the discussion's initial words are from the great Taoist philosophic classic, the *Tao Te Ching,* no doubt borrowed to emphasize the inauspicious nature of warfare.

The military theorists, perhaps because of their personal experience of the horror and miseries of warfare, frequently included reminders about the danger of being deluded with aggressive campaigns as an incontestable means to profit and glory. Naturally, as material civilization advanced and the rewards for victory rapidly escalated—both for aggressive states and their individual soldiers—their warnings were less heeded. Perhaps the most famous statement on the dual aspects of warfare and the need for a balanced understanding is the *Art of War*'s opening sentence: "Warfare is the greatest affair of state, the basis of life and death, the Tao to survival or extinction." A century and a half later Sun Pin summarily expanded his ancestor's thoughts:

> Victory in warfare is the means by which to preserve vanquished states and continue severed generations. Not being victorious in warfare is the means by which to diminish territory and endanger the altars of state. For this reason military affairs cannot but be investigated. Yet one who takes pleasure in the military will perish, and one who finds profit in victory will be insulted. The military is not something to take pleasure in; victory not something through which to profit.

Sun-tzu decried prolonged campaigns because they economically debilitated the state, but he also warned against wantonly mobilizing the army:

> If it is not advantageous, do not move. If objectives cannot be attained, do not employ the army. Unless endangered, do not engage in warfare. The ruler cannot mobilize the army out of personal anger. The general cannot engage in battle because of personal frustration. When it is advantageous, move; when not advantageous, stop. Anger can revert to happiness, annoyance can revert to joy, but a vanquished state cannot be revived; the dead cannot be brought back to life. Thus the unenlightened ruler is cautious about it; the good general respectful of it. This is the Tao for bringing security to the state and preserving the army intact.

The *Wei Liao-tzu* echoed his views: "The army cannot be mobilized out of personal anger. If victory can be foreseen, then the troops can be raised. If victory cannot be foreseen, then the mobilization should be stopped."

Virtually everyone agreed, at least in theory, that frequent battles deplete a state, and—surprisingly—that numerous victories equally prove injurious. Thus even the great Wu Ch'i, who reputedly went undefeated in scores of encounters, said:

> Being victorious in battle is easy, but preserving the results of victory is difficult. Thus it is said that among the states under Heaven that engage in warfare those who garner five victories will meet with disaster, those with four victories will be exhausted, those with three victories will become hegemons, those with two victories will be kings, and those with one victory will become emperors. For this reason those who have conquered the world through numerous victories are extremely rare, while those who thereby perished are many.

Accordingly, Sun Pin also remarked:

> The army's victory lies in selecting the troops. Its courage lies in the regulations. Its skill lies in the strategic configuration of power. Its sharpness lies in trust. Its power lies in the Tao. Its wealth lies in a speedy return. Its strength lies in giving rest to the people. Its injury lies in frequent battles.
>
> If in ten battles someone is victorious six times, it is due to the stars. If in ten battles someone is victorious seven times, it is due to the sun. If in ten battles someone is victorious eight times, it is due to the moon. If in ten battles someone is victorious nine times, the moon has sustained him. If in ten battles someone is victorious ten times, the general excels, but it leads to misfortune.

The historical illustration summarizes the Sui dynasty's rapid destruction through attempting three ruinous invasions of Korea from 611 to 615 A.D. In each case the number of men mobilized probably exceeded a million, with additional hundreds of thousands in support, thereby severely disrupting the agricultural industry in the northeast, largely depopulating it, and causing severe economic chaos. Even more tragic, the Sui had just brilliantly succeeded in reuniting China after centuries of brief, often contending dynasties that had ruled over fragmented areas. Unfortunately, the emperor was not only enthralled with warfare, he foolishly undertook impossible missions that proved disastrously unsuccessful and never had the pleasure of grappling with the problems that victory might bring. While victory may be problematic, defeat certainly proves so.

Another negative aspect of large-scale and frequent warfare is the danger posed by the thousands of troops mobilized and then concentrated under the command of effective generals to whom they feel a direct allegiance. The ancients emphasized performing standing down ceremonies in order to reemphasize civil virtues (as discussed in the next chapter) and control, and presumably to remove the general as a potential threat to the ruling house. (This threat is why loyalty suddenly became emphasized as an essential qualification for generals during the Spring and Autumn and subsequent Warring States periods. Many revolts throughout Chinese history were launched by ambitious, successful generals confident in the personal loyalty of their troops, particularly when they felt their power was threatened or they had not received adequate recognition and rewards.) Accordingly, the *Ssu-ma Fa* discussed procedures to be followed not only to excise the commander's military authority but also to recivilize men brutalized by the experience of war, to ease their transition from a harsh, violent world into a peaceful, orderly agricultural society:

> When the soaring birds have all been slain, then good bows are stored away. When enemy states have been extinguished, ministers in charge of planning are lost. Here "lost" doesn't mean they lose their lives, but that the ruler has taken away their awesomeness and removed their authority. He enfeoffs them in court, at the highest ranks of his subordinates, in order to manifest their merit. He presents them with excellent states in the central region in order to enrich their families and bestows beautiful women and valuable treasures upon them in order to please their hearts.
>
> Now once the masses have been brought together they cannot be hastily separated. Once the awesomeness of authority has been granted it cannot be suddenly shifted. Returning the forces and disbanding the armies after the war are critical stages in preservation and loss. Thus weakening the commanding general through appointment to new positions, taking his authority by granting him a state, is referred to as a hegemon's strategy. Thus the hegemon's actions incorporate a mixed approach of Virtue and power. Preserving the altars of state, gathering those of character and courage, both are encouraged by the strategic power of the Middle Strategy. Thus to exercise such power the ruler must be very secretive.

100 Forgetting Warfare 忘

Tactical Discussion

The Sage remains conscientiously alert not to forget danger when secure or chaos when well ordered. When the realm is free from military affairs, the martial cannot be neglected. If every aspect isn't pondered, one will lack the means to defend against the violent. It is necessary to internally cultivate culture and virtue while externally making strict martial preparations. When embracing and being conciliatory toward distant peoples, guard against the unanticipated. Throughout the four seasons one must practice the martial rites in order to show that the state has not forgotten warfare. One who has not forgotten warfare teaches the people not to neglect their military training. A principle from the *Ssu-ma Fa* states: "Even though the realm is at peace those who forget warfare will inevitably be overturned."

Historical Illustration

When T'ang Hsüan-tsung ruled, he inherited a long heritage of peace in which the weapons had been destroyed, the horses put out to pasture, the generals dismissed, and the army rested. The state knew nothing about military preparations; the people nothing about warfare. When the rebellions of An Lu-shan and Shih Ssu-ming suddenly erupted, the civilian officials were incapable of acting as generals and the city dwellers inadequate to the tasks of combat. The very altars of state were endangered, an inheritance long protected largely lost. Alas, can warfare be forgotten?

Commentary

"Forgetting Warfare" addresses the tendency of states and nations to completely relax when peace is attained, to forget the desperate times of warfare and grow unwilling to continue self-discipline and the material expenditures necessary to maintain a ready force. (One need not look beyond America's attitudes and experiences both before and after the two World Wars and the Korean debacle, all of which began with outmoded weapons, untrained troops, and little will to fight, for poignant examples.) China particularly suffered from such myopic vision even though major battles were fought either on its territory or along the borders almost every other year, and it was constantly plagued by rebellions, millenarian movements, and border clashes with nomadic peoples. The bureaucratic penchant to disdain the profession of arms while believing in the all-transforming power of superior virtue, coupled with the pressing needs for the state's public works—as well as the monetary drain requisite to sustaining an opulent imperial lifestyle—compounded the problem and increased the competition for scare resources and manpower.

In antiquity, when populations were small and warfare was mainly fought by the nobility, annual hunts and other group exercises, as well as each warrior's ongoing personal training, sustained the military's readiness. However, when armies shifted from exclusively chariot-based forces to chariot and infantry components, and later cavalry and infantry, the formations, command and control, deployment of weapons groups, and similar military essentials demanded extensive training and full-time professional officers as well as a core of permanent soldiers. Men were forced to serve involuntarily, often for up to three years, a heavy burden upon their families and possibly a fatal hardship for them. Every man who abandoned agriculture work to become a soldier lessened the productive labor force and thus reduced farm yields, while larger armies naturally wrecked ever-greater destruction over the countryside. Clearly there were many disincentives to maintaining a strong, numerous force, and the state was easily surprised by bold nomadic powers who, if not confronted, had to be appeased.

Many military strategists, famous generals, and even a few court officials (when enemies threatened) fervently spoke about the need to contemplate both present and future danger and undertake intensive preparations. For example, the T'ai Kung apparently commented to King Wu of the Chou:

> Today the Shang King knows about existence, but not about perishing. He knows pleasure but not disaster. Now existence doesn't lie in existence, but in thinking about perishing. Pleasure doesn't lie in pleasure, but in contemplating disaster.

Chinese theorists believed warfare, a result of human conflict, was inherent in the human condition. Sun Pin, for example, graphically conveys this point in "Preparation of Strategic Power":

> Now being endowed with teeth and mounting horns, having claws in front and spurs in back, coming together when happy, fighting when angry, this is the Tao of Heaven; it cannot be stopped. Thus those who lack Heavenly weapons provide them themselves. This was an affair of extraordinary men. The Yellow Emperor created swords and imagized military formations upon them. Yi created bows and crossbows and imagized strategic power on them. Yü created boats and carts and imagized tactical changes on them. T'ang and Wu made long weapons and imagized the strategic imbalance of power on them.

Some of the philosophers believed it resulted from competition among a growing populace for limited goods and attempts to fulfill ever-increasing desires. Insofar as their views naturally influenced the military thinkers, many of the latter stressed that only a strong, well-ordered, economically prosperous state can furnish the minimal basis for warfare. The *Wei Liao-tzu* particularly emphasized economic strength as a deterrent:

> Control of the army is as secretive as the depths of Earth, as dark and obscure as the heights of Heaven, and is given birth from the nonexistent. Therefore it must be opened. The great is not frivolous; the small is not vast. One who is enlightened about prohibitions, pardons, opening and stopping up will attract displaced people and bring unworked lands under cultivation.
>
> When the land is broad and under cultivation the state will be wealthy; when the people are numerous and well ordered the state will be governed. When the state is wealthy and well governed, although the people do not remove the blocks from the chariots or expose their armor, their awesomeness instills order on All under Heaven. Thus it is said "the army's victory stems from the court." When one is victorious without exposing his armor, it is the ruler's victory; when victory comes after deploying the army, it is the general's victory.
>
> Land is the means for nourishing the populace; fortified cities the means for defending the land; combat the means for defending the cities. Thus, if one concentrates upon plowing, the people will not be hungry; if one concentrates upon defense, the land will not be endangered; if one concentrates upon combat, the cities will not be encircled. These three were the fundamental concerns of the Former Kings, and among them military affairs were the most urgent.

With this foundation, the people could be motivated to fight, and the court might overawe its enemies. Conversely, Wu Ch'i pointed out to Marquis Wu that being incapable of fighting meant that the ruler had failed his people (and would of course be at the mercy of other states):

> In antiquity the ruler of the Ch'eng Sang clan cultivated Virtue but neglected military affairs, thereby leading to the extinction of his state. The ruler of the Yu

Hu clan relied upon his masses and loved courage, and thus lost his ancestral altars. The enlightened ruler, observing this, will certainly nourish culture and Virtue within the domestic sphere while, in response to external situations, putting his military preparations in order. Thus when opposing an enemy force if you do not advance, you haven't attained righteousness. When the dead lie stiff and you grieve for them you haven't attained benevolence.

Even the *Huang Shih-kung,* which was heavily influenced by Taoist thought and perhaps written at the end of the Warring States period, espoused the same strong view:

The Sage King does not take any pleasure in using the army. He mobilizes it to execute the violently perverse and punish the rebellious. Now using the righteous to execute the unrighteous is like releasing the Yangtze and Yellow Rivers to douse a torch, or pushing a person tottering at the edge of an abyss. Their success is inevitable! Thus when action should be taken one who hesitates and is quiet, without advancing, seriously injures all living beings. Weapons are inauspicious instruments, and the Tao of Heaven abhors them. However when their employment is unavoidable it accords with the Tao of Heaven. Now men in the Tao are like fish in water. If they have water, they will live; if not, they will die. Thus the ruler must constantly be afraid and not dare lose the Tao.

Warfare was still thought to have a moral basis and in fact be imperative upon the state to eliminate evil and staunch the perverse (as asserted by the Ssu-ma Fa):

In antiquity taking benevolence as the foundation and employing righteousness to govern constituted uprightness. However when uprightness failed to attain the desired objectives they resorted to authority. Authority comes from warfare, not from harmony among men. For this reason if one must kill people to give peace to the people, then killing is permissible. If one must attack a state out of love for their people, then attacking it is permissible. If one must stop war with war, although it is war it is permissible. Thus benevolence is loved, righteousness is willingly submitted to, wisdom is relied upon, courage is embraced, and credibility is trusted. Within, the government gains the love of the people, the means by which it can be preserved. Outside, it acquires awesomeness, the means by which it can wage war.

Within this coherent view there were different means to achieving victory, implying varied approaches to preparation. For example, at an early stage in warfare the T'ai Kung discussed the similarity of farming tools and their methods of employment with ordinary military requirements. However, the *Wei Liao-tzu* offered a broader, synthesized late Warring States view:

> In general, in employing the military there are those who gain victory through the Tao, those that gain victory through awesomeness, and those that gain victory through strength. Holding careful military discussions and evaluating the enemy, causing the enemy's *ch'i* to be lost and his forces to scatter, so that even if his disposition is complete he will not be able to employ it, this is victory through the Tao.
>
> Being precise about laws and regulations, making rewards and punishments clear, improving weapons and equipment, causing the people to have minds totally committed to fighting, this is victory through awesomeness.
>
> Destroying armies and slaying generals, mounting barbicans and firing crossbows, overwhelming the populace and seizing territory, returning only after being successful, this is victory through strength. When kings and feudal lords know these, the three ways to victory will be complete.

Perhaps one of the main problems, well recognized by the *Ssu-ma Fa,* was the distinctive, vividly discordant value systems of the martial and civil, the military and the bureaucracy. Against the highly stratified, minutely detailed ceremonial form governing the atmosphere and procedures of the court and bureaucracy, the army required an "uncivil" brusqueness that made it alien and antagonistic to the chief administrators and therefore unlikely to receive support:

> In antiquity the form and spirit governing civilian affairs would not be found in the military realm; those appropriate to the military realm would not be found in the civilian sphere. If the form and spirit appropriate to the military realm enter the civilian sphere, the Virtue of the people will decline. When the form and spirit appropriate to the civilian sphere enter the military realm, then the Virtue of the people will weaken. In the civilian sphere words are cultivated and speech languid. In court one is respectful and courteous and cultivates himself to serve others. Unsummoned he does not step forth; unquestioned, he does not speak. It is difficult to advance but easy to withdraw.
>
> In the military realm one speaks directly and stands firm. When deployed in formation one focuses on duty and acts decisively. Those wearing battle armor do not bow; those in war chariots need not observe the forms of propriety; those manning fortifications do not scurry. In times of danger one does not pay attention to seniority. Thus the civilian forms of behavior and military standards are like inside and outside; the civil and martial are like left and right.

Just as asserted in the chapter's tactical discussion, the military writers realized that both aspects were equally necessary, both fundamental to the state and crucial to its survival. Thus, in a passage that again cites the famous clause from the *Tao Te Ching* seen in the last chapter, "weapons are inauspicious implements," the *Wei Liao-tzu* states:

> Weapons are inauspicious implements. Conflict is a contrary Virtue. All affairs must have their foundation. Therefore when a true king attacks the brutal and chaotic he takes benevolence and righteousness as the foundation for it. At the present time the warring states then establish their awesomeness, resist their enemies, and plot against each other. Thus they cannot abandon their armies.
>
> The military takes the martial as its trunk and takes the civil as its seed. It makes the martial its exterior and the civil the interior. One who can investigate and fathom the two will know victory and defeat. The civil is the means to discern benefit and harm, to discriminate security and danger. The martial is the means to contravene a strong enemy, to forcefully attack and defend.

Thus "not forgetting warfare" was known to require a concerted effort to meld civil measures with military preparation, to avoid the tendency to laxity and ease, embarking upon a course of self-discipline and willing hardship.

Appendix: Historical Characteristics of Chinese Warfare

Neolithic Through the Hsia

Warfare emerged, marked by conflicts at the village level and the construction of defensive walls, one of the chief characteristics of Chinese military engagements thereafter. Weapons were crafted from stone, bone, and, in the late Hsia, perhaps bronze. Arrows and spears composed the missile weapons; combat axes, knives, and staffs, the shock weapons. The newly rising nobility furnished the warriors (or probably the nobility become empowered through being warriors), and combat occurred between limited forces of a few hundred to a few thousand; individual, somewhat ritualized clashes may have been the chosen mode.

Shang

The Shang overthrew the Hsia by force, although the combatants only numbered in the thousands. During the Shang, bronze weapons were perfected; the chariot, manned by three men, became the focus of military organization; battles largely resolved into individual combat; campaigns of a few weeks became more common, but engagements generally lasted less than a day. Several thousand warriors composed a field army, but the number mobilized approached fifteen thousand for one or two campaigns, requiring supporting troops conscripted from the lower classes. Disparate materials were employed for weapons—stone and bone, especially for arrowheads, continued, but the nobles, fighting on behalf of the state, drew bronze weapons, helmets, and some armor. Short swords appeared and were countered by overlaying wooden shields with bronze; several hundred chariots might be employed in an encounter; an effective military organization with a hierarchical command structure developed; the primary chariot weapon was the halberd, supplemented by fighting axes and a variety of hand weapons. The compound bow was also prevalent, allowing great power and range. The size and strength of the chariot continuously improved and, since they were badly outnumbered (although by a demoralized and divided foe), the Chou may have conquered the Shang through increased mobility and the employment of more powerful four-horse chariots.

The chief protagonists in the Shang-Chou conflict were King Chou of the Shang, depicted in traditional literature as evil incarnate; King Wen, the benevolent, cultural king who presided over the Chou's rapid expansion; King Wu, King Wen's successor, who capitalized upon their power to overthrow the Shang dynasty at the famous battle of Mu-yeh, probably in 1045 B.C.; and the T'ai Kung, an elderly sage advisor who probably defected from the Shang and is portrayed as formulating the strategies and tactics pivotal to the Chou's conquest.

Early Chou

Rather than dramatic breakthroughs, technology and weapons advanced slowly but relentlessly, including the sword, which evolved to attain its final length and shape. Infantrymen, organized around the focal chariots, increasingly undertook a supporting role. Leather and metal-working skills advanced, allowing better, sharper, and sturdier weapons and armor. Armies increased both in size and number as the central Chou government declined and peripheral states grew restless. A stylized martial code continued to govern engagements. (No important figures emerge during the period, nor are any battles cited in the *Unorthodox Strategies* from it.)

Spring and Autumn Period

Warfare evolved significantly: the number of chariots increased dramatically, from one thousand early in the Spring and Autumn period to four thousand by the end of it. Campaign armies similarly expanded, from ten thousand to forty to sixty thousand, as the infantry developed and became an important component force, eventually operating independently rather than centered on the chariots. By establishing the squad of five as the basic organizational unit, articulation, segmentation, and deployment into varying formations became possible. Weapons groups were specialized but mixed in employment. Form and civility were abandoned as warfare became a matter of survival.

The Eastern Chou period began when the capital was shifted to the east under barbarian pressure, signifying the end of the Chou's long-fading domination. Thereafter the strongest states contended for power and influence, fighting among themselves to establish their hegemony over the realm while still nominally acknowledging the righteous authority of the Chou house. One of China's epoch battles, that of Ch'eng-p'u (summarily portrayed as the historical illustration for Chapter 45), occurred, and Sun-tzu appeared in the state of Wu about 513 B.C. By the end of the Spring and Autumn period innumerable states had perished, while major engagements constantly erupted among the larger survivors.

Warring States

Warfare rapidly escalated to an unimaginable scale, with campaign armies approaching 600,000 or more men in the last century. Infantry forces dominated, but limited cavalry units also began to appear in the third century A.D.; chariots were counted by the thousands, up to six thousand being fielded at a time, although in an increasingly reduced combat role; complex tactics evolved and were employed, being embodied in military writings; the crossbow was invented and used for massed volley fire at the battle of Maling under Sun Pin's direction in 341 B.C. with devastating results; the halberd was replaced with a shorter version with a pointed tip as an infantryman's weapon; campaigns and sieges required months, and battles extended over several days. Objectives changed from simply subjugating enemies and confiscating their riches (or enslaving them) to seizing territory and exterminating enemies. Fortified cities become important targets, difficult to reduce, stimulating the development of siege warfare. Casualties rose dramatically, often totaling a hundred thousand or more per side in single battles. Iron weapons appeared but seem not to have been an important factor. The state of Ch'in, the eventual victor from among the seven strong states that began the period—Ch'in, Ch'i, Ch'u, Han, Wei, Chao, and Yen—reunited China for the first time since the Chou's disintegration to establish the brief Ch'in dynasty.

The Warring States was a period of both military achievement and intellectual ferment. Many famous generals distinguished themselves in command of vast armies, including Sun Pin, Pai Ch'i, Yüeh Yi, and T'ien Tan. (Chapter 90 of the *Unorthodox Strategies* briefly recounts the interrelated exploits of Yüeh Yi and T'ien Tan.) Philosophers such as Shang Yang, Hsün-tzu, and Mo-tzu formulated new doctrines that dramatically affected both statecraft and outlooks and came to have a significant impact on military thought and practice as well.

Former and Later Han Dynasties

Cavalry completely displaced chariots and thus became the critical component force for maneuver warfare, including in the massive expeditions against the steppe "barbarians" initiated by Han Wu-ti that required a hundred thousand cavalrymen at a time. The sword became a slashing weapon, and other forms, particularly shorter versions suitable for mounted use, evolved. Iron weapons fully displaced bronze weapons except for highly prized officers' swords, while the ordinary infantryman also became better armed with mass-produced, inexpensive cast-iron weapons. Clashes were mainly with border peoples; subjugating internal fiefdoms required smaller forces than in the Warring States, but both Han dynasties suffered extensive, religiously based revolts that engendered extremely destructive warfare.

The period began with widespread fighting as remnants of the old states previously vanquished by the Ch'in, as well as other spontaneously arising forces, sought to reassert their power in the chaotic years of Ch'in's collapse and disintegration. The main contenders finally became Liu Pang, who eventually founded the Han dynasty, and Hsiang Yü, who identified himself with the state of Ch'u. Both frequently appear in the historical illustrations, as do some of their subordinates in command of secondary armies.

Three Kingdoms

Three states struggled to control China: Shu (or Han) in the southwest, under Liu Pei; Wei, the nominal successor to the Han dynasty under Ts'ao Ts'ao, in the north; and Wu, in the east, ruled by Sun Ch'üan. By this period weapons and forces essentially attained their final forms. However, the cavalry employed heavier armor even though mobility became the critical factor in most engagements. Fixed defenses, complexly articulated and integrated tactics, and logistical concerns predominated. One hundred thousand- man armies were the norm, but several important battles were fought with significantly larger and smaller forces.

The triangular strife among the contending parties produced many romantic myths and great figures, several of whom appear in the *Unorthodox Strategies.* Ts'ao Ts'ao became the dominant leader in the north after defeating Yüan Shao at Kuan-tu in the fading years of the Later Han dynasty (as recounted in the historical illustrations for Chapters 23, 28, and 89), while

Ssu-ma Yi distinguished himself as a commanding general. Liu Pei in Shu enjoyed the brilliant strategic counsel of Chu-ko Liang and the outstanding generalship of Kuan Yü, later apotheosized as the God of War, both of whom frequently appear in the historical illustrations. Finally Sun Ch'üan in Wu benefited from a strong corps of generals, including Lü Meng, as may be seen from the historical illustrations for Chapters 21, 22, 37, and 97.

Northern and Southern Dynasties

Warfare in the north remained essentially unchanged, although armies stressed unorthodox tactics and mobility and therefore adopted lighter armor. Clashes in the south, where the populace rapidly increased and the economy began to prosper as refugees fled the north, required adapting to the wetter, heavily vegetated terrain, as well as crossing rivers and streams; therefore, the main fighting, being initiated by "barbarian invaders," occurred in the north, involving numerous border peoples who consistently exploited their mobile striking potential to successively wrest control of northern China and dominate it through several short-lived dynasties. The major conflicts thus originated between seminomadic or nomadic peoples capable of fielding 30 to 40 percent of their population and sedentary agriculturalists dwelling in nuclear cities replete with immovable assets, weakly defended by a much smaller percentage of the population.

T'ang and Sung

The main clashes arose between dynastic forces and the border peoples, with the T'ang dynasty generally being successful early in its rule but weaker in the second half, as the historical illustrations will reveal. The revitalized Sung failed to project power beyond its borders, which increasingly shrank, and warfare became constant (although no conflicts are cited in the *Unorthodox Strategies* from this period). Internal, debilitating rebellions plagued them both. In the Sung, infantry assumed a disproportionately important role and the western border peoples even incorporated Chinese infantry into their own forces.

Indexes

The indexes that follow cover all three parts of the hundred chapters of translated text—the tactical discussion, historical illustration, and translator's commentary. Only the general introduction, being contextual, has not been included, while the references are to the chapter numbers themselves.

In determining the entries for Index I, "Strategic and Tactical Principles," the emphasis has been upon significant tactical principles and fundamental military concepts, and upon illuminating passages rather than full comprehensiveness. (Examples cited from the historical illustrations may illustrate the tactic either from the observer's or enemy's viewpoint.) In using the index, reference should also be made to related concepts. While some tactical principles have been explicitly noted, in most cases there are varying possibilities for any particular situation—such as being outnumbered—and therefore only a general category has been indicated. Where general agreement upon an issue exists, such as "severing enemy supply lines," the principle itself is concretely identified. Fundamental concepts, such as "configurations of terrain," invariably entail numerous tactical possibilities and are therefore classified under "concepts" rather than the associated principles.

Index II reprises the names of historical figures, geographic places, books, and a few special items, such as romanizations of Chinese characters and vital military terms. Index III lists all the chapters in which the individual military classics are actually quoted, not just cited, arranged in probable chronological order by composition date.

Index I: Strategic and Tactical Principles

Essential Military Concepts, Theories, and Practices

Essential Tactical Principles

Commonly Encountered Situations with Selected Tactics

Offensive Measures

Defensive Measures

Index II: Names, Places, Books, and Special Terms

Index III: Quotations from the Military Classics

Chapter citations for quotations from the eight essential military writings known as the *Seven Military Classics* and the *Military Methods,* arranged in probable chronological order by composition date.